THE WILD WEST
OF FILM

Advance Reader Copy

THE WILD WEST WEST OF FILM

OTESSA MARIE GHADAR

Advance Reader Copy

20/20 PRODUCTIONS

Washington, DC

The Wild West of Film

Published by 20/20 Productions. 2020 Connecticut Avenue, NW, Washington, DC 20008.
Copyright © 2013 20/20 Productions. All rights reserved. No part of this book may be reproduced in any form without prior written consent of 20/20 Productions.

ADVANCE READER COPY

ISBN-13: 978-1492966906
ISBN-10: 1492966908

www.TwentyTwentyProductions.com

ACKNOWLEDGEMENTS

Thank you so much to my friends, family, and colleagues for their tireless help and support in this immense and intense endeavor

Special thanks in particular to the following:

Lis de Tuerk Ghadar — Contributing Writer and Editor
Ashley Mumford — Contributing Writer and Editor
Kathleen Loughran — Contributing Writer and Editor
Elizabeth Parker — Contributing Writer
Helga Thomas for her guidance and support with the book.

Allison Bailey — Researcher and Editor
Jorge Franzini — Researcher & Editor (Social Media)
Zachary Young — Researcher (Post-Production)
Joy Turner — Researcher (Tumblr)

Contents

About the Author   1
Introduction 3
New Media: Why Bother?   9

CHAPTER ONE   15
Script and Story   15
Writing for the New Short Format   16
Principles of Story   19
Structuring Story for the New Format   21

CHAPTER TWO   25
Shots, Scale, and Cinematography   25
Picking the Right Shooting Style   25
Visual Design and Aesthetics   25
Considerations of Scale   26
Revisiting the Keystone Method   30
Shot Choices   30
Shot Lists   41
Exercises   44

CHAPTER THREE   51
Rounding Up Your Resources   51
How to Build Your Team   52
Equipment   64
Production and Costume Design   67
Locations   70
Tips, Tricks, Tools   72

CHAPTER FOUR   73
Planning and Scheduling   73
Breakdowns   73
Scheduling   80
Shot Lists   85
Storyboards   87
Floorplans   87
Insurance and Permits   88
The Callsheet   90

CHAPTER FIVE   95
Money, Budget Allocation, and (Crowd) Funding   95
Crowdfunding   100

CHAPTER SIX   105
Ready, Set, Go   105
Tips, Tricks, and Tools of the Trade   105
Craft Services   117

CHAPTER SEVEN   125
Post-Production   125
Need to Know: Software for the New Frontier   127
Editing Tips, Tricks, Tales from the Trenches   139
Post-Production Music   144

CHAPTER EIGHT   149
Social Media   149
Demographics   157
Social Networking Websites and Apps   164
Video Sharing Websites   214

CHAPTER NINE   229
Analytics   229
Google Analytics   230
YouTube   241

Vimeo   245
Blip   247
Facebook   248
Twitter   253
Link Shorteners and Trackers   255
Pinterest 257
Instagram   258
Tumblr   258

CHAPTER TEN   261
Self-Distribution and Festivals   261
Self-Distribution   261
Festivals   285

CHAPTER ELEVEN   289
Self-Publishing   289
Platforms   290
How to Prepare Your Book Files   294
Marketing Your Book(s)   296

CHAPTER TWELVE   297
Best Practices for Your EPK and The Literary Pitch   297
The EPK (aka Electronic Press Kit) 297
The Literary Pitch 303

CHAPTER THIRTEEN 307
Web Site Basics and Web Design   307
Basic Structure of Web Page   307
Website Layout   310
Search Engine Optimization   314
Website Hosting   315

Choosing and Registering a Domain Name   318
How to Install Google Analytics   319

CHAPTER FOURTEEN 321
Forms, Paperwork, and Important Documents 321
Acting Exercises   321
Agreements   323
Pre-Production and On-Set Documents 331
Craft Services   338

About the Author

Otessa Marie Ghadar, a Washington D.C. native, is an independent film maker and web series creator on the rise. She was an early pilgrim to New Media's "Wild West" of filmmaking and has become an acclaimed pioneer of the of the web series format. She is the creative force behind "Orange Juice in Bishops Garden (OJBG)," a project that started out as her graduate film school thesis and became one of the oldest and longest running web series. She continues to foster the I-TV medium as the Founder and President of 20/20 Productions, a new media company that consults, produces, and distributes independent new media productions. Otessa has been named as a recent Filmmaker of the Month by the Washington, D.C. Office of Motion Picture and Television Development and has been recognized as an I-TV Innovator. She organized and hosted the First DC Web Series Festival in April 2013 and arranged for the first screening of web series at the 27th Annual Washington, DC International Film Festival (Filmfest DC). Her show, "Orange Juice in Bishop's Garden," continues to rise in popularity and has gained viewership in over 140 countries around the world. Film and new media courses in schools across the U.K. have used her show as a successful case study for web production. Her show is also a Telly Award Winner, three time LA Web Fest Winner, two time Webby Award Official Honoree, and has had screenings at The OUTlander Project at SXSW, Dinah Shore Weekend, and other web festivals. The Human Rights Campaign has also recognized her show for making a positive contribution to the the LGBT community.

Whether in film or fiction, at her core, Otessa is a storyteller. Returning to her roots, "Orange Juice in Bishop's Garden" is an example of "writing what you know." It's part recollection, part urban legend, part pure fiction, and completely inspired by her own memories of growing up on the cusp of the Internet era. Her stories embody the rebelliousness of the '90s grunge era while tackling social issues that surround youth, such as sexuality, bullying, peer pressure, and intolerance. The first four seasons of OJBG are available in paperback and as ebooks online. The special edition "Director's Notebook" containing the script books to Seasons 5, 6 and 7 will include special illustrations, behind-the-scenes photographs, and director's notes. She has also published several creative short stories, which are also available in paperback and as ebooks.

Introduction

Dear Readers,

I remember the advent of the Internet in the '90s. I remember feeling like we were on the cusp of something weird and wonderful, and new. And we were — and still are. The rules for the web are largely still unwritten and precariously being defined by the millions who use and add to it. When I began the journey as an independent artist and web series creator, I had no idea what I was getting into. I never knew, never even suspected, when I first put pen to paper and fingers to keypad, what would result.

Much of what I learned in formal classes and film school has been tremendous in shaping me as a filmmaker and in fine tuning my skills, aesthetics, and work ethic. My professors and fellow students were inexpressibly inspiring. On the other hand, much of what I learned was irrelevant to me as an independent producer for the web with limited resources. I now realize there is an unfulfilled demand for educational tools created for students growing up in the 21st Century digital age and outdated information being taught in traditional film studies. My endeavor with this book is to provide you the first, most current and comprehensive book on independent, small screen filmmaking for the web. It's something I dearly wish I had when I first started out! It would have saved me countless hours, headaches, and heartaches. But all that experience has brought me here and has made me able to share what I learned with you.

Before delving in, I first want to thank you for reading this book, taking a chance on new media, and for wanting to add your story to the chaotic and marvelous mix of content on the web. True, there is no set "plan" for creating a web series — it's all custom to your own resources, unique abilities, and, most importantly, your passion. But there is a method to the madness — and I will show it to you! You must be passionate about the story of yours because you're here, reading this, ready to marshal a great amount of your time and energy into learning about how to make it a reality. Your passion will come across on-screen and will be the factor in setting your passionate story apart from the cacophony of content online.

With gratitude and excitement, I wish you happy reading and successful producing!

Sincerely,
Otessa Marie Ghadar

A web series is more commonplace now, but in 2007 it was bizarre. It was weird. No one understood what the word even meant. It was kinky, strange, and ill-advised. But I did it anyway. And my fans, and cast and crew came with me. My web series *Orange Juice in Bishop's Garden (OJBG)* is now one of the oldest and the longest running series on the web.

I was an early pilgrim to New Media's "Wild West" of filmmaking. *OJBG* started as a glint in my graduate student eye as my thesis film package. The web was new, the cutting-edge of the digital arts. What also really grabbed my heart about it was the DIY element, the grass roots up-start-ness of it all. The web was something that hearkened back to my teenage years — to riot grrl, to zines, to analog mix tapes and dubs. There was something very hand-done about this form of digital that reminded me of my '90s youth. So, I set out to make this janky analog/digital blend: a web- series about the pre-internet era.

So many film school students go into debt creating one short film that they hope will go to Sundance, and at the end of the day, their film just ends up being a business card. One of the most expensive business cards that could ruin the next fifteen years of their lives if their film doesn't pay off. It's terrifying! With the web series format, I found a place where I could be creative, explore the things that I'm interested in, and do so in a way that wasn't going to break the bank.

In my film student days, when I first started *Orange Juice in Bishop's Garden*, I would hear a lot about the decline of the box office, which I think we're still continuing to see today. Interestingly enough, though, when I began doing a little more research I noticed that people, especially in the under 30 bracket, were actually consuming and watching more media every year. They just weren't getting it in the theaters. With this in mind, I thought that the best way to reach people was to reach them through the web, through the Internet. So I got into Internet television and I ended up, quite luckily, being right about that. The web was — and in many ways still is — the Wild West of filmmaking. There are no rules. It's not inscribed. It's a perfect space for nontraditional stories and nontraditional storytellers.

I think the kind of stories that I was really interested in telling were about people who were largely underrepresented in mainstream media. They need stories, too! And many aren't seeing them. Using the web was the way I chose to reach people. And being out there at the forefront and taking a chance to tell unique stories on a new and emerging medium was worth it. When I began taking steps to actualize my story from an idea into a web series, the biggest problem I constantly ran into was people asking, "What the hell is a web series?" In 2007, there weren't very many web series. *The Guild*, the one web series you can now reference and everyone knows, didn't exist yet. The only web series in existence at that time were *Homestar Runner*, *Quarterlife* and *lonelygirl15*. And, honestly, without the latter two, *OJBG* probably wouldn't have even existed. Those were really the early web series that inspired me to pursue producing for the web. I wrote, directed, and produced the web series, which is the case for a lot of us web series creators. We take the big ideas and ask, "Is this scalable?," which is something you don't really learn in film school.

In terms of preparation, though, there was really nothing for me to use as a model. There was no guidebook, there was no rulebook. No one was teaching how to write short form content for the web. Film studies teach how to write a three act feature, or a five act television script, but no one taught the best writing format for web series. I had to figure all of it out by myself through trial and error. The way I prepared my first season was very different from how I prepared for seasons two, three, four, five, six, and seven. I built my preparation in later seasons off of the mistakes I made from season one. There were a lot of things that I did which were not for the best, and I later discovered newer, better ways.

This first season was made by sheer force of will. There was very little money. (So little that when I told people the budget they would laugh in my face and tell me it couldn't be done.) I would like to state for the record that it can be done. It WAS done. And I would like to encourage others to do the same. That said, things happened that could have completely derailed production. The original AC (assistant camera person) was hit by a train. A man on PCP tried to steal our equipment. A faulty generator cost us two days of shooting. There were liars, and cheaters, and only five when it should have taken village. There was even a flasher.

A lot of the obstacles I encountered were strangely a result of me having to unlearn things that I had been taught in film school that just weren't applicable for the web. There are now more web series online than I can name, but there still isn't a guidebook to help creators, like myself, who had a story, the passion to tell it, and no budget. This book is my way of sharing the things that worked for me, tips and tricks, and general web know-how.

Besides the information I'll be providing in the book, the one piece of advice that I would give to creatives is just go out and do it. Really go out and do it. Make it happen. Use your phone or a webcam. Even if you don't know what you are doing, it doesn't matter. Make it happen. I would say: "start small." Don't spend money that you don't have. That's number one, because I've seen a lot of people make that mistake, and that is dangerous, and you don't want to do that. Start with the resources that you do have. Look at what you have, and build a story around it. If the pieces look broken, or don't look like they will add up, change your perspective. Find the angle, whereby they are actually secretly the pieces to make some different, but better. If you think it's not enough, let me tell you: people were always saying I was trying to do was impossible, year after year, after year. And yes, it sounded impossible, but we did it. We did it. And we won oodles of awards. And I'm very proud of the show.

Overall, the thing that I learned most from undertaking this web series journey was how to PREVAIL. To exist and persist. To take the tattered remnants of a plan, and find the way that those shreds were actually the secret pieces to something even better. The first time you do something it's probably going to be a little wrong. So, all the more reason to work your kinks out. So don't be afraid of failure, because people have learned very little from success. I think it's from failure that we learn how to truly make things better. My experience has been that you always run into limitations and restraints–it's how you deal with them that is artistic and creative and even more organic.

New Media: Why Bother?

Knowing that creating and producing for the post-internet world defies many traditional production, distribution, and marketing methods, why even bother? Why aim for a low-budget or independent web series rather than a million dollar blockbuster feature film? And why should seasoned filmmakers bother to re-learn or revisit their trade? Why should anyone learn the best practices of social media? Because not only is the industry changing, but the world is as well. The ways in which we access information, learn, communicate, socialize, and entertain have all changed post-internet. Like it or not, there is a new frontier, and a largely not inscribed one, with both opportunities and pitfalls. The world will continue to change with or without you, so stake your claim!

Media and entertainment entities in Hollywood have become large institutions with large budgets to match. They're also filled with their own missions, bureaucracies, and rules. While they're giants of entertainment, their gigantic stature also poses creative limits. To digital creatives with stories to tell, being small and self-represented can be an advantage. If being independent, low-budget, online, digital, marginal, or new seems an impossible battle to win in the face of the monied mainstream, you are quite frankly wrong. Defeat is hardly inevitable: David versus Goliath is hardly a new tale. And we can take a page from the principles of guerrilla warfare. Build your strategy around your strengths. With limited resources, a small group can effectively stand a chance against large and lumbering institutions like Hollywood. They move slowly. You are light and flexible. You can turn on a dime.

With a shorter chain of command and with freedom from entrenched policies for approvals, you can more easily and quickly adjust to changing circumstances and incorporate new concepts into your work. On the other hand, being a large entity is like having a heavy center of gravity. The further this entity extends outside of its comfort zone, the more elements need to be coordinated — and the weaker and less primed for success it becomes. With so many moving parts, these entities become massive entertainment beasts with a bad turning radius and a limited range. Sure, your budget will most certainly be bigger if your pitch is one of the lucky ones to be picked up by a big production company or mega-corporation. In the end, however, you may end up sacrificing significant creative control over your artistic expression.

The free artistic reign for your content online is one of its biggest appeals for content creators and viewers alike. There's room for nontraditional stories and storytellers. What was previously in the margins of traditional or mainstream storytelling can come to the forefront on the web. While the lumbering beast of Hollywood and tradition can have massive bottom lines and a mainstream focus, their strategy is to make as many sales as possible by entertaining and engaging as many people as possible. But the mainstream does not describe us all; it barely even describes its own audience. Where do the rest of us go for our stories, our own representations, and for our own voices? This is what has brought so many people online, as creators and as viewers: we are filling a void. The niche and the peripheral can take root and flourish in the digital soil. There is a demand for such stories and Hollywood is not producing enough of them, but on the web, YOU can.

The web series format is a fortunate one as it allows viewers and individuals all over the world to feel acknowledged and represented, whether they're from Saudi Arabia, Iran, Sri Lanka, Senegal, or beyond. You're not segmented to one market at a time. For example, the global availability of content online is especially important when considering government censorship of media and social discourse or traditionally taboo topics. *Orange Juice in Bishop's Garden* has received acclaim from viewers around the world who say the show fills a huge void in their lives. The LGBT storyline in the show was particularly instrumental in the show going viral because many of the countries where people were viewing the show actually have laws against viewing LGBT content online, or laws restricting the freedom of individuals and certain lifestyles. For marginalized or persecuted identities, new media pushes the boundaries of what is acceptable, exposes people around the world to new communities, and creates forum for discussion and change. People can log on and feel less alone.

Additionally, audiences can tire of rom-com repeats, repetitive repackaged plots, and Hollywood happy endings. There's a significant portion

> **WOULD YOU LIKE TO KNOW MORE?**
> **When Popular Meets "Non-traditional"**
>
> 1. THE GUILD, Felicia Day
>   *A show centered around the personal lives of avid, bordering on obsessesive gamers in the "Geek"/MMORPG community*
>
> 2. AWKWARD BLACK GIRL, Issa Rae
>   *Minorities, contemporary African-American female experience*
>
> 3. ORANGE JUICE IN BISHOP'S GARDEN, Otessa Ghadar
>   *LGBT, urban youth coming-of-age, nostalgia culture for Gen X/Y*
>
> 4. ANYONE BUT ME, Tina Cesa Ward and Susan Miller
>   *LGBT, post 9/11 coming-of-age*
>
> *Traditionally, the beauty and makeup industries have pushed a certain standard of beauty that is both unhealthy and unattainable to most people. The Internet provides a place for the rest of the world to access and create tutorials relating to themselves.*
>
> 5. DESTINY GODLEY
>   *DIY, African-American how-to maven for the the online beauty community*
>
> 6. FASHION BY ALLY
>   *DIY; fashion, beauty, and Asian eyes specific makeup tutorials*
>
> ALL OF THESE SHOWS ARE SPEAR-HEADED BY WOMEN, AND MOST ARE ALSO MINORITIES, TWO GROUPS THAT HAVE TRADITIONALLY BEEN UNDER-REPRESENTED IN THE LARGER FILMMAKING INDUSTRY

of the population who do enjoy watching these movies and shows, but they're also watching other content online, and probably more often, too. Hollywood and mainstream entertainment companies have tried to capitalize on the indie market and have had an especially difficult time in "taming" the web and getting into web viewing. The number of web series created outside the entertainment hubs of LA and NY also attest to the fact that viewers and content creators are looking outside of established entertainment moguls for the latest video content.

A large part of the answer to the question, "why the web?" comes down to the fact that the web promotes a democratization of film. The web has been instrumental in pushing forward the evolution of cinema. It's easier to take a risk and experiment with different stories and techniques on the web. Thus, more filmmakers are allowed to enter and change the industry. It's the arena for the underdog. It's also a space where viewers themselves can become critics and commenters, and thereby authors. The public can be directly engaged with the creator.

> ### A Further Look
>
> Korean filmmaker Chan-wook Park, director of films like *Oldboy* and *Thirst*, filmed his 2011 movie *Paranmanjang* (aka *Night Fishing*) on an iPhone 4[1]:
>
> > "'There are some good points of making a movie with the iPhone as there are many people around the world who like to play and have fun with them,' Park Chan-wook said. Compared to other movie cameras, the iPhone was good 'because it is light and small and because anyone can use it.'"
>
> ---
>
> 1 "Park Chan-wook's Newest Film Shot Entirely On iPhone," Reject Media, LLC, http://www.filmschoolrejects.com/news/park-chan-wooks-newest-film-shot-entirely-on-iphone.php

In an era where the cost of attending movie theaters has increased significantly (3D, concessions, etc.), frugal minded audiences are deterred from watching many movies and are more likely to be selective with the ones they do see. This also leads audiences to have higher expectations for a movie they do pay for and can be extremely disappointed when these expectations aren't necessarily met. Coupled with the fact that movies move in and out of theaters more quickly, and are almost instantly available for viewing via pirated downloads, video-on-demand (VOD), or rental, theaters are becoming a venue for special viewings where a large screen and a quality audio system are valued.

AVERAGE MOVIE THEATER TICKET PRICES

Year	Avg. Price	Adjusted to Inflation Rate*
2013	Est.$7.94	$6.89
2012	$7.96	$6.79
2011	$7.93	$6.65
2010	$7.89	$6.45
2009	$7.50	$6.35
2008	$7.18	$6.37
2007	$6.88	$6.13
2006	$6.55	$5.96
2005	$6.41	$5.78
2004	$6.21	$5.59
2003	$6.03	$5.44
2002	$5.81	$5.32
2001	$5.66	$5.24
2000	$5.39	$5.09
1999	$5.08	$4.93
1998	$4.69	$4.82
1997	$4.59	$4.75
1996	$4.42	$4.64
1995	$4.35	$4.51
1994	$4.18	$4.38
1993	$4.14	$4.27

Average Price Source: MPAA (current year estimated by Box Office Mojo)
*Adjusted according to the general US inflation rate, based on 1992 average ticket price of $4.15

However, for the most part, people are opting to watch at home, on their TVs or mobile devices. Especially with modern TV set ups and mobile devices becoming increasingly sophisticated, why pay for movie tickets when you can watch it cheaper online? Why go to the theater when you can watch thousands of other content without leaving your home?

Lastly, the web is largely free — and who can argue with that? It might not be the immersive experience of the movie theater but it is also not an immersive experience for your pocketbook. The web also allows for <u>personal viewing</u> in the sense that it allows you to watch at your convenience, not at preset theater schedules. Video content can fit into the chinks and cracks of your life, like say a commute, or while waiting at the DMV. No Hollywood movie is coming to you at the DMV.

Given these factors, why bother producing for anywhere other than the web?

Chapter One
SCRIPT AND STORY

Preparing for an ultimately small screen production has its peculiarities that require nontraditional methods and practices. How you would prepare for a feature film to screen in theaters is radically different from how you would prepare for a web-based video. In fact, the entire psychology of viewership and creation is shifted when you move to the small screen. Initial receptiveness and perception of your content is altered when you're disassociated from a well-known mainstream media entity or production company and are representing yourself as an indie artist on the web. How you set yourself apart will begin in pre-production and will require you to re-imagine every step of your process in the post-internet digital age — from script, shots, breakdowns, funding, social media, and beyond.

Everything on the web is shorter, faster, and cheaper; and people's expectations follow accordingly. How people want content drastically changes when it comes to the web. First, you're not screening at a theater with limited film options. Your viewers are not necessarily in a darkened room, viewing your content on one large screen with a group or community of viewers. We've lost the captive audience of the movie palaces and living room sofas. With people now watching video content on their smart phones and tablets, there has been a shift away from communal viewing to more personal viewing. The interplay of emotions between the viewer and content in relation to the surroundings has changed. For example, the infectious laughter during a comedy in a theater is absent when viewed alone on a phone and this influences how funny the comedy is perceived. Most likely, your audience will be alone, distracted, and viewing your content on a small screen. People now watch content on their phones on the go and in full daylight, during their commutes, in the waiting room, etc. With the near-limitless viewing choices in the digital age, your viewer's setting and environment now play different roles in how you create your content to capture and hold your viewer's attention.

Outside the theater you're competing with thousands of other online and offline content readily available at the viewer's fingertips. You'll need to grab them fast! And don't bore them! And, if possible at all, make it easy to watch (this includes maybe even making it free!). Because you're competing to grab and hold viewers' attention, the length and pace at which your story flows will greatly differ. In this section, I'll provide you with tips to help you create content specifically for the web and to do it well.

WRITING FOR THE NEW SHORT FORMAT

So you have your story, or perhaps just an idea for a story. First things first, before you even write the first line of your script, how long should that story be? How do you compose this into digestible pieces or episodes? Simply put, how do you structure your narrative?

Standard "old school" formats were originally dictated by elements outside of anyone's creative control, and these trends continue today. For movie theaters, they were, and are, looking to cover their overhead or "house nut". It is preferable for them to fit more screenings into a day. Clearly, you can fit more screenings in a day with shorter length films. Ever notice how few movies there are that run past the 2:20 mark? This partly has to do with considerations of how many showings can be packed into a theater's viewing roster.

For television, the considerations have traditionally been — and continue to be — largely advertising based. Even the act structure of TV writing is built around the ad breaks. Just think of all those pre-advertising-break cliffhangers that make you want to sit through the commercial just so you can find out what ends up happening. Additionally, television writing must build a narrative that supports not only this ad-centered structure, but also very particular programming lengths. For non-premium channels, a 30-minute time slot is actually around 22 minutes of actual programming and in a one-hour slot there is approximately 42 minutes

Script and Story 17

of programming[1]. And of course, don't forget about the content rating system for movies and television...

But all of this has nothing to do with you! Online you have virtually no limitations set on your story, whether it be by rating, length, or format. So how do you carve out a structure from that infinity of possibilities — and how do you pick one that works?

There is a "sweet spot" of programming length for the new "small screen." Much of your viewership can come from mobile views and smartphones — and not just that it "can", but also that it should. You want to encourage as much viewing as possible, across as many platforms as possible. Given this, do not clog up bandwidth or deter what can be a highly viable market. Current smartphone streaming and bandwidth abilities put a programming sweet spot under ten minute mark; six to seven minutes is ideal.

AVERAGE MOBILE CARRIER DATA SPEEDS
July - December 2012

Carrier	Download Speed (MBPS)	Upload Speed (MBPS)
Verizon	13.4	7.9
ATandT	12.2	5.5
T-Mobile	7.3	1.9
Sprint	2.1	0.9

Figure 1.1

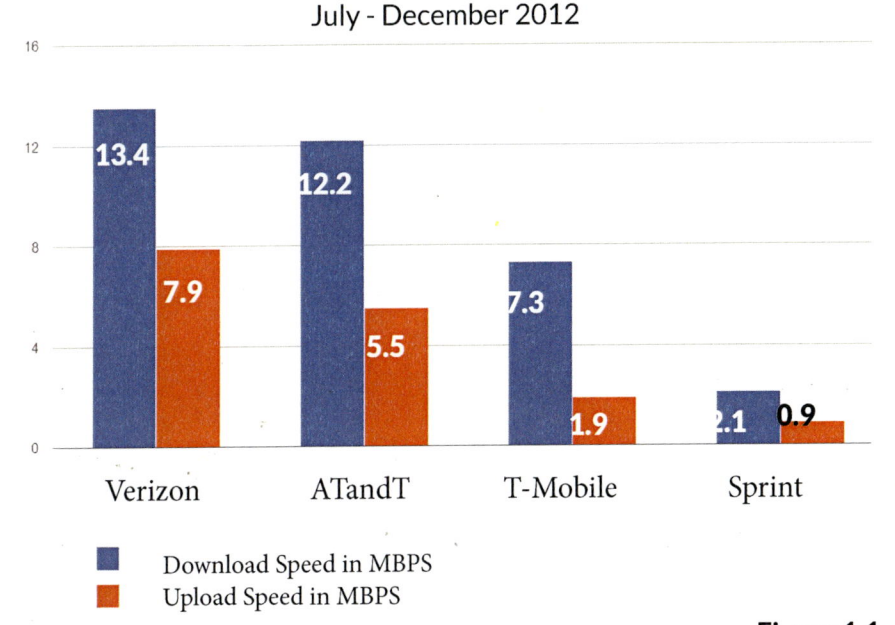

Average Mobile Carrier Data Speeds Source: RootMetrics

---

[1] "Television Ads Are Taking Over Our TV Hours," http://brusimm.com/television-ads-are-taking-over-our-tv-hours/

Given that one page of screenplay corresponds to approximately one minute of screen time (yes, there is a method to the madness, in case you didn't know that before). This means you want to aim for a six to seven page script per episode.

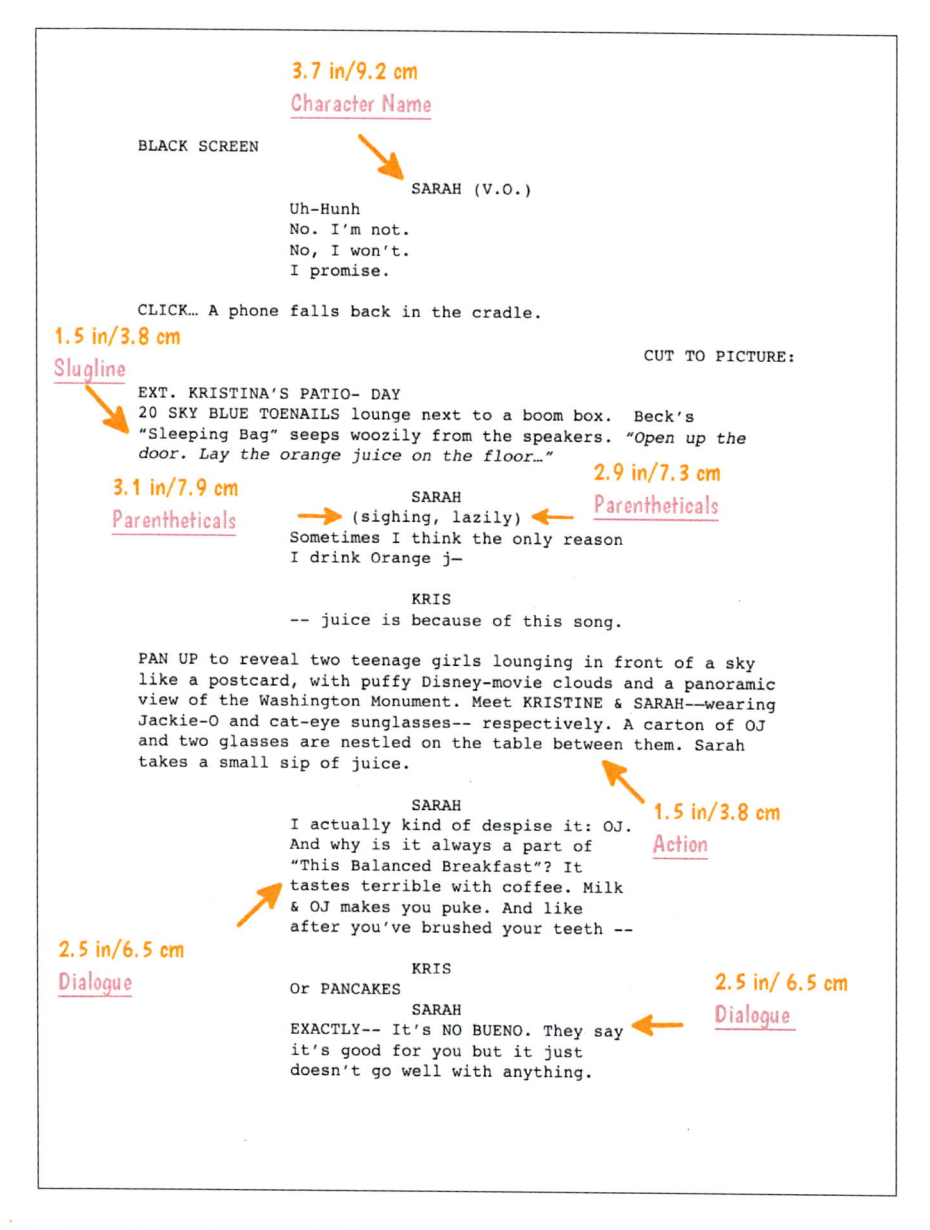

```
                              3.7 in/9.2 cm
                              Character Name

            BLACK SCREEN
                                      SARAH (V.O.)
                              Uh-Hunh
                              No. I'm not.
                              No, I won't.
                              I promise.
            CLICK... A phone falls back in the cradle.
1.5 in/3.8 cm
                                                      CUT TO PICTURE:
Slugline
            EXT. KRISTINA'S PATIO- DAY
            20 SKY BLUE TOENAILS lounge next to a boom box.  Beck's
            "Sleeping Bag" seeps woozily from the speakers. "Open up the
            door. Lay the orange juice on the floor…"
                                                    2.9 in/7.3 cm
    3.1 in/7.9 cm                SARAH
                              (sighing, lazily)     Parentheticals
    Parentheticals    Sometimes I think the only reason
                      I drink Orange j—

                                      KRIS
                              -- juice is because of this song.
            PAN UP to reveal two teenage girls lounging in front of a sky
            like a postcard, with puffy Disney-movie clouds and a panoramic
            view of the Washington Monument. Meet KRISTINE & SARAH--wearing
            Jackie-O and cat-eye sunglasses-- respectively. A carton of OJ
            and two glasses are nestled on the table between them. Sarah
            takes a small sip of juice.

                                      SARAH
                              I actually kind of despise it: OJ.       1.5 in/3.8 cm
                              And why is it always a part of           Action
                              "This Balanced Breakfast"? It
                              tastes terrible with coffee. Milk
                              & OJ makes you puke. And like
                              after you've brushed your teeth --
2.5 in/6.5 cm                         KRIS
Dialogue              Or PANCAKES
                                      SARAH                            2.5 in/ 6.5 cm
                              EXACTLY-- It's NO BUENO. They say        Dialogue
                              it's good for you but it just
                              doesn't go well with anything.
```

Figure 1.2   A properly formatted screenplay with margin markers

Having discussed that viewability across all platforms is a must, the corollary of that is that people like having options as well. If your full season of episodes can be strung together as a feature length experience, this will open up your content to more viewers, and also more platforms of both viewing and sales. For example, some sites, like Amazon, are generally disinclined to show web series as such. Instead they will take a web series if it is strung together in a form that is more recognizable to them and the mainstream viewing population. It's the same content, but being able to market it in multiple ways is a boon. Definitely consider the power of including and planning for bonus content, which can be super short and ancillary. People enjoy having a variety of options and methods for consuming and curating content. Diversification is optimization. Also, try to think of ways in which your bonus content can build upon or further unfold your creation — avoid mere repetition: make it special.

Different models work for different platforms; if you want your video content to have the maximum exposure, this means embracing multiple platforms. More and more filmmakers are embracing smartphone and tablets as new, exciting, and viable mediums for showcasing their work.

A Further Look

For example, Olivier Assayas, the director of the acclaimed film *Carlos*, used the different advantages of various platforms to work in his favor regarding distribution and user-experience. Assayas shot the film as a TV miniseries then re-edited it by restructuring the plot, changing the shot composition and pacing to create a two-hour theatrical version[1]. It's the same story told in two different ways.

---

1   "Does the Smartphone Spell the Death of Cinema?," Omar Ayoub, Art Direction & Design, http://blog.omarayoub.com/post/27000477483/does-the-smartphone-spell-the-death-of-cinema

PRINCIPLES OF STORY

Feature films generally revolve around the three act screenplay principle. Television shows usually follow a five act paradigm. But what about the web **(Figure 1.3)**?

Figure 1.3   Three Act and Five Act structures

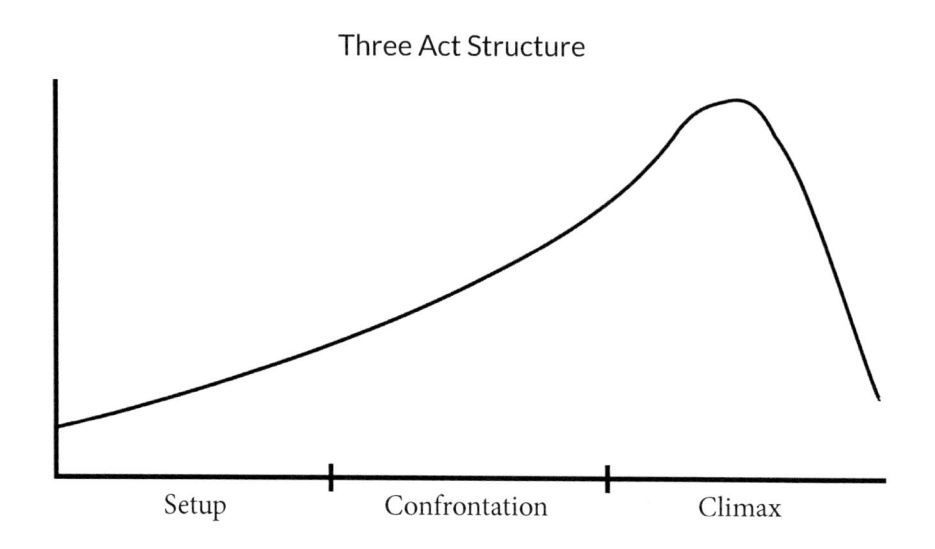

Three Act Structure

Setup | Confrontation | Climax

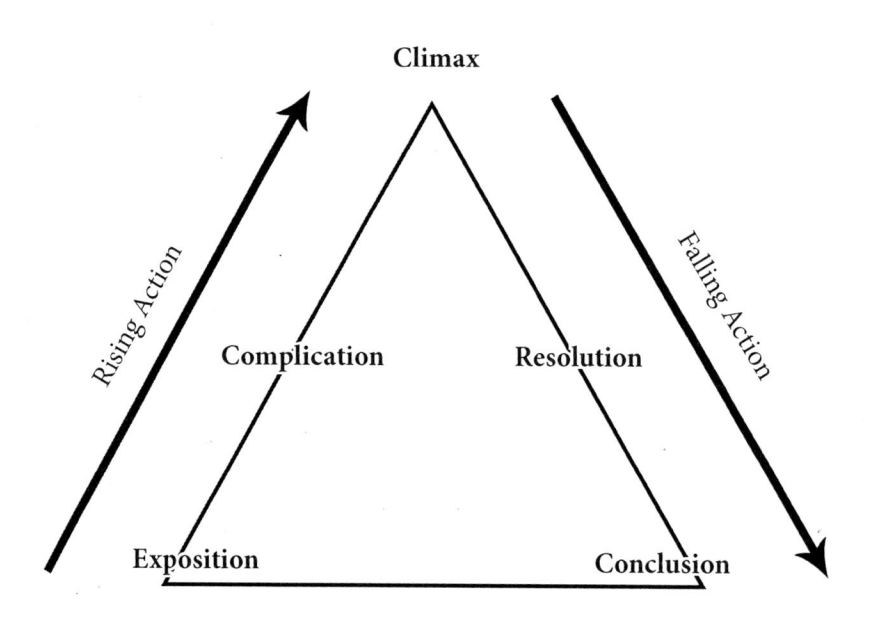

Five Act Structure

Climax

Rising Action

Falling Action

Complication

Resolution

Exposition

Conclusion

Script and Story   21

With such a short format, under 10 minutes, you don't want to cram too much into one episode. Let it breathe, people! At the same time, move too slowly and you end up with the what I like to call the "Soap Opera Conundrum" where one event can go on for two weeks.

> **WOULD YOU LIKE TO KNOW MORE?**
>
> *One Life to Live (OLTL)* is an American soap opera that was broadcast on ABC's television network for more than 43 years. The show held a special and interminable "Go Red Ball" Valentine's Day event that would make for weeks of episodes in a long drawn out plot. *OLTL* was cancelled in 2011 due to low ratings, high production costs, and viewers' changing tastes. Like other canceled soap operas, the show was scheduled to make the jump from on air to online as a web series in early 2013. It will be interesting to note if over time their story pacing speeds up as a result of the new format.

So if we want to avoid the ADHD-ification of content and also avoid the slow-as-molasses-style of soap operas, this still leaves a vast swathe of in between-ness.

Let's break it down.

STRUCTURING STORY FOR THE NEW FORMAT

It's recommended to think of each episode as an act, or a beat, in itself. Each piece should move the plot forward, and yet also *hinge* compellingly on the next installment. Within each act, build an inciting incident — some moment or revelation or new piece of information — that the entire episode is both moving to and away from. It should be the hinge on which the episode functions — **the "Keystone"**, if you will.

Consider then also, that each episode should have an external or **"Extra-**

dos plot and the internal or ***"Intrados"*** plot. On first viewing, the plot is moving along on the surface (extrados), where you think you understand what is going on in the story, but perhaps do not see the internal machinations. After the inciting incident, when the new information is made clear, or upon repeat viewing, the intrados story arc becomes clear. While we thought one story was happening, there was an additional hidden

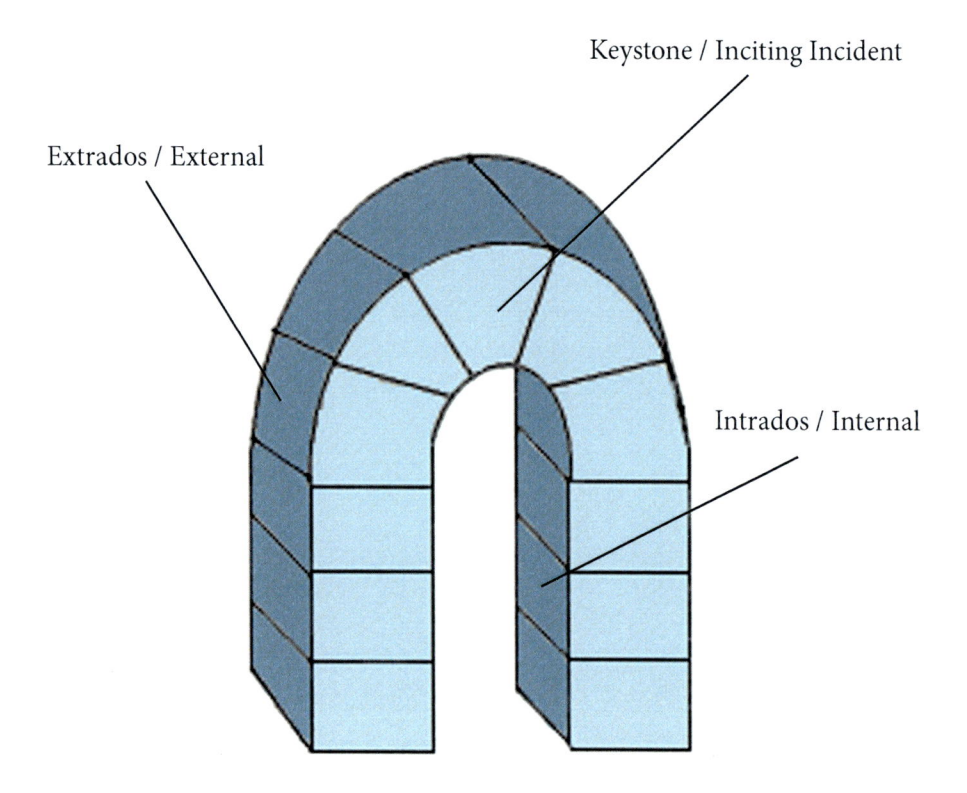

Figure 1.4 Arch with Extrados, Intrados, and Keystone indicted.

story serving as the support and guide for the larger arc of the extrados story.

Note that the keystone or inciting incident need not take place at the middle mark of an episode **(Figure 1.5)**. Indeed, it can be unexpected and intriguing to move this far forward toward the beginning of an

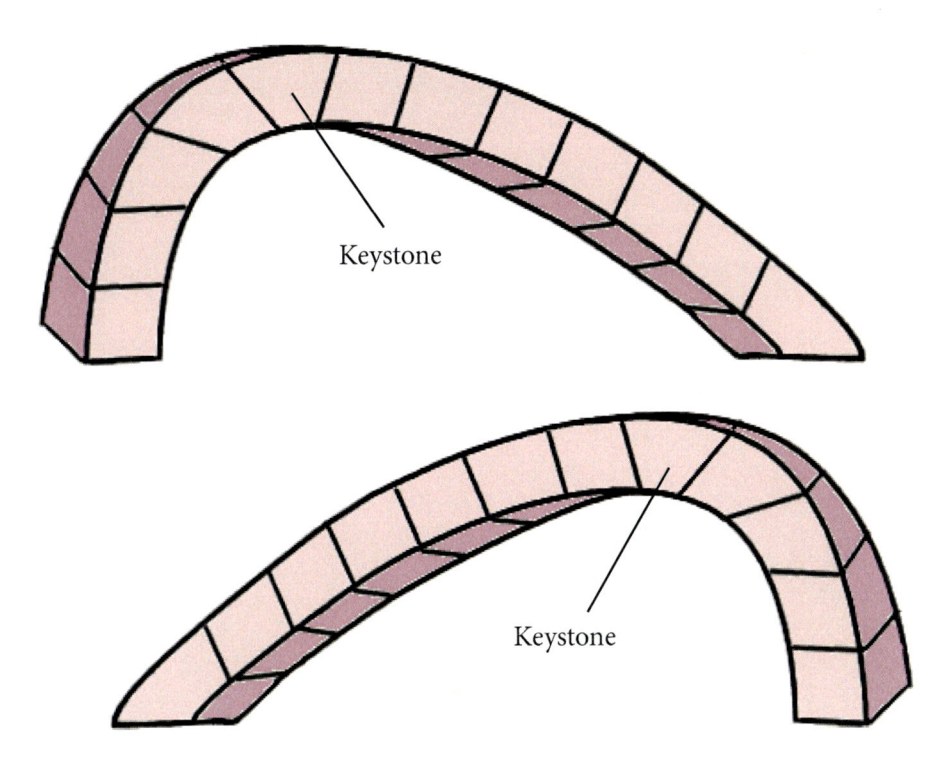

Figure 1.5 Arch, top-left, with Keystone toward the beginning of the story. Arch, bottom-right, with Keystone toward the end of the story.

episode, or back toward the end of an episode. As long as everything is firmly rooted and supportive of this placement, the story arc succeeds.

For more information on the Keystone Method, see "Revisiting the Keystone Method" on page 30 ▶

Consider also the elegance of pairing story arc with one's shooting style or shot choices.

For more information, see "Shot Choices" on page 30 ▶

Chapter Two
SHOTS, SCALE, AND CINEMATOGRAPHY

PICKING THE RIGHT SHOOTING STYLE

Think of the conventional shooting strategies used in Hollywood. These can be anything ranging from cinematic, where you have moving shots and a moving camera, to a sitcom where you have multiple cameras shooting at different angles. With a more reality or documentary style, you can opt for a handheld camera following the action. Or if it's vlog format, you can use a webcam. You'll have to decide what is the shooting strategy for your series.

First thing to address: what is your shooting style?

Exercise:

Compile a list of inspiration art. What shots, lighting, mood, and feel do your favorite works share?

Are there many different cuts, many different angles? Or are they reliant on more single shots and moving cameras? Know who you are as an artist and know the needs of your story.

VISUAL DESIGN AND AESTHETICS

Choose the best color palette for the style of your show. A saturated look is achieved through using complementary colors (warm colors against cold colors and vice versa). That will make colors pop. How does the color scheme inform your story? Do you want rich bold saturated colors? Or are you making something gritty like "Scarface," in which case a desaturated look will make everything look the best. In that case you're pulling the color out of your world and trying to keep all the colors in the same family.

Narrow the palette, so it is controlled via your production design: wardrobe, walls, set dressing. This will really define the look of your series. Even if you can't paint the walls, you can bring in plants or artwork with the colors that you want. Put together a binder or book that represents your production design. Put in references like shots from other movies or just color swatches. They can be digital files that will then be shared with the cinematographer and production designer.

It's all about what you bring with you. Think about what your characters will wear. When talking with your cinematographer, also discuss the colors of light that will be done using gels. Gelling can add color to locations that might not have a lot of color.

Exercise:

Go back to your inspiration art list and note the colors. Take screen-captures as references for your visual design. Use a color wheel to line up complementary colors. Identify the feel and explain how it is affected by the color, temperature, and saturation.

An important thing to note is to always record horizontally on smartphones rather than vertically. Viewers become apoplectic when they feel as though they are cut-off from personally recorded action. Rookie mistake — always remember to get as wide a physical shot as possible.

CONSIDERATIONS OF SCALE

Terms like the "new format" and "small screen" get bandied about frequently, but it is worth a keen, critical view past the verbalese. Upon closer inspection, shooting for the small screen is an even greater departure from form than perhaps initially suspected.

Consider the size of an average laptop... now a tablet... now a smart-

Shots, Scale, and Cinematography 27

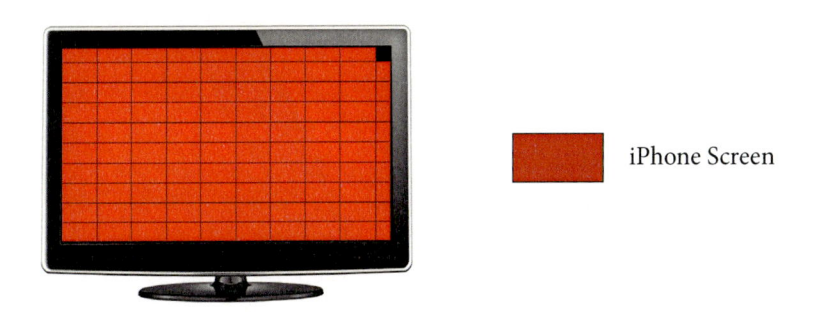

iPhone Screen

Figure 2.1   90 iPhone 5 screens fit inside the screen of a 38" HD-TV

phone... Now compare this to the size of a contemporary HD-TV or a traditional movie theater screen. The ratio for a 38" sized HD-TV is 950% larger than an iPhone 5 **(Figure 1.6)**.

Now, let's place a standard Close Up of someone's face.

	Movie Theater	38" HD-TV	MacBook Pro15"	iPhone 5
Aspect Ratio	1.85:1	16:9	16:10	16:9
Diagonal	34 ft	38 in	15.4 in	4 in
Width	30 ft	33.12 in	13.06 in	3.49 in
Height	16 ft	18.63 in	8.16 in	1.96 in

Figure 2.2   Comparsion of close up from Orange Juice in Bishop's Garden in different aspect ratios

You see that? The impact has VASTLY changed.

Consider now what a EWS shot looks like on a 1). movie theater screen.

Figure 2.3

2). TV screen.

Figure 2.4

3). laptop.

Figure 2.5

4). smartphone.

Figure 2.6

OK, now you see that?

Importance of CLOSE UPS in web format and new media

Consider how the screen size has affected our visual and emotional response to media. What was previously over-sized and potentially overbearing on a movie theater screen, or even a TV screen, has instead become personal and relatable on the "small screen" of your computer or smartphone. It all comes down to scale; what was human-sized and comfortable on a large movie screen is certainly not on your smartphone.

Shots, Scale, and Cinematography   **29**

Those wide shots instead become miniaturized, as though one is viewing a Polly Pocket toy.

The ability to feel the same size as the characters you are watching has a psychological importance for your viewers. Additionally, when you have a wider shot, know that a lot of the detail will be diminished when viewed on the small screen. Keep these facts in mind when you consider your use of close-ups in web format and new media, and consider the scale while you put together your shot list.

Michaelangelo's David
Ideal Proportions

To illustrate the psychological influence of magnitude, envision Michaelangelo's David. It is a statue of ideal proportions on a super-sized scale. His sheer super-human size makes him a representative paragon of form. Towering at a height of 13 feet and 5 inches and positioned on top of a pedestal, in its presence, the David is over-powering and awe-inspiring. It is no longer human; he is a almost god-like. By contrast, peering into a Polly Pocket is like looking at a ant-hill. Now... let's put David in his new home.

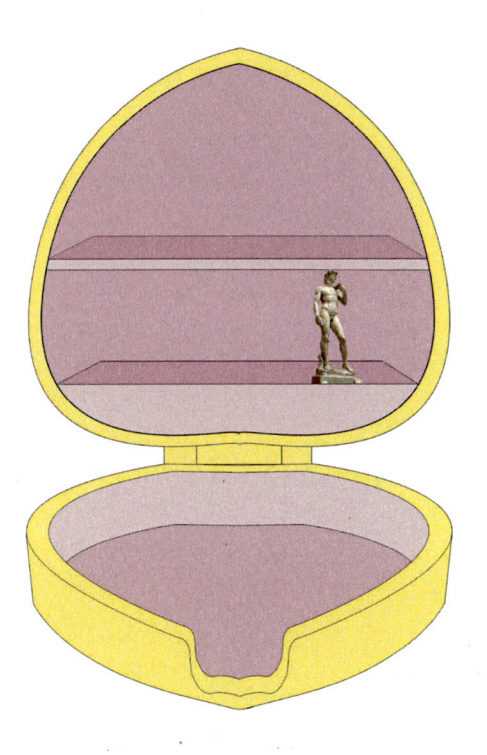

Look how cute he is! Safe to say, the meaning imbued and the psychological response has been altered. What was classical and timeless art has turned into a comedic parody, a laughable joke, due to size alone.

REVISITING THE KEYSTONE METHOD

The Keystone Method of Shooting (See Figures 2.7 & 2.8)

With this new format, and its attendant story differences, the next logical question is: What does this mean for shooting style and shooting plan? Considering the "Keystone Method" and its *one act story structure*. You can build on this foundation through shot-listing. Structuring both your story and your shots to hinge around the keystone moment are of tantamount importance and can lead to powerful visual storytelling.

Other examples:

- Moving from long takes to short takes and back again.

- Or, shooting on one side of the line, and then crossing (to re-establish the line) to highlight your inciting incident — and then continuing from the re-established side thenceforth.

- Or, consider shooting in a "standard" or traditional shot-reverse-shot style, but using it as a counter-point to the use of a more fluid, lyrical, or subjective style.

SHOT CHOICES

Camera Shots (Figure 2.9)

Shot: A unit of film that encompasses the moment a camera starts filming/recording, to where it cuts and ends.

XLS/WS (Extreme Long Shot/Wide Shot): A shot where the subject itself takes up very little of the image, while large backdrops take up most of it.

LS (Long Shot): Closer in on the subject than an XLS, but the subject remains small, usually taking up the height of the frame at most.

Shots, Scale, and Cinematography   31

Figure 2.7   Example of the "Keystone Method" from *Orange Juice in Bishop's Garden*

> Season 6, Episode 1 demonstrates a change in perspective through the type of camera shots used when a tense moment occurs. This episode is marked by a move from a subjective camera style, where we are seeing events through Sarah's eyes, to a more objective style, where we are viewing her instead. The marked shift from the subjective and lyrical style to the objective and traditional "shot-reverse-shot" style allows the audience to see the story through her perspective, and then see her within context of the story at large. The hinge point in this episode is when she is walked in on by Adrian and she realizes the actuality of what she's doing — cuckolding Adrian with his fiancee, Chloe. As soon as Adrian walks in, the shift in tone and style takes place. The viewer sees Sarah as others in the story see her. This causes Sarah to face a moral dilemma, whereas before she was in her own head, unaware of the moral ambiguity of what she was doing. She, and the viewers, are able to see how her actions appear from the outside. **Watch episode online:** http://OJinBG.com/6-1-summer-of-97-continued/ ▶

Figure 2.8 Example of the "Keystone Method" from *Orange Juice in Bishop's Garden*

In Episode 1 of Season 5, the keystone is marked by a change in color grading, shifting from a cool, realistic tone to a cross processed style. This stylistic change conveys that the underwater, dream scene appears more realistic than reality itself. In context of the story, this translates as the character's (Sarah's) dreams alerting her to very real issues that she then ignores in her waking life. The cinematography demonstrates the keystone visually with the character's dreamy and clouded thinking represented through an altered reality. **Watch episode online:** http://OJinBG.com/5-1-summer-of-97/ ▶

Shots, Scale, and Cinematography

XLS/WS

LS

MLS

MS

MCU

CU

ECU

Establishing Shot

Master Shot

Figure 2.9 Examples of camera shots from *Orange Juice in Bishop's Garden*

MLS (Medium Long Shot): Shot where the subject is seen from the knees up, also referred to as a three-quarters shot.

MS (Medium Shot): Subject takes up a good amount of the frame, shot from the waist up.

MCU (Medium Close Up): Between a medium shot and close up, subject is usually shot from the chest up.

CU (Close Up): Shot tight on subject so a specific part of them, like their head, takes up most of the frame.

ECU (Extreme Close Up): Shot is so tight on a subject, it's almost uncomfortably close, usually highlighting a specific detail, like an eye.

Establishing Shot: A shot of the setting or building in which the following scene is about to take place, to give viewers a sense of space and location.

Master Shot: Wide shot that covers all the characters and potential action, within the specific scene.

Camera Angles (Figure 2.10)

Bird's Eye: An overhead angle, as if from the viewpoint of a bird. Gives viewers a large, if not full-scale view of all the action, in a god-like fashion, looking down upon the scene's subjects.

High Angle: An angle shot from slightly above the subject, looking downwards. Usually intended to make the subject look smaller, insignificant, or powerless. Often used in horror movies to depict victims in times of crisis.

Low Angle: The opposite of a high angle, shot below the subject, looking upwards and intended to give power to the subject. Often used in horror movies to give a menacing power to the slasher or killer.

Eye Level: A neutral shot, where the camera rests on even level with the subject.

Shots, Scale, and Cinematography

Dutch (or Canted) Angle: An angle that isn't perfectly vertical, and is tilted off to the side, creating a somewhat disorienting sense.

High Angle

Low Angle

Eye Level

Dutch Angle

Bird's Eye

Figure 2.10 Examples of camera angles from *Orange Juice in Bishop's Garden*

Camera Movements (Figure 2.11)

Pans: A movement where the camera physically stays in one place, but scans the scene from left to right or right to left.

Tilt: Like a pan, the camera stays in the same physical space, but scans up and down.

Dolly: The camera is placed on a moving platform in order to follow the subject through a scene. For complicated dolly shots, track will be laid down for curved movements, instead of just following a subject from left to right, or vice versa.

Figure 2.11 Examples of camera movements from *Orange Juice in Bishop's Garden*

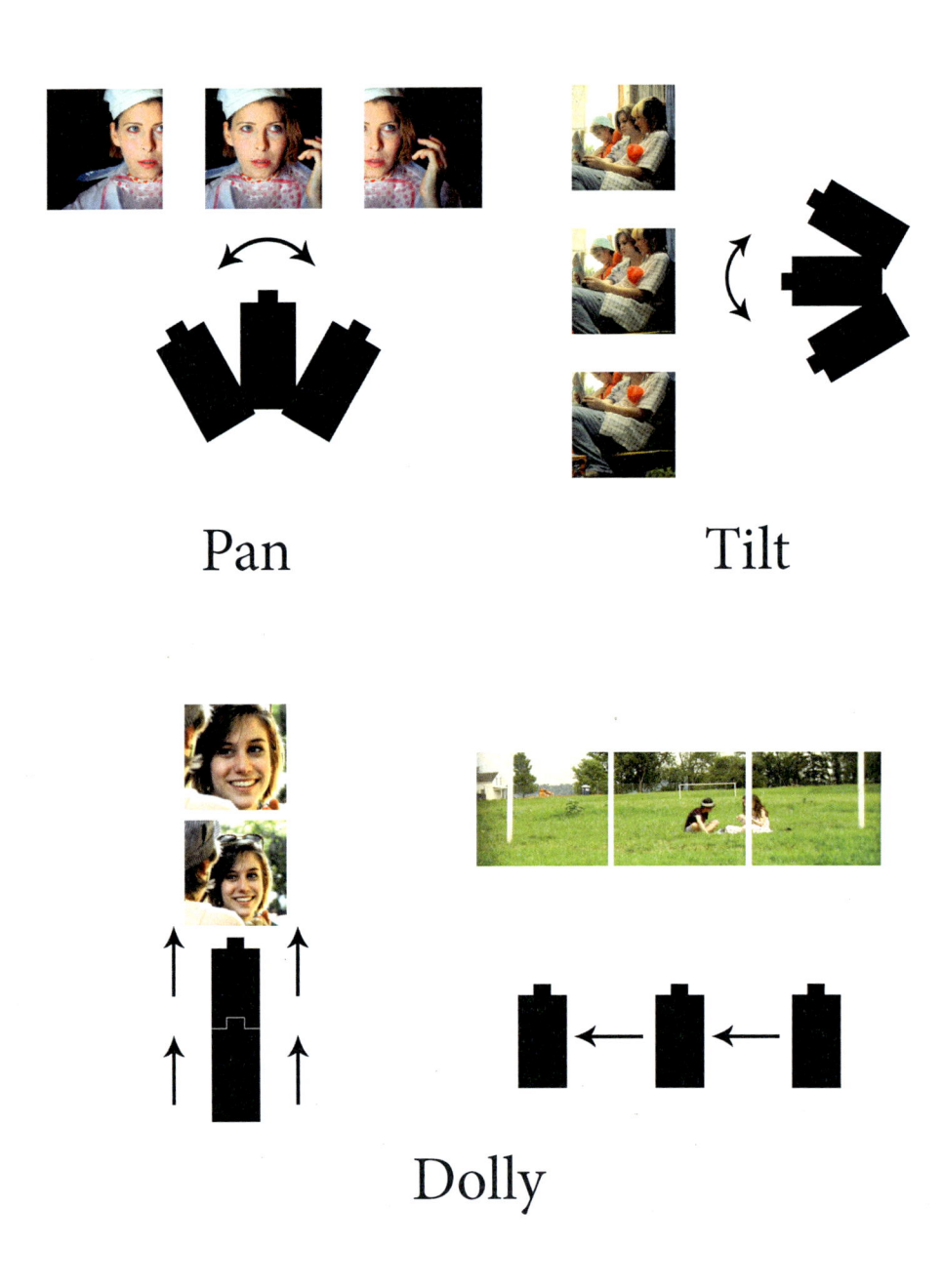

Pan

Tilt

Dolly

Shots, Scale, and Cinematography

Hand-Held Shots: Shots that are captured through hand-held photography. Movements are meant to be portrayed as realistic or natural, as if the viewer were present in the scene. They can sometimes be intended to look as if the camera were being held without a tripod or stabilization, sometimes referred to as "shaky cam."

Steadicam Shots: A Steadicam is a harness or rig that straps to a person's chest, which allows the camera to be stabilized but still move independently. Steadicam shots smoothly and evenly follow the operator's movements, while the rig's armature absorbs the shocks of any bumps, jerks, and shakes. Steadicam shots are thus noted for having an even and fluid movement.

Crane Shot: Somewhat of an aerial dolly, the camera is placed on a heavy crane/jib, which allows the operator to move the camera freely in a 3D space.

Boom (or Jib) Shot: Not to be confused with a crane shot, a boom shot appears more similar to that of a boom microphone, where the camera is attached to a large pole and able to move in large vertical or horizontal movements, but not entirely free like a crane shot. With booming up and down (unlike tilting), the camera does not stay in the same physical place.

Zoom Lens: With the help of a camera's zoom lens, the camera is able to grab a closer shot to the subject, without actually moving, thanks to a series of adjustable lens, which magnify the subject.

Aerial Shot: An extreme version of what a crane shot accomplishes, usually taken from a helicopter, aerial shots are able to focus on large subjects and move around them with ease. Aerial shots are not necessarily downward bird's eye view shots.

ETC:

Long Shot vs. Long Take: The two can often be confused. A long shot refers to the actual picture or image intended to be captured by the camera, while a long take is a longer than usual amount of uninterrupted shot being recorded by the camera. Think picture versus duration.

Depth of Field vs. Depth of Focus: These two similar terms are often confused and misused for one another. Depth of Field is the range in which an image will stay in focus. If an entire image is in focus, including the background, that image has a large depth of field; if only what is closer to the camera, like the foreground, is in focus, and not the background, it has a smaller depth of field. Depth of focus, on the other hand, is a calculation of where a certain lens will have a subject in focus, in relation to its position.

The Line and the 180 degree Rule: The "line" refers to a basic principle of capturing images on screen. It has to do with the on screen spatial relationship of people (and things) and how to capture images so that the spatial representation remains a logical representation of layout for a viewer of the final product. To better understand this principle, it helps to imagine a "line" or "axis" running from one character to another, which connects them. For example, pretend Jack and Jill are looking at each other and conversing about whether to climb the hill behind them. When capturing this conversation, it helps for Jack to consistently be looking the same direction when speaking with Jill, and for the hill to either always be present behind him or for it to never be present behind him. The same goes for Jill. If Jill is on the right and Jack is on the left, staying on one side of the line makes certain that they are consistently represented as being on their sides. However, if you "cross the line," Jill will suddenly be on the left and Jack would be on the right. This can be disorienting to viewers because, if not careful with the line, it can look like Jack and Jill are talking away from each other, and as though the hill is magically and mysteriously disappearing and reappearing. That said, sometimes that confusion or disorientation created by crossing the line can actually be a stylistic choice that works. And last but not least, do keep in mind that "crossing the line" is different from "re-establishing the line."

Re-Establishing the Line: When re-establishing the line, you are making a conscious choice to cross the line, and to start shooting consistently on the other side of the line. This can be done to highlight an emotional change, or a point of drama in the scene, or even to reveal something that may have previously been hidden — say, Jack and Jill's hill (**Figure 2.12, Figure 2.13**).

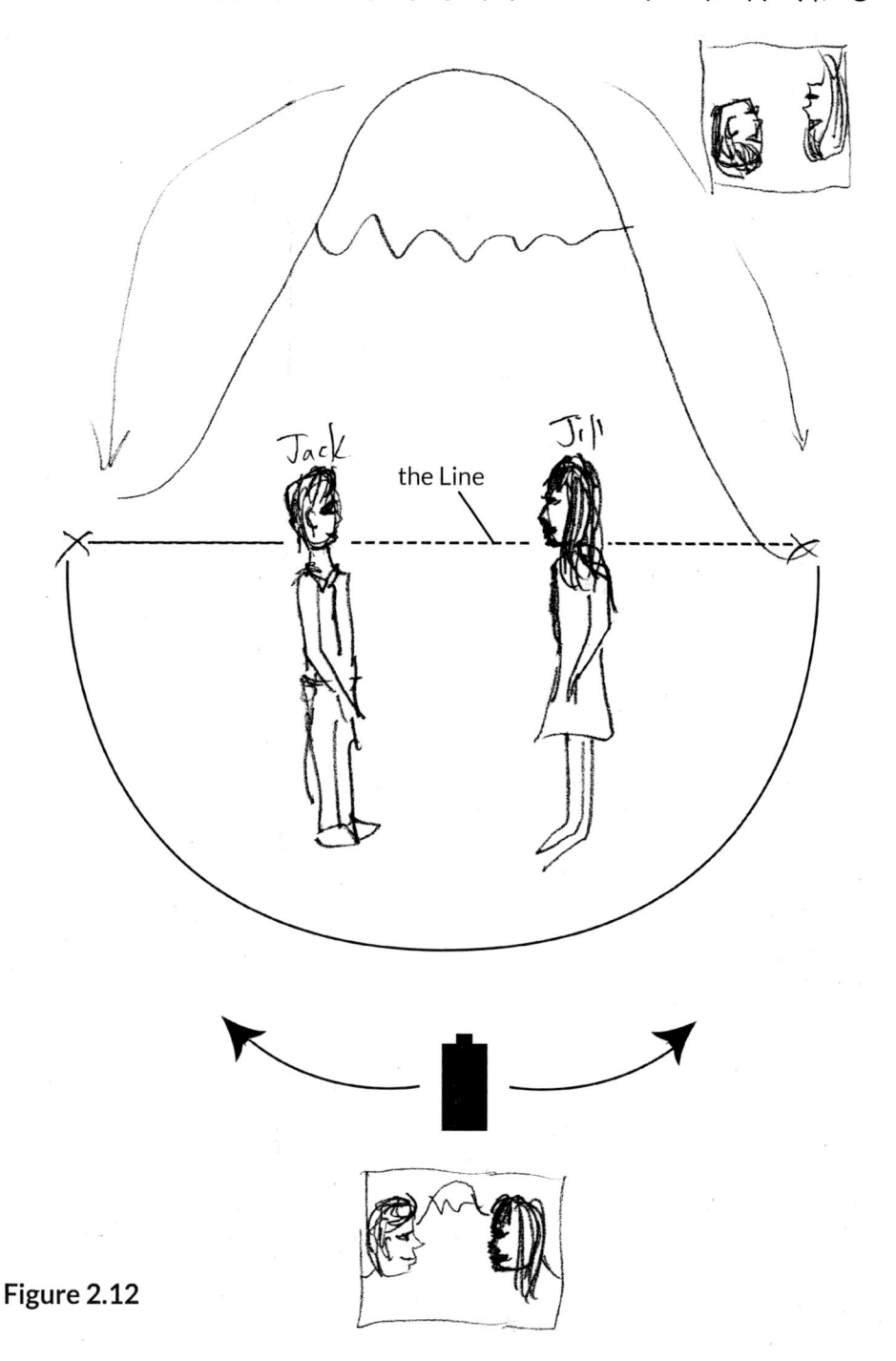

On this side, there is no moutain in the background, Jill looks screen right, and Jack looks screen left.

Figure 2.12

On this side of the line, Jill looks screen left, at Jack. Jack looks screen right, at Jill.

Figure 2.13 Example of the changes in perspective and background on different sides of the line.

SHOT LISTS

Even though new media renders many older elements of pre-production obsolete, making a shot list is still an important step in the process. This is in large part because it improves collaboration, letting key crew members sync their creative visions and allowing other people in the cast and crew to be fully aware of what this vision entails.

Your DP should definitely be informed and included in your shot list process. Other crew members working on lighting or set design can also be consulted in this process, as they might be able to contribute ideas based on what their own work will be.

> **TALES FROM THE TRENCHES**
>
> Some people will tell you that the shot list is largely the product of the cinematographer, which is discussed and worked on with the director. That may be true on mega-budget productions, but I have always built my own shot lists. It insures consistency in your vision. And also, bear in mind that if you aren't paying your crew the going rates, they may not have the time to donate to building the shot list with you from the ground up.

Actually building the shot list is relatively easy, leaving a lot of room for creativity. In a traditional shot list, scenes should be numbered numerically (1, 2, 3...) and set-ups alphabetically (a, b, c...). Here is an example of this format with a single camera documentary-like set-up.

Tapestry – Kate Jenkins & The Intentional – Shot List

1. Interview with Kate

    a. MS – Mid – Handheld - Kate sitting down and getting comfortable, maybe taking a drink of water. Shift camera around a bit to get wider perspective of interview set-up.

    b. LS – High – Handheld – Quick long shot of interview set-up to get accustomed. Sort of an establishing shot. Kate looking around and getting comfortable again. No talking.

c. MS – Mid – Tripod – Main interview set-up. Locked in. Kate on a thirds line, from the shoulder up, with minimal headroom. Stay for entire interview.

d. CU – Mid – Tripod – Re-shot introduction (name, occupation) now as a close-up. Only her face.

2. Tour of Apartment

a. MS – Mid, OTS – Handheld – Following Kate around the apartment. Over the shoulder while she walks, moving a bit left or right, and sometimes higher, depending on what she is looking at. Move in on specific objects if mentioned by her.

b. LS – Low – Tripod – Kate walking past the camera, first going towards it and then walking away from it. Camera locked on ground.

c. MLS – Low, Profile – Tripod – Variation on past shot (different location in apartment). Kate walking past the camera in profile, left to right and then right to left.

d. CU - Mid - Handheld - Kate looking out a window, at a bookshelf, or at something that seems to provide her with inspiration. Rack focus between her face and the object.

Within each set-up is a description of the shot. If it is close, medium, long, or somewhere in-between; low to the ground, mid level, or high up; handheld or stationed on a tripod; and a general description of what it will include. This final, general description includes the most freedom, as any sort of detail can be put into it. Lighting, visual effects needs, physical movements, etc. The more that is put in it, the more helpful it will be on the day of shooting. This format can even be tweaked to emphasize different needs, as evidenced by shot lists from Orange Juice in Bishop's Garden:

Figure 2.14 (on page 43)   Example of the shot lists from *Orange Juice in Bishop's Garden*, Episode 1 of Season 5, "Summer of '97 Continued"

Shots, Scale, and Cinematography

43

DAY one Monday 6/27/11

1. WS Sarah's POV of the post-party

2. dolly toward Chloe as Sarah is talking to Chloe -- Sarah enters her POV

3. CU of Chloe w/ compact & lipstick --rack focus from her frown -- to the lipstick-painted smile-- back to Chloe's (real non-reflected face) for when Sarah gets Chloe's attention & starts talking to Chloe...
   ... then run Chloe's CU master shot of the whole scene from this set-up (and dont forget to have Chloe "squish" Adrian's head in this shot too

4. ECU of sir-marks-a-lot face in Chloe's compact

5. CU's of sailors w/ ink & such

6. ECU's of other people asleep

_____turn around_____

7. Chloe's POV of Adrian --play w/ perspective & scale -- Chloe's fingers "squish" Adrian's head -- then Paul wakes Adrian up

8. CU of Paul & Adrian (from Chloe's POV)

9. ECU of sir-marks-a-lot face in Chloe's compact

10. Push out & zoom in on Sarah -- waking up from mermaid dream -- reveal sleeping bag -- then settle into CU of Sarah through her sitting up and locking eyes w/ Chloe...then Sarah crawls out of frame

11. dolly back *(away from Sarah as she crawls toward Chloe) (end dolly move before "I'd actually really like that..."

12. CU of Sarah talking -- in 2nd position

13. CU of Sarah talking -- w/ rack focus to people groaning & eye-rolling -- in 2nd position

14. CU Drew -- though his marks-a-lot action and through Tamsin-wake-up too. This becomes a dirty single of Tamsin too-- then when Drew leaves -- we see Ryan (looking skeptical in frame) and then Ryan exits frame too.

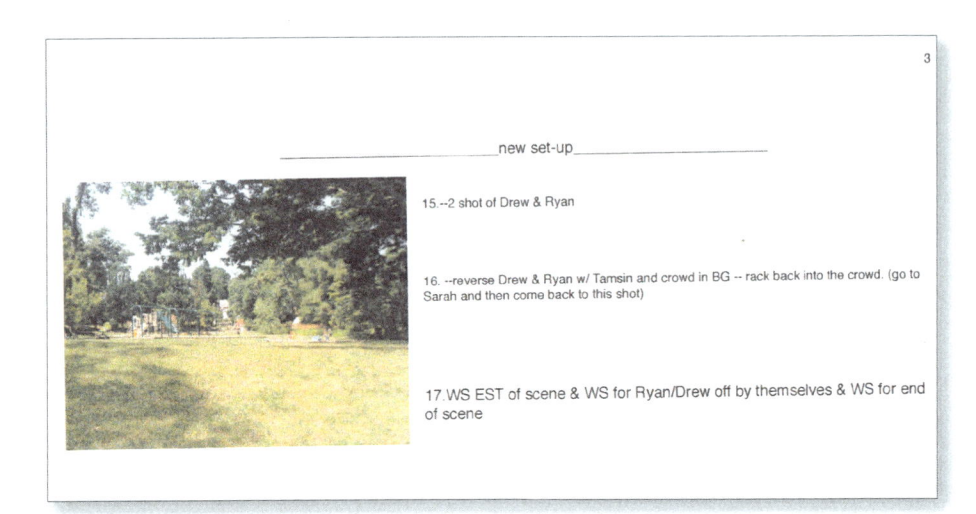

```
                                    new set-up

    15.--2 shot of Drew & Ryan

    16. --reverse Drew & Ryan w/ Tamsin and crowd in BG -- rack back into the crowd. (go to
    Sarah and then come back to this shot)

    17.WS EST of scene & WS for Ryan/Drew off by themselves & WS for end
    of scene
```

Shot lists can then be shared with the entire cast and crew on the day of the shoot, letting them get a very clear idea of what they will be doing for each scene. The boom operator will know when to go in closer or to stay further back, the actor will know when the close-up is coming, and so on. It is certainly fine to add shots to the shot list on the day of shooting, and unpredictable elements like set changes or weather might require it to be tweaked, but getting everything on the shot list will help ensure proper coverage. A shot list provides an opportunity to check that there is appropriate coverage and shot variety. If a crew simply shoots off the cuff without one, inadequate coverage will often not be clear until the editing stage. The shot list also provides a platform for the key crew members to really think about their roles before they get on set, and that can be an invaluable step in making their work successful.

Exercises

Build a rough scenario and a mock-up of a shot-list based around the script in **Figure 2.15**.

Things to consider:

- When do you want to be close, and when do you want to be far away?

- When do you want to be subjective or "in someone's head" and when is it preferable to be objective, or even clinical?

- Are you looking up or down at the material and subjects — and to whom do you want the viewer to look up or down at?

Figure 2.15   Excerpt from the Season 5, Episode 1 script of *Orange Juice in Bishop's Garden*

```
2.  EXT. DAY, GRADUATION LAWN (BEACH PARK) - MORNING:

    Sarah is in a sleeping bag -- her legs are twisted up in it. Her
    "tail" is caught.

    MORNING AFTER EPIC PARTY: 1997. THE AFTERMATH. EVERYONE IS THERE.

    Sarah's surrounded by ADRIAN, the sailors, Ryan, Chloe, Drew,
    Brianna, Alex, Tamsin, Sheen, Rob, (Strawberry?)

    Adrian has magic marker scrawled all over his face.
    etc..."FUCKTARD" "SIR BUTT SNIFFER" that kind of stuff. dirty.
    Adrian sleeps by sailors with goofy-sleep-grin.

    Sailor Paul with inky nose. Drew, Ryan ("I LOVE/HATE SAILORS" on
    their foreheads. have some inside joke that they develop...),
    Bri by the sailors--passed out.

    PAN TO CHLOE

    The only other one awake is CHLOE. and she is looking in her
    compact mirror...

    Chloe looks in the mirror. Frowns. On the verge of tears. She
    takes a tube of red lipstick, smears it onto the mirror. Paints
    a happy face over her frown. She watches her wristwatch.
                    CHLOE
              FUCK.

    Sarah way-lays Chloe...
```

                              SARAH...
                         shy but bold
                    I just had a dream that I was a mer-
                    maid. Swimming was..like flying in the
                    waves... And Gwen, my girlfriend was
                    there. I miss her so much. But am so
                    proud of her. Moving by herself to NY
                    was so brave.

You would think this would annoy Chloe but instead it acts to
remind her that there is something that doesn't suck in the
world. And the mindless love-talk is a much needed distraction.
Chloe smiles.

                              CHLOE
                    So I'm not sure if you know, or I guess
                    you would have to, but -- I'm sublet-
                    ting Gwen's place & you can stop by if
                    you ever want to be in her familiar
                    space. Her stuff's all there & it might
                    make you miss her less.

                              SARAH
                    i'd actually really like that. a lot.
                    thank you for thinking of me like that.

                    I just miss her but she needs to be in
                    NY now because she is destined for
                    greatness. I just want all the world to
                    conspire in her favor.

Her voice escalates, waking people up-- they roll eyes

CHLOE stares at Adrian (still asleep) and ROLLS her eyes. Sailor
Paul wakes Adrian-- they POUND fists.

Adrian points to Paul's nose. Chloe shows him with compact mir-
ror. He lifts a magic marker from his pcket...starts SNIFFING.

                              DREW
                    Heyy-- Sir Marks-A-Lot.

Sailors/Drew/Ryan laugh. inside joke= new friendship.

Tamsin= still asleep. DREW, flirtatiously, takes a blade of
grass-- tickles the end of Tamsin's nose with it. She wakes up &
sneezes.

Shots, Scale, and Cinematography

3

                TAMSIN
What the hell Drew? Ugh I want coffee.

DREW--very much INTO Tamsin. She doesn't reciprocate.

                DREW
      I'll go get it for you.

Tamsin USES HIM LIKE A PUPPY DOG-- pats his head. Drew goes to rush off.

Ryan side-steps Drew --

                RYAN
    Look, I know you like her, but don't
    mug yourself.

                DREW
    Don't mug myself? wha?!

        beat
    Is it that obvious--

                RYAN
    Don't let her treat you like a pet. If
    she doesn't respect you, she'll never
    be into you. I'm just saying from per-
    sonal experience.

Bri eavesdrops--

                DREW
    But maybe it's different with Tamsin.

                RYAN
    Don't reward her when she dismisses
    you. If you do, it'll just bring out
    the worst in everyone, including Tam-
    sin.

                DREW
    I'm going for coffee.

PAN OFF of DREW, Back to the lawn--

                SARAH
    So I've been thinking about expanding
    "my act" from the whole solo singer

```
                                                                    4

            songwriter thing... I want a band. a
            full band.
Everyone is excited... want to be in the band. Ryan esp.
                    SARAH CONT
            I'm going to be holding auditions soon.

                                            HARD CUT TO BLACK

                                                END EPISODE.

                                        3 & 2/8 pages   total


THE GIST-->

Chloe doesn't like Adrian anymore. Adrian loves the navy. Sail-
ors are friends with Drew & Ryan (& Bri). Drew likes Tamsin.
Tamsin doesn't like him back. Sarah is starting band. Ryan tries
to be friendly-- Sarah is iffy. Chloe is nice to Sarah.
```

Watch episode online: http://OJinBG.com/5-1-summer-of-97/ ▶

Further Considerations and Exercises

Build a narrative sketch around these shot and story themes:

1. What if, during a confrontation or fight scene, you were to slowly tilt or boom up on one of the speakers? — Consider what that would do for their standing in the scene. If you move from low to high, you can elevate someone's position, literally and figuratively. And if you move from high to low, you can "cut someone down to size" as it were.

2. Additionally consider that looking down from a high angle can have an almost CCTV panopticon-like connotation. When would that be of particular narrative advantage or disadvantage?

Sometimes you can completely subvert these generalized interpretations, and doing so can also be a meaningful choice. For example, when is being low and looking up actually a position of power? Is a monster under a bed in a position of power? Yes, certainly.

3. Think of other examples of both traditional, in-stream (or cis-expressions) of shots AND counter-stream (or trans-expressions) of shots. Think of ways you can express or subvert expectations visually.

Simply put, it's all about using some cinematic virtuosity to underscore your keystone. These are merely suggestions, but do consider the importance of aligning your story with your shots. Story and shots should be in conversation with each other and riffing on these themes can create an interesting confluence or divergence in your work.

4. Come up with your own example of this.

Chapter Three
ROUNDING UP YOUR RESOURCES

Imagine a world where everything could be completed virtually. You might think we're there already, but films aren't created over Google Hangouts and Facetimes. At least, they aren't yet. So, in the meantime, you'll still need to be prepared for physical production. And this means you'll need to secure your tangible resources, whether they be cast, crew, locations, equipment, or wardrobe. Though this may seem like it's something that's either too old school or too innate to be discussed in a new media textbook, *do not be fooled*! There are incredibly important new elements and shades of meaning to consider in the Wild West of Film, especially because many of these projects will be completed with a low budget. And, hey, even if you think you already know everything there is to know about the set experience, still take a gander at this chapter for some pretty wild tales from the OJBG trenches.

As for the budget that makes this all come to life, see "Shot Choices" on page 30 ▶

First things first, use all the resources at your disposal. Remember that you do not need to start from scratch, and not everything needs to be secured or purchased. You already have resources, some of which you may not even be aware.

It is all about collaboration. In addition to your physical resources, take a look at the people you know. What are the relationships you can rely on for creating your series? What are the assets that you have on hand for shooting? These can be locations; cast members; people who can do sound, camera, wardrobe, or design; even people who can pick up lunch, so you can work at being a producer. These people can be friends or family. As for location, you want to pick a place you are able to control. Use your personal relations.

Task: What do you have? Tally up all the resources you have at your disposal. These can be people, locations, cameras, webcams for vlog format, software, gift cards to Costco… you name it. Now, what kind of story can you create from these building blocks?

Remember that sometimes you have to work with what you have, and that doing so can be the most meaningful, creative exercise there is.

HOW TO BUILD YOUR TEAM

Cast

The most important element to building your cracker-jack team actually has nothing to do with people at all. It is all about *time*.

Get your cast and crew *early*. Find those who have a real passion or an expertise in their field. You need people with some experience and creativity, and finding them takes time.

As for your acting talent, you'll need to gather them as soon as possible. You want them committed, with paperwork signed, and schedules locked. You want to book them early enough so that you and your project are something they schedule around, not something they try to fit into the cracks. More time also means more rehearsals and more time for you all to work to successfully realize the artistic vision.

For examples of paperwork needed for cast, see "Forms, Paperwork, and Important Documents" on page 321 ▶

Cast people who are professional and serious about their craft. Many actors are looking to expand their reel/portfolio and would love to work on your project because it helps them build their reel. There is so much talent, especially new or undiscovered talent, and taking a chance on each other can be the beginning of a fruitful union. Only working with your friends or people in your circle may feel safe but it will not give you the best performances.

> **A Note on Working with Talent in the Post-Internet Age**
>
> It has been posited that people are losing verbal and interpersonal skills in our digital world. I agree with this sentiment. And, truly, while it is key to cultivate and build strong digital skills, it is folly to do so at the loss of the verbal and personal.
>
> The loss of verbal and in-person skills may be considered systemic across all ages. However, today's youth have grown up post-internet. For them, social media, texting, and cell phones are first languages: they are positively fluent.
>
> When it comes to working "post-internet" and with the younger generation in particular, here are some tips.
>
> Don't just rehearse: throw mixers and hang-outs. Insist on phone calls over texts. Get to know them, and have them get to know you. Become a physical, tangible presence in each other's lives.

Don't forget to cast that net wide: you should explore online casting sites and also reach out to local theater departments, community theaters, and acting classes. All of these will help get the word out and build buzz. (See a list of resources further in the chapter.)

Once you have reached out to this network, schedule auditions in a regimented way. Try to schedule a few days of auditions so that people have a higher likelihood of being able to make at least one of the days. Each audition should be short, say 15 minutes max. This is only round one. Save the in-depth meetings for your callbacks. Ideally you want to spend the time with the actors who had a real chemistry for the material and of whom you wanted to see more.

Once you have your audition schedule, create accounts on casting websites and contact local theater troupes, etc... Include catchy, but descriptive one line hook, or log-line, to describe your project. Know who your characters are — and know them backwards and forwards. It is important to know your characters before looking for the actors to portray them. Still, *be open minded: you may find someone who doesn't fit your original vision but is perfect for the part.* That said you will still be required to create character breakdowns, which describe each character by age, gender, and possible ethnic background. Remember to also give a

---

A Note on Working with Teens and Youth

With teens in particular, you may not be able to have them simply show up, work on a scene, and leave. Or, you can, but it might not be as successful as you were hoping. That level of focus and professionalism is something that is often built over time.

You will benefit from learning to listen to them -- from learning from them. Who are they? What are their interests?

Look for both verbal and non-verbal cues. What do they argue/fight/complain about? And what do they rave about? How do they speak? What do they wear? What do they eat?

Ask questions. What do they do with their free time? Where do they like to hang out? What classes do they enjoy the most and the least? Do they have pets? Favorite band and why? Who is their best friend and why? What was the best day they had in recent memory?

Teenagers' minds have recently gained the capacity for abstract thought and they are reveling in this ability and actively organizing their own selves and the world around them according to these meta-principles.

If you learn how to read them and how to listen to them, you will have better luck communicating with them. Communication is not just talking: it is learning to listen, so that others are inclined to do the same for you.

Especially when it comes to difficult scenes or artistic endeavors, your young actors may not have the emotional experience to grasp all scenes. However, if you have the tools to communicate, you can help lead them to a type of personal understanding that unlocks the scene for them.

short blurb, per character that explains what makes him or her tick and who s/he is as a person. Print sides, which are short excerpts from the script that sum up who the characters are and provide salient insight into the project. Have many (more than you think you'll need) copies available at the audition and use these for your audition material.

For acting excercises, see "Important Documents" on page 246 ▶

Crew

For your crew, the "Keys," or heads of each department, are the most important people to find and should be chosen first. The earlier they're brought on, the more they can positively inform any decisions that you're making, like gear, shooting schedule, and feasibility. Make sure they care about your project, not just their craft or their reel. You want to make sure they are creating what you need, and not just what would look really cool on their show reel or website. And, of course, make sure that they can work within your budget. Find people who solve problems and don't just try to bleed your budget dry. These are the people who will help you succeed.

Your cinematographer is important to help you craft all the visuals, so bring him or her on first. S/he is in charge of all things camera and lighting related. S/he knows the technical info and gear you will need, so ask him or her for an equipment "Want List" and also a "Need List" that is based on your project. Also find a good sound recordist, somebody who has experience with production sound, which is different from concert recording or studio music recording. Sound is crucial: without good, clean audio, people cannot understand your work. So, don't just put a boom in your sister's hands and hope for the best. The quality of your audio is a key factor that determines whether a work is perceived as professional or amateur. Also find somebody with good production and costume design skills as s/he is also essential for overseeing the visuals of the series. From props to set dressing itself, s/he determines what goes in front of the camera and should work to create a cohesive world. It would help for him or her to have a design and art background.

Finally, identify a first assistant director (AD), someone to handle all the logistics and scheduling for the shoot. It is not an aesthetic position, but it is *crucial* for the shoot. Getting people to the set on time, making sure call sheets go out, and mostly just getting everyone unified and informed about the shoots: a good AD keeps you all afloat. S/he lets the director focus on the style and informs the director about how s/he is doing in terms of following the set schedule. ADs make the set as productive as possible.

> **WOULD YOU LIKE TO KNOW MORE?**
>
> Because most web series don't have a big Hollywood budget, crew members must deviate from the traditional Hollywood route by wearing multiple hats. Although the Coen Brothers (*Fargo, The Big Lebowski, No Country for Old Men*) are big time filmmakers, they have been known to multi-task and to take on various positions on their own crew. Joel and Ethan Coen have worked as film directors, producers, screenwriters, editors, and cinematographers. While it may seem like taking on so much responsibility for one project would make things difficult, the Coen Brothers are proof that multitasking can be done, and that it can be done well.

Crew Terms and Definitions

There is no set formula for the responsibilities the crew will have because it depends on who is multitalented and in what areas, but the following is an idea of how crew responsibilities tend to break down in a web series:

First things first… ABOVE THE LINE versus BELOW THE LINE.

Above-the-line refers to those people who realize and foster the creative actualization of your production, and to the expenses associated with the above. These are generally fixed costs, i.e., if you cut or alter the project, the above-the-line costs remain the same.

These roles include, but are not limited to, the screenwriter, producer, director, casting director, and actors.

Below-the-line refers to everybody else and the associated expenses incurred. These costs are flexible, i.e., if you alter the script, shooting style, or schedule, these costs can fluctuate.

Glossary of Terms

The **director** is in charge of the creative transition from the script into visual images paired with audio recordings. He or she chooses and sets up individual shots in addition to directing the actors.

The **producer** is generally the go-to for all tactical and practical things, some examples being the budgeting and scheduling of the project.

The **writer** writes the script, delineates the plot, and is in charge of the use of thematic technique and development.

Creator is a term that can denote several different roles. Often in independent or web series realms, this is shorthand for a "slashie," as in a Producer/Director/Writer. In TV, the creator is slightly different and is the thematic adapter of the original storyline. (e.g. Josh Schwartz, who created "The OC" and David Milch, who created "Deadwood".)

Actors breathe life into the written roles; they give personality and relatability to the descriptions laid out by the script.

The **1st Assistant Director** (AD) corrals and manages all the crew and acts as timekeeper for the day. He or she should also be involved in script breakdown and scheduling in pre-production (although in the indie and low-budget worlds these responsibilities may fall far more heavily or entirely on the producer or director). The 1st AD is short for first assistant director, and as you can imagine, the AD is, in many ways, a key go-to for the director and producer.

The **2nd AD** corrals and manages the cast and extras, and creates and distributes the callsheets. (*Indie tip: If you don't have a 2nd AD (and not all projects do) then your 1st AD will most likely be creating the callsheets.)

A **script supervisor** is responsible for maintaining the film's internal continuity and ensuring that filming follows the script. He or she keeps detailed notes on all filming and records a project's daily progress in shooting the script. These notes and maintenance ensure that the final project has been fully shot and covered, and that these pieces can be successfully cut together.

The **editor** edits the final shots and ensures the correct sequencing and cohesion.

Sound records and mixes the on-set audio recordings so that your picture isn't a silent movie or TV static.

Your **production designer** handles the sets, the scenery... the overall LOOK of the visual spaces in your work.

Costume designer handles the wardrobe and the visual manifestations of the world you are attempting to create through apparel and accessories.

Make-up and **special effects** (the people that create fictitious settings) are self explanatory, and they work closely with production and costume designers to make sure that the look is cohesive and that they are not at departmental odds with each other. They report directly to the above-the-line crew, such as the director and producer.

Craft Services ensures that everyone is fed and that you don't have a hunger-related mutiny.

DP, or director of photographer, works closely with the director to build and to visualize the shots, cinematography, and lighting.

1st Assistant Camera (AC) pulls focus for the DP and takes care of the camera gear's maintenance and upkeep.

2nd AC is in charge of changing and charging camera batteries, changing lenses, operating the clapper board, filling out and filing all camera sheets, and dumping footage.

The **gaffer** oversees the lighting and electricity of the overall production.

Grips provide camera support and handle the moving, staging, rigging, and setting up of heavy equipment.

Cast and Crew Resources to Know

Can you even imagine a pre-Craigslist world? What started as Craig's personal pet project in his hometown has single-handedly revolutionized how people find gigs, housing, furniture, and each other.

In the digital age, the casting and crewing up process is one of the arenas that has seen great change, and Craigslist is just one facet of this process. Simply put, do not be afraid to use online listings to find talent and don't forget about your social media resources as well.

Find out how to recruit via "Social Media" on page 108▶

Mandy
http://www.mandy.com/
Mandy is a Film TV Broadcast Production resource for film television production jobs, casting calls, facilities listed by territory, equipment classified ads, and film sales.

Craigslist
http://www.craigslist.org/
Craigslist is a an international, online classifieds site.

Breakdown Express (for LA/NY)
http://www.breakdownexpress.com/
Breakdown Express allows you to submit and to receive pictures, resumes, and video submissions online.

DragonukConnects
(for the Mid-Atlantic)
http://www.dragonukconnects.com/
DragonukConnects.com is a professional networking community and jobs site, covering Pennsylvania, Southern New Jersey, Delaware, Maryland, Washington DC, Virginia, and the surrounding outskirts.

National Americans for the Arts
http://www.americansforthearts.org
Americans for the Arts is the nation's leading nonprofit organization for advancing the arts in America.

Arts Journal
http://www.artsjournal.com
Each day, Arts Journal features links to stories culled from more than 200 English language newspapers, magazines, and publications with writing about arts and culture.

Creative Capital
http://www.creative-capital.org
Creative Capital, a New York City-based nonprofit organization, acts as a catalyst for the development of adventurous and imaginative ideas, by supporting artists who pursue innovation in form and/or content in the performing and visual arts.

Dance/USA
http://www.danceusa.org
Dance/USA is the national service and leadership organization for profession-

al dance in the U.S.

Film Arts Foundation
http://www.filmarts.org
Film Arts Foundation (Film Arts) is a non-profit leader in the media arts field, providing comprehensive training, equipment, information, consultations, and exhibition opportunities to independent filmmakers.

Fractured Atlas
http://www.fracturedatlas.org
Fractured Atlas is a non-profit organization that serves a national community of artists and arts organizations. They help artists and arts organizations function more effectively by providing access to funding, healthcare, education, and more.

Independent Feature Project
http://www.ifp.org
IFP is a 28-year old, not-for-profit membership and advocacy organization that supports and serves the independent film community, by connecting creative talent with the film industry.

International Theatre Institute
http://www.iti-worldwide.org/
ITI aims to promote international exchange of knowledge and practice in theatre arts in order to consolidate peace and solidarity between peoples, to deepen mutual understanding, and to increase creative co-operation between all people in the theatre arts.

National Alliance for Media Arts and Culture (NAMAC)
http://www.namac.org
NAMAC is a nonprofit association whose membership comprises a diverse mix of organizations and individuals dedicated to a common goal: the support and advocacy of independent film, video, audio, and online/multimedia arts.

New York Foundation for the Arts (NYFA)
http://www.nyfa.org
The New York Foundation for the Arts (NYFA) gives more support to artists and arts organizations in all disciplines than any other private organization in the country.

The Actors Fund
http://www.actorsfund.org
The Actors Fund offers a broad spectrum of programs designed to address the needs of the entire arts community, which includes comprehensive social services, health care services, employment, training, and supportive housing.

The Field
http://www.thefield.org
The Field's mission is to serve independent performing artists on a completely non-exclusive basis. This means that everything it does is open to artists from all aesthetic viewpoints, cultural backgrounds, and levels of development.

The Foundation Center
http://www.fdncenter.org
Established in 1956 and today supported by more than 600 foundations, the Foundation Center is the nation's leading authority on philanthropy. It connects nonprofits and the grantmakers supporting them to tools they can use and to information they can trust.

The New York Public Library for the Performing Arts
http://www.nypl.org/research/lpa/lpa.html
The New York Public Library for the Performing Arts in the Dorothy and Lewis B. Cullman Center houses the world's most extensive combination of circulating and non-circulating reference and research materials on music, dance, theatre, and recorded sound.

Theatre Communications Group
http://www.tcg.org
TCG's mission is to strengthen, to nurture, and to promote the professional not-for-profit American theatre.

Theatre Without Borders
http://www.theatrewithoutborders.com
Theatre Without Borders is an informal, volunteer, virtual community that shares information and builds connections between individuals and institutions interested in international theatre exchange.

Working Today
http://www.workingtoday.org
Working Today is a national not-for-profit organization dedicated to providing low cost health insurance for individual artists, freelancers, and small 501(c)3 organizations.

THINK LOCALLY
Try contacting nearby troupes and theaters or the film department of your major's office.

Tips, Tricks, and Tales from the Trenches

1. Working with crew: the importance of pre-production meetings. During these meetings, you should make sure people are clear on what their roles are, what expectations are, with whom they will be working, and to whom they will be reporting. You may not have the luxury of a full crew or of a crew that has 5+ years of experience. You may be cobbling together your crew from a mixed bag or from a wild collection of scrappy people. Consider holding mini boot-camps before you start shooting, to train or to polish up those who need some extra training. This allows them to brush up on their roles, responsi-

bilities, and how-tos in a safe space, before the pressures of the on-set experience.

2. Communication is the key to collaboration. When possible, meet and talk with your team in person rather than only relying on email and text. Things like humor and sarcasm struggle to come across in written forms. Talking in person is always best...and remember to talk with people, not at them.

3. It is important to have people sign their paperwork and releases and, if they have not, make sure it is a prerequisite, before they start their scenes or work with their departments.

4. Consider obtaining a definite commitment from your actors, before you totally write your final, locked copy of the script. You do not have the benefit of a five-year contract, so this might save your sanity. This applies, in particular, to work that is in process, say a multi-season storyline that is coming back for season 2.

5. Check up on people's resumes.

OTESSA'S TALES FROM THE TRENCHES
Horror Story

In *OJBG* Season 1, there was a young woman whose resume was too good to be true. She had applied to be our first AD, and her resume listed AD experience and AP experience for one of the TOP, TOP news stations (yes, that's right, one of the three letter giants of the biz). I called her in for an interview: she seemed bright, capable, and competent. Unfortunately what I did not do was check up on her reference at the major news station. On Day One of our shoot, it became painfully clear that this young woman had no idea what an AD was, nor had she ever been one. I then called the station listed on her resume, only to learn that no one knew her name, but (and I quote) "perhaps she had been an intern for a short time." Of course, by this time, the damage had been done, and we were short an AD.

Lesson learned: if someone seems too good to be true, he or she probably is. And lesson #2: check those references.

Rounding Up Your Resources

6. Have youth? Be prepared for more trials and tribulations... and to be more involved. Being a teenager is hard. Also, remember that when hiring minors, you are not merely hiring the child actor, you are also hiring his or her parents, so make sure you are all copacetic.

OTESSA'S TALES FROM THE TRENCHES
A Note About Energy Drinks

Season 1 of *OJBG* relied heavily on exterior night shoots (a mistake I learned from quickly). Now, the teen-aged cast loved energy drinks and they used anything as an excuse to drink them... and night shoots, in particular, were everyone's favorite excuse to ride the bull. This was before the FDA's findings came out, before the world knew many energy drinks led to cardiac arrhythmia, and before you legally needed to be of a certain age to buy them. But even before all that came to light, it was clear as day to me that the bull was trouble. Energy drinks can create a crash and burn to put coffee to shame. Its blood sugar and energy spike was no good for maintaining a long-term meta-stability and it also seemed to get in the way of some actor's "instruments," like some sort of beta-blocker for listening, ability, and talent.

Needless to say, we put a kibosh on the underage energy drink consumption! Of course, even then, they would sneak off to the 7-11 to buy cans, which they would then chug really fast behind tree trunks when no one was looking. We literally had to be on patrol, making sure they weren't getting "loaded" on the "fruit of the bull." This of course goes for all stimulants on set, too; be careful about relying on caffeine for focus. It's a short-term fix to a long-term problem.

Keeping a hyper-vigilant eye on caffeine consumption (and altering your craft service table accordingly) will manage stress-levels and sleep deprivation. You want your cast and crew at their best, not tweaked out.

See more on how to mange "Craft Services" on page 117 ▶

---

7. Be wary of an excess of night shoots. They really will take a toll on your cast and crew. People's circadian rhythms are set to and based

around sunlight. Too many night shoots create a certain "vampirification" that is not advantageous to mere mortals. Also, consider when you are filming. Summer days have the most hours of sunlight per day, so this is not a convenient time for night shoots but is excellent for exterior, day shooting.

8. Avoid cats, dogs, and performing animals unless absolutely necessary. Enough said.

EQUIPMENT

Film-specific stores and businesses may often be the priciest options for securing gear and other resources. So, don't be afraid to look off the beaten path and to cast your net a bit wider. Do some research ahead of time and use this as a springboard. Many companies won't list prices online, so call around to find the best deals, being sure to keep track of prices for comparison. Another option is to try smaller establishments, like production companies, that may have equipment for rent or sale. Avoid securing your deals on the web; instead, try speaking to an actual person at the company. Having a conversation, being personable, and telling him or her about your production could help you secure a special deal. It's also a great way to build relationships that could benefit you in the future.

If you can purchase equipment for a reasonable price, that you'll be able to use in future productions, great! But it's also important to be aware of when renting is the better choice. Renting will sometimes be the most cost effective option, especially with pricey items or unusual gear that you want only for a specific scene. When renting, don't just ask for day rates, inquire about weekends. Renting for a weekend is often the cost of "one day." Also, if you do an extended rental (say a week or two weeks), you can frequently receive a much better deal on that bulk period of time. One week's rental can easily come out to a three-day rental.

Websites like eBay and Craigslist are also useful alternatives. They can provide great deals on things that are generally much more expensive—just remember to be aware of product ratings on sites like eBay, as this

Rounding Up Your Resources   65

will shed light on how reputable the sellers are. If your budget is super tight, DIY (do-it-yourself) may be your best bet. For example: Pick up a few work lamps at Home Depot, in replacement of expensive lighting kits (even china balls are beautiful, inexpensive, and provide a gorgeous, soft, and even light. Better yet, they are so attractive that you can even use them in your home after you're done shooting. Win/win.)

Figure 3.1 Example of china balls being used as lighting from *Orange Juice in Bishop's Garden*

In addition to physical equipment, also keep in mind the software you'll need on-set and in post-production. Something super high-end may not be required, and you could instead opt for some of the many inexpensive and free programs available. Even pre-packaged software, like iMovie or Windows Media Maker, may be able to suite your needs, but if you can use Final Cut Pro (FCP), Avid Media Composer, Adobe Premiere Pro, or other high-end software, use it. And do consider that for the pro-sumer (professional consumer) market, FCP has become something of an industry standard, as it provides a good flashpoint of ease-of-use and processing power.

You may find that some of the equipment and software you need is owned by friends, colleagues, and members of your crew, so ask around to see what you can borrow, buy, or rent from the people you know.

Production Software for Your Camera

Software is not a big step in the production process; almost all cameras run on built-in programs. The one large exception to this is Magic Lantern, a free piece of software designed to improve the video functions on certain Canon DSLR cameras. Currently available for the Canon 5D Mark 2, 50D, 60D, 500D, 550D, and 600D (with more coming soon), Magic Lantern runs off SD or CF cards and builds on the firmware that comes with the camera. It has not been approved by Canon, and (be forewarned!) installing Magic Lantern does technically break the warranty of the camera, but it is easy to revert back to the default firmware. Though Magic Lantern represents a risk to your warranty, there are benefits to be considered as well, and the program has a good track record.

The enhancements themselves vary a great deal depending on what you want, as the possibilities are far reaching. The most popular features it includes are: letting you turn off Automatic Gain Control, a default function meant to regulate audio volume that often mistakenly makes audio levels unstable; displaying zebra stripes on and over underexposed areas of the video feed; showing focus peaks on the parts of the image in focus; and displaying waveforms, histograms, or vectorscopes over the live-view feed. This only scratches the surface, with everything from Audio Gain to complex crop marks just a few clicks away on the Magic Lantern menu.

The install process usually takes around fifteen minutes, though it is good to leave more time to learn the new features and to see how everything works. Even if only a couple of the features are put to use, it's still a valuable free tool to have in your arsenal. The DSLR revolution helped users achieve high quality images from low cost cameras, and Magic Lantern helps bridge the features gap that still separates them from the likes of RED, Arri, and higher-end Canons.

As an additional note, you should definitely make sure you have and know how to use the XDCAM suite, if you are shooting on the Sony EX-1. It streamlines the processes of browsing and transferring your footage.

PRODUCTION AND COSTUME DESIGN

In many ways, the new frontier of storytelling is vastly divergent. When it comes to Costume and Production Design, in particular, there are both similarities and differences.

In some ways the old ways continue to relate to the new format. In terms of transparency of information, this is particularly true. Taking photos of props and wardrobe, creating croquis, drawing make-ups faces — all of these things build a road map for your vision — a road map that anyone (regardless of department or training) can understand. These are tools that make it easier for others to help you and your work. These are not vestigial. They are not anachronistic. They continue to inform and to assist in the new and emerging arts.

While designing your wardrobe and planning the props, think about how the clothing and items will appear on screen. This does not mean that the items need to be expensive, just that they are appropriate and believable. Work with your costume and your production designer to decide the best way to translate your "look" into an outfit or a set. Put these ideas and designs onto paper or into your computer.

The considerations of scale continue to be particularly relevant. The importance of close-ups means that your props and wardrobe and scenery — and everything that makes your mise-en-scene real — should all hold up under fine viewing. You need it to look good up close. ("All right, Mr. DeMille, I'm ready for my close-up.") By contrast, your wide shots can be more forgiving. The small screen scale means that extreme scrutiny is quite difficult in the wide. This can be particularly relieving; that cheap polyester dress you have in mind for the actress to wear as she crosses the Golden Gate Bridge (wide shot) will be perfect.

When planning a budget for wardrobe, remember that there is no need to buy designer. Look for deals at places like consignment shops and thrift stores. Don't forget to raid your own closet and to borrow from your friends and loved ones. Your actors may have appropriate clothing, which they might be willing to wear for the scenes. This can be a great solution— the clothes will fit and so will the cost. Finally, if you have basic sewing skills, get cracking.

The same concepts apply to set design. Do you really need to turn an empty room into a living room? Can you film in your sister's living room instead and is she willing to allow you to do that over the number of days that you require? If the answers are "yes" then you do not need to head out to your nearest Target to purchase a couch. You or your friends probably own many of the items you need to dress a set. Those borrowed objects will have the "lived in" look that will make your set realistic.

For low-budget and independent creators, the likelihood of having a full-force team for Costume and Production Design is low. Most likely you, and those you rely on, will wear many hats. As a result, it is particularly important to keep the departmental elements transparent, for the benefit of both pre-production and on-set. For example, in addition to having the Wardrobe Department keep its own "bible" or book, include an extra column in your breakdown, describing and picturing the costumes scene-by-scene. Take photographs of the outfits and, if possible, the actors dressed in their outfits. It also helps to have a photograph of all of the costumes in each scene, especially if you plan to film in a non-linear (discontinuous) format. You want as many people as possible to be able to understand the scene information by department because, quite frankly, you may need to share PA's between departments. Or you may simply be understaffed!

tal Minors:	10	# Total Extras:	4		
	DESCRIPTION	CAST		EXTRAS	PROPS, ANIMAL, VEHICLES, STUNTS, EFX
ise, om	Beth's parents pack, slam suitcases shut. Mom leaves note: "the Rules"	Mom, Dad		0	Dresser-w/-drawers, suitcases, clothes, toothbrush, notepad, pen
room	Sarah worries to Beth re: Maggie	Sarah, Beth		0	
rway	Mom & Dad leave. Beth and Hunter fight. Adrian shows up.	Mom, Dad, Beth, Hunter, Sarah, Adrian		0	Note/"Rules" list, envelope w/ cash, suitcases, arm-cast
	Beth, Sarah raid Hunter's room, try on clothes, steal bras, spit in perfume.	Beth, Sarah		0	Many many bras, vanity table, jewelry clothing, CKone bottle
hen	Beth faces Hunter. Adrian	Beth, Sarah, Hunter, Adrian		0	poptart, brown liquor bags, two 40's,

Figure 3.2 Wardrobe column in a script breakdown from *Orange Juice in Bishop's Garden*

Day

Ep7 Sc 1

Episode 7 Scene 1
Alex/Davis,

Sam, Tamsin, Libby

Figure 3.3 Example of wardrobe photos, by scene, from *Orange Juice in Bishop's Garden*

It is also worth noting that all of these additional materials (like pictures from wardrobe fittings) can make excellent behind-the-scenes content and social media fodder/fuel. These pre-production and on-set tools have a secret life that it is well worth considering and allowing to live to the fullest. Viewers love seeing behind-the-scenes — whether this be in a social media post, when you are trying to get the word out about your work. Or, whether this is in the very beginning of pre-pro, when you are simply aiming to crowd-fund. These photos, drawings, etc. all create a LOOK — they imbue meaning to others and they can be shared, liked, blogged, and more for success.

LOCATIONS

When it comes to finding and securing your dream locations, there are a variety of factors that need to be considered. First, you need to know what look you need. What environment serves the story and the emotional undercurrents of your work?

Make a "Want List" and a "Need List" for your locations, similar to what you have done for your equipment. It is advantageous to think in terms of your dreams, but equally so to think about what realities and foundations those dreams are based upon. If you have a date scene, yes, you could shoot it in a five star restaurant, or one of those sky-bars with the revolving floors. But what kind of date is it? Is it, at its heart, meant to be grandiose or simply romantic? Because romance doesn't necessitate the fancy restaurants and the big bucks, it could be a romantic picnic outside, on a beautiful day, with a gorgeous backdrop featuring nature's own scenery. And, if you really do need that fancy restaurant, remember that you can keep the space small and the shots tight… this makes it easier to fill the space believably and more cheaply. You could even create it yourself in part a friend's apartment. All you would need is an elegant corner to set dress, and perhaps a fancy waiter to enter the table-space.

Remember that many states and counties will provide free or inexpensive location permits. This means that you will have a vast arsenal of exterior locations and even some interiors, of which you may not yet be aware. In addition to this, there is of course your social network, your friends, families, and loved ones. They may well allow you to film in their spaces. And don't be afraid to reach out to businesses and locations. The worst thing they can do is say "no," which is no great loss to you because it is not like you had the location to begin with and if they say "yes," you win. Nothing ventured, nothing gained.

Rounding Up Your Resources

Compare smaller locations nearby that you will have control over versus bigger locations where you'll have to travel more. Remember that travel time will cut into your shooting time, but if it's a great location, it might be worth it. When a place seems great, remember to consider all factors. Will there be a lot of traffic outside? Will it sound great?

If you can, bring your key crew members to check out the location to see if it's going to work. This is called a "technical scout." It's crucial to check it out at the time that you're planning on shooting. Otherwise you might get the wrong impression. A place could be quiet in the day but loud at night. Shooting at an airport will ruin the sound. This is why you need all the key crew members, sound, and cinematographer especially. Shots with complex gear can't be filmed in really tight spaces, and only the cinematographer might notice that.

Do preliminary scouts at locations to see if it's even feasible for shooting, but also consider doing something in studio to change things to look however you want. Making it easy for you to control things can be a big plus. Think about a studio or apartment space you have access to. Can't shoot at a liquor store? Try making one somewhere else with a lot of empty bottles. You might be able to pass it off with the right sound design in post.

Otessa's Tales from the Trenches

This scene from OJBG was completely fabricated by the Wizard (aka my mother the Production Designer) because no liquor store would allow us to put an 8-year-old behind the counter of its store. So, we improvised. We took an empty storage closet and dressed it to the nines to make it look like a real, live liquor store. We asked all of our friends and family to save their empty liquor bottles over the course of several months. And we printed out the signage, based on photos of counters at real liquor stores. And, most importantly, we kept it small and tight. A smaller set means less needs to be dressed and that saves time and money).

TIPS, TRICKS, TOOLS

Locations — need locations?

Remember the power and importance of physically dropping by in person! Showing up means that you take up physical space. It is hard to ignore you. Someone must speak with you and if you end up being an outrageously pleasant human being with an interesting request… you may well have a new location at your disposal. An articulate, polite, and well-timed drop-by can do wonders for convincing a place of business or other public location that it needs to be a part of your creation.

And, also, don't forget the importance of using social media. As wonderful as "in-persons" are, you absolutely must consider and use new technology methods as well. Yes, you can secure locations and resources through Twitter — I've seen it happen on my own shoots! In 140 characters or less you can sufficiently grab someone's attention.

And one more note, don't forget that to many people, art and filmmaking are exciting. They may be curious and you can use this as a selling point. Would they like to be in the background? Do they have a niece, nephew, son, or daughter that wants to be in pictures? Would they like a special "thank you" mention in the credits? Offer perks…there is nothing quite like the mutual scratching of backs.

Chapter Four
PLANNING AND SCHEDULING

There is no set "plan" for creating art in the digital world. It's all custom to your own resources, your own unique abilities, and, most importantly, your passion.

Where do strategies for planning come from? In the example of a web series, these principles come mostly from the film industry. And in the example of independently published ebooks, these principles come from the traditional world of publishing. But all of these are filled with old school techniques that can be irrelevant to you as an independent producer with limited resources.

Why a web series? Why digital art? Why an indie ebook? You must be passionate about that story of yours because you're going to have to marshal a great amount of time, energy, and money into producing it. That passion will come across on the screen and will be the difference between other projects and your passionate story.

There are several steps that are specific to creating a web series or online video, which are expounded upon here.

For more on digital and non-traditional publishing and web-design, see "Self-Distribution" on page 261, "Best Practices for Your EPK and The Literary Pitch" on page 297297, and "Web Site Basics and Web Design" on page 307 ▶

BREAKDOWNS

The breakdown is what allows you to (you guessed it) break down your screenplay for shooting.

If you are lucky, the breakdown will be done by a line producer or some such similar person. However, it may well have to fall to you as well. The breakdown is one part of a larger mechanism that makes sure nothing slips through the cracks. It is better to have the breakdown done well, rather than for it to merely "not be your problem". If it's not done properly, it will most certainly be your problem.

The breakdown takes a screenplay and breaks the script down into its constituent elements, scene by scene. Anything that appears in a scene will need to be marked and figured out so that, on the day of shooting, you have everything you need.

Why breakdown? We work in a visual medium. Everything written in the screenplay appears on the screen. For example, let's say you have a scene with teenagers getting positively sick from drinking "jungle juice" (aka—a quarter inch of everything from their parents' liquor cabinet mixed together). Well, you'll need to make sure you have the "jungle juice". Oh, and will you need vomit with that? You need to know! And you need to have it with you on set.

How do you breakdown? Take a screenplay and mark it up scene by scene. Each scene is denoted by a script's slug line and takes up a certain physical amount of space on the page. Going scene by scene, you must measure each scene into 1/8ths of a page. If a scene takes up half a page, it is 4/8ths of a page. Note that you do not turn these fractions into least common denominators: you always leave them in 1/8ths. The number of 1/8ths is then marked in the top corner of the scene and circled. If a scene lasts longer than eight 1/8ths, it is converted to 1. Thus, a scene lasting twelve 1/8ths is marked 1 and 4/8ths.

Marking Elements

Marking 1/8ths is just the beginning; you must also color-code your script. One for cast, one for extras, one for picture cars, another for props and anything *physical or tangible* that a character will interact with, another for special effects, and so on and so forth. There is a standardized form for this color coding (see below); however, this may prove to be overkill for your needs. If you decide to simplify, just make certain that

Planning and Scheduling 75

you and your team are clear on what your system means.

Remember also that props, extras, et cetera are not just everything that is written explicitly but also things that are *implied*. Implied means not just things (like vomit) but also people. If you wrote "Graduation: Class of 1996," then you need to have *extras*, like proud parents, teachers, and kid sisters. Props include anything actors handle and the attendant accessories for those things. For example, at your graduation, you will need flowers, balloons, graduation presents. And of course, since it is 1996, be certain that nothing seen on the screen is anachronistic.

Exercise: First, grab your highlighters and go through your script. Mark up each scene according to the color coded chart. Keep in mind your talent, your props, et cetera. For special effects, mark if you need smoke, rain, lightning, or anything that will have to be done on set.

Figure 4.1   Standard color codes for marking a script during the breakdown process. Source: Wikipedia, http://en.wikipedia.org/wiki/Breaking_down_the_script

Element	Shape or color	Description
Cast	Red	Any speaking actor
Stunts	Orange	Any stunt that may require a stunt double, or stunt coordinator.
Extra (Silent bits)	Yellow	Any extra needed to perform specifically, but has no lines.
Extra (Atmosphere)	Green	Any extra or group of extras needed for the background.
Special Effects	Blue	Any special effect required.
Props	Purple	All objects important to the script, or used by an actor.
Vehicles/Animals	Pink	Any vehicles, and all animals, especially if it requires an animal trainer.
Sound Effects/ Music	Brown	Sounds or music requiring specific use on set. Not sounds added in during post.

Element	Shape or color	Description
Wardrobe	Circle	Specific costumes needed for production, and also for continuity if a costume gets ripped up, or dirtied throughout the movie.
Make-up/Hair	Asterisk	Any make-up or hair attention needed. Common for scars and blood.
Special Equipment	Box	If a scene requires the use of more uncommon equipment, (e.g. crane, underwater camera, etc.).
Production Notes	Underline	For all other questions about how a scene will go, or confusion about how something happens.

Okay, so you've used your script like a coloring book... now what? Take the highlighted items from your breakdown and turn them into breakdown sheets for every single scene. This organizes all the elements you highlighted into a list and spreadsheet. Now that the information is presented in a logical way, all necessary components can be compiled for each individual scene **(Figure 4.2)**.

Why do this? With scripts with many scenes in multiple locations, breakdown sheets will help you keep track of what you need on each different day of shooting. It will help you work efficiently, bring only what you need on set, and have actors on set for only the scenes for which you need them. This maximizes shooting time with the added benefit that your cast and crew will feel confident that you're well-prepared and that you're considerate of their time.

Do you need a breakdown sheet for every single scene? Yes. You will most likely be shooting discontinuously (more on that in scheduling), and you will not always be able to shoot out your locations. Sometimes you will have to re-visit them. Sometimes you will be rained out. Sometimes you will have to plan around an actor's schedule. All of this means that you really do need to think of things scene by scene.

Planning and Scheduling 77

> **TALES FROM THE TRENCHES**
>
> While major motion pictures etc will have their Costume Designers manage their own "Book" or "Bible" — on an indie production like, say, a web series, this may not be the best method for you. People wear many hats on a web series production, so the more you can keep the costume information in-stream and congruent with your breakdown, the better. I add an additional column at the end where I include all costume information and then I attach a picture as well. You may also want to consider adding pictures of props.

Figure 4.2   Example of breakdown sheet from *Orange Juice in Bishp's Garden*

Producer: Otessa Ghadar (917) 327-5169   Directors: Rebecca Conroy (917) 690-9793 & Otessa Ghadar
UPM: Michelle Hora (716) 445-2227
ilm Title: **ORANGE JUICE IN BISHOP'S GARDEN Season 2**   Episodes 1, 2, 3, 4
ogl The bad things we do, the things we get caught for—and how they are never the same. Like a Wonder Years fo

ist of locations/Total shoot days:

1 School Classroom	6 Kalorama Circle	11 Rock Creek Park- w
2 School Auditorium	7 Diana Spencer's Deck	12 Rock Creek Park- gl
3 Back-steps- school	8 Laura-the-Goth's bedroom	13 Rock Creek Park- gl
4 School Hallway	9 29th St. Place cul-de-sac	14 Sarah's Bedroom
5 Chinatown	10 Woodley Park	15 Rox's Bedroom

Total Cast: 19   **# Total Minors:**   6   **# Total Extras:** 2

EPISODE ONE

CE NE	PAGE COUNT	INT/EXT DAY/	TIME PLOT	LOCATION	DESCRIPTION	CAST	EXTRAS	PROPS, ANIMAL, VEHICLES, STUNTS, EFX	W
1	4/8	INT/DAY	10am 6/15/95	School Classroom	Travis/Laura-the-Goth see Teaacher expell Jake/Trip	Travis, Laura, Teacher,	2 (stand-ins for Jake & Trip)	Black beanie, smurf hat, blue striped hoodie	
2	7/8	INT/DAY	NOON 6/15/95	School Auditorium	Principal berates school	ALL	10	flourescent lights	
2	1 & 7/8	EXT/DAY	2:07 PM 6/15/95	Back-Steps - School	Sarah & Gwen talk	Gwen, Sarah	0	back-steps	Sar Gw

Exercise: Break down this scene from OJBG. Go scene-by-scene, to create a breakdown sheet. From these breakdown sheets, determine how many extras you will need. Then, create a sample shopping lists for all props, wardrobe, and special effects.

Figure 4.3   Excerpt from the Season 5, Episode 3 script of *Orange Juice in Bishop's Garden*

EXT. GRASSY LAWN OR PORCH, LATER, IN PERSON:

TAMSIN, LIBBY and REMI chat-- Remi with an ace-bandaged arm. They all lie down on a blanket, looking up at the sky, and we circle them as they speak. Ring-around-the-rosey.

>   TAMSIN
> I can't believe you sprained your arm in a TRUSTFALL!!?
>
>   REMI
> Thanks. The irony has **not** escaped me.
>
>   LIBBY
> So, what, they didn't catch you when you fell or something?
>
>   REMI
> More like they were so jumped up about it, they attacked.
>
>   TAMSIN
> But camp OK otherwise? Must be nice to get back for the weekend though. Hot showers much?
>
>   REMI
> More like doctor's appointments!! My mom didn't trust the camp to fix it right.
>
>   TAMSIN
> So you hanging out with Davis a lot at camp??

Remi --SQUIRMING. Tamsin looks at her as if to say-- GO ON, what?

>   REMI
> Well in the beginning yea. I mean we didn't really know anyone else

> at Bramblewood... and it was fun,
> but then Davis kinda went off in
> another direction. He doesn't seem
> that into Alex anymore. He's been
> umm, exploring, with another guy.
>
>   TAMSIN
> But Alex?!
>
>   REMI
> He hasn't told her, as far as I
> know, he's in the closet.
>
>   LIBBY
> Well then why are you telling us
> and not her?
>
>   REMI
>   (*ignoring*)
> It's kinda like he wants to have
> his cake and eat it too?
>
>   TAMSIN
> He's probably just scared. Doesn't
> make it right though. God. Poor
> Alex. Boyfriend's in the throes of
> a "sexual awakening".
>
>   REMI
> Why am I always single? I'd rather
> have this kind of drama, than none
> whatsoever.
>
>   LIBBY
> You're being stupid. I'd rather NOT
> have some loser following me
> around.

Watch episode online: http://OJinBG.com/5-3-secrets-lies/ ▶

SCHEDULING

Ahh... the principles of scheduling. Scheduling can be the most infuriating and also the most important part of your entire production. Lackluster scheduling can doom your project before it has even started filming.

> **OTESSA'S TALES FROM THE TRENCHES**
>
> I was extremely lucky to have an unparalleled professor to teach me about the principles of scheduling. Professor Richard Brick was and still is an incredibly insightful producer and a tremendous teacher. I owe him MUCH. He was also a stickler for things like production strip boards.

A Production Stripboard functions like a visual language. Each strip piece conveys a font of information, and together they tell not just the story of your film, but also the story of your schedule and your films on-set needs. It is in many ways like Quipu (aka. "talking knots" or the ancient Incan language, which was not word based at all— but instead thread and fiber based. Each knot, color, and pattern held a meaning.) Think of your Production Strips the same way.

Figure 4.4   Side-by-side comparison of quipu and production strip

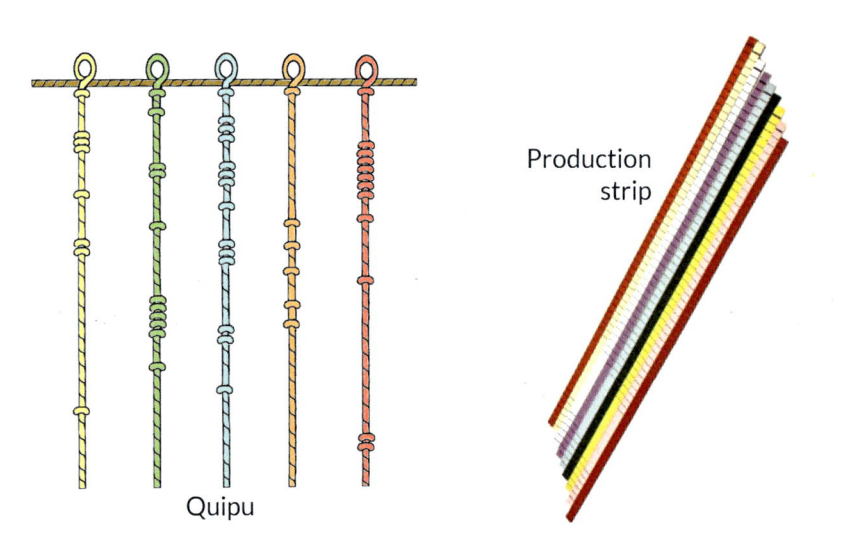

Planning and Scheduling

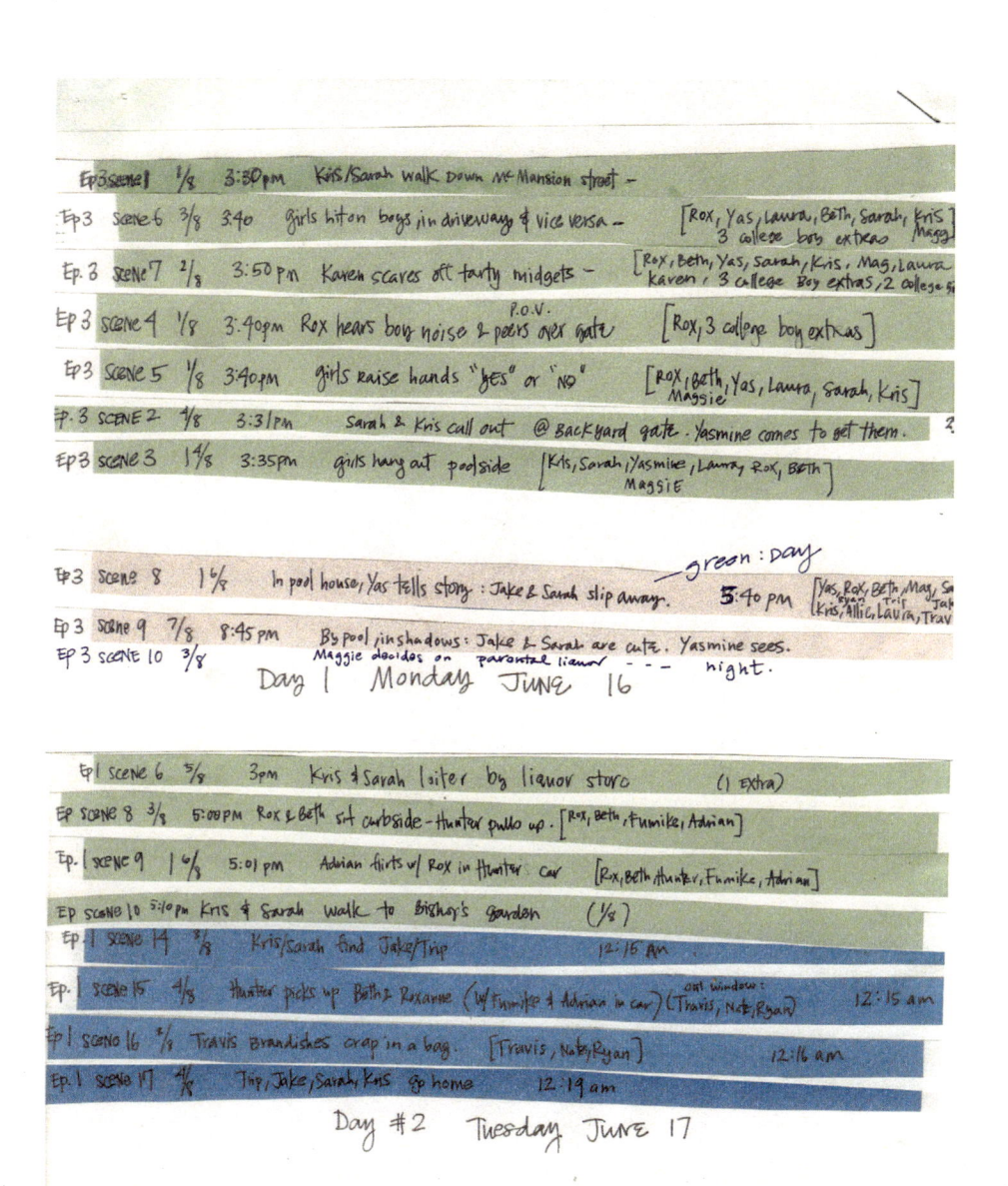

Figure 4.5 Examples of production strip board from *Orange Juice in Bishop's Garden*

Note the information to put on each strip:

- Day/Night/Dawn/Dusk

- Exterior or Interior

- Scene number

- Number of Pages or Page count — this is always in 1/8ths. It just is. No you don't express these in a lowest common denominator. It is 4/8ths not 1/2. It just is.

- Main Characters (e.g. not extras) — each one is denoted by a number

- Music

- Special Effects

- Special Equipment

- Animals

- Cars

- Numbers of Extras

- One-line description of scene

PRODUCTION STRIP BOARD KEY:

Green: exterior day
Blue: exterior night
White: interior day
Yellow: means interior night
Pink: exterior dusk/dawn
Black (or a flipped over strip): end of day/break between shoot days
Black followed by white followed by black: week ending

> **OTESSA'S TALES FROM THE TRENCHES**
>
> There are some fancy computer programs out there that function as production budgeting and scheduling software. (EPBudgeting and EPScheduling come to mind). There is also some great free-ware, like Celtx. But, you don't necessarily need any software at all. I am old school and tactically driven — I also find it helpful to physically have a scanned copy of my production stripboard on set. This way, if we don't "make our day"— or if we get rained out — we can immediately re-schedule on set, using the strips in my on-set notebook as a guide. You can certainly buy production strips et cetera; however, I frequently just cut up colored paper on my own from home.

Some basic principles of scheduling to consider:

1. *Schedule your exterior shots at the beginning.* You want to "shoot out" your exterior shots first. That way, if you run into inclement weather and have to postpone an exterior, you will still have days remaining in which to do so. The last thing you want is to film your interiors first, then move to exteriors at the end of your shoot — only to find that it is raining and thundering and you are stuck up a creek without a paddle, as they say.

2. *Shoot your DAY scenes first, then move to NIGHTS.*

3. *Turnaround time* — you must give your cast and crew 12 hours of "turnaround time" before you call them to set again. Turnaround time starts after their travel time. So, if you wrap at 5 p.m., you cannot call people at 5 a.m. because this doesn't grant them time to get home. You generally include one hour of travel time. So, if you wrap at 5 p.m., the soonest you can call people to set again is 6 a.m.

   Yes, you can break this, but there can be penalties to do so— not the least of which is exhausting your team — which prevents them from giving you their best. Mass sleep deprivation can really bite back.

4. *Do difficult scenes toward the beginning of your shoot (say, a scene with lots of extras).* This way it's out of the way early: people have lots of

energy at the beginning; and you'll need that energy for a demanding scene with lots of moving parts.

5. *Now, as for romance scenes, there are generally two differing schools of thought*:

    1). Do it in the beginning and just get it over with — use any awkwardness of your actors not quite knowing each other yet to its advantage, in that they get to know each other quite quickly.

    2). Do the scene later — in effect waiting until the actors have sufficiently gotten to know each other.

    Typically, if it is a first-time love scene (e.g. neither the actors nor the characters have been together before), then I will schedule the scene early. Any awkwardness or lack of being completely physically acclimated to each other fits both the story, the characters, and the actors. It just makes sense.

    However, if it's supposed to be a scene where the characters really know each other and have a longstanding rapport, (but the actors do not yet) then I will generally wait until I feel the cast has that rapport with each other. It should look completely natural and being acclimated to each other's mannerisms et cetera is a part of that. Although ideally, if you do your work in pre-production, your cast should be ready as soon as Day 1.

6. *Sometimes you will only have access to a location or some type of resource for a limited amount of time — say one day.* In these instances, you will have to use the above principles, while also scheduling around this limitation.

7. *Ideally, your cast members will be completely available. However, they may not be.* In these instances, you will have to schedule around them, while also seeking to maintain balance with the principles of scheduling. Especially if you are just starting out with your show, make sure you don't leave it dead in the water before you've even begun by attaching cast members whose lack of availability would

be debilitating to your shoot. Also, (especially for later seasons of an ongoing show) many consider the availability of their cast of characters and use that knowledge to inform their writing process. It can circumvent scheduling disasters and can be especially useful in a field where we do not generally have the luxury of five year contracts. There is no guarantee that if you write it they will come.

8. *Consider the complexity of your shooting style and how it affects the number of pages you can shoot in a day— typically called a page count.* In a classic television show on broadcast network, they are often shooting up to eight pages a day. Keep in mind they have full union crews with highly experienced professionals. Don't feel bad if you cannot necessarily shoot that many pages. By contrast, in feature films that include very complex scenes, they may only shoot two pages a day. Have a vlog, cooking or reality show? You may be able to shoot many pages in a day. However, you will have more content to go through, which means many days in the editing room, finding the best shots and cutting everything together.

Once you have compiled your all elements and have scheduled around them, it is time to do more planning…

SHOT LISTS

You must conceive of your shot list. But you can make it easier by breaking your story down scene by scene. It helps to start on a smaller scale. If possible, meet with your cinematographer to talk about which shots you need by going through the script and breakdowns. Go scene by scene and decide what is actually necessary to shoot. What do you need to see in each scene? They will give you ideas and insights. However, also be prepared that on a shoestring production, your DP/cinematographer may not have the time or ability to hold your hand in this way. So be prepared. Have your own strong artistic vision and creative plan. You may well have to come up with you shots and lighting schemes on your own, and then meet to discuss with your key team members afterwards, once things are more "gelled" in the mold. Especially if people are donating their time, they may not be able to give you all the time in the world, so be considerate and be prepared for this.

When creating your shot list make sure you have a wide variety of shot types. You don't want the viewer to get bored. Also, make sure that the shots properly express the moment and feel of each beat of the script. And, of course, number your scenes accordingly. Each scene will have various set-ups. So for scene one, you will have shots 1A, 1B, and so forth.

And if you need a refresher on the basics, see **"Shot Lists" on page 41▶**

Figure 4.6 Example of the shot list from a scene in what later became Season 3, Episode 3 of *Orange Juice in Bishop's Garden*, "Escape to Candyland"

STORYBOARDS

Choose whether or not you want to make storyboards. You could just do simple stick figures on index cards or do something really nice. Or use reference pictures from something else you admire. It's more of a reference to get you on the same page, so they can give ideas on camera movements, lighting textures, etc. The visual component of the storyboard can certainly help ensure you have a wide variety of shot types. They can also help get your ideas across to visual learners. Not everyone processes information in the same way, and sometimes a picture can be worth those thousand words.

FLOORPLANS

The floorplan is another visual tool that allows your team to understand your shots and cinematographic style. It is a bird's-eye-view of your location, with stylized and standardized drawings that reflect where the camera is, how it moves, where your actors are, and how they move.

Figure 4.7   Example of floor plan from *Orange Juice in Bishop's Garden*

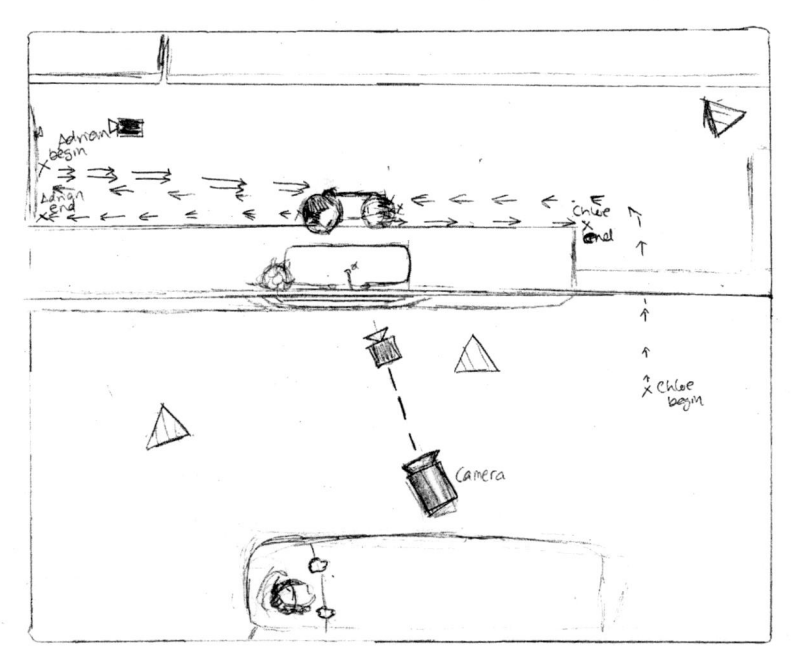

INSURANCE AND PERMITS

(Because clearly you do not have nearly enough paperwork already.)

As tempting as it may be to curb time and costs by forgoing insurance and proper permits… DON'T do it. It's just a silly and stupid thing to do. You need insurance because otherwise you don't have a safety net. No one reputable will rent to you. And what happens if your equipment breaks? What do you do if someone is hurt and you do not have workers' compensation? Ohh, and you want to obtain location permits without insurance? Forget it; it's not possible.

Okay, so you get the picture. Insurance takes a bite out of your budget, but it is essential. With it, you can protect your team, yourself, your equipment, your props, your locations…virtually everything. But where do you find that insurance? A reputable company that will underwrite your production insurance is the Film Emporium. A short search online can help you find other options as needed. But be certain to compare prices and check reputations.

In addition to buying insurance, it's also important to have the proper location permits. Before obtaining permits right away, consider the different extremes of permit applications' processes. Not all states and counties have the same fees or processes. Some permit applications will be easy to fill out, and the permits may be free. Other areas may have inexorable application processes and expensive daily permits **(Figure 4.8)**. Figure out which are the most user-friendly for your needs. It may be that a slightly longer drive to a location is actually worth it in the long run.

Also, don't forget to think about the fact that, frequently, with your location permits, you receive parking for productions vehicles and picture cars. On set time is money, and unnecessary parking moves and feeding meters will cut into your artistic process and work flow. You don't want to be moving cars when you should be making art. And you don't want to be wasting any of your budget on parking tickets.

Yes, we all do run-and-gun footage on occasion, but that should be the exception to the rule, not the norm. When going the "run-and-gun" route though, always be prepared with a cover set, in case you get kicked out of

Planning and Scheduling 89

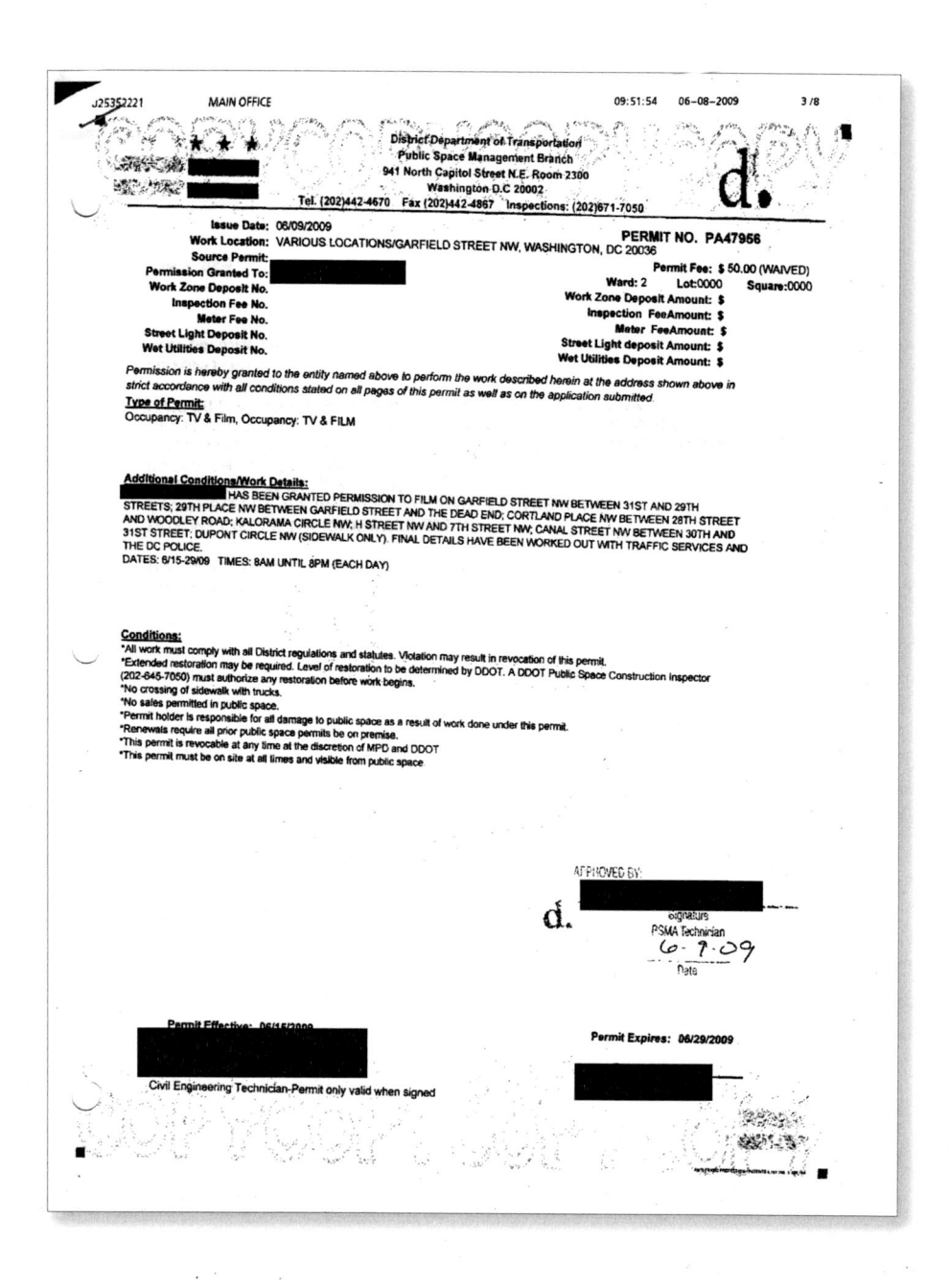

Figure 4.8 Example of Washington, DC Office of Motion Picture and Television Development film permit

your first location.

THE CALLSHEET

(You've made it...you are finally ready to start filming...and guess what? There's more paperwork.)

The callsheet will be part of the skeleton supporting your on-set experience. It's the life-line to your day. It should include sunrise, sunset, weather report, location directions, nearest hospitals, nearest restrooms, the scenes that will be shot that day, the one-line description of the scenes, the cast members needed (with their needed arrival times), the crew needed (with each of their arrival times), the list of who is whom for the day's cast and crew, and a list of on-site contact numbers.

You may also want to consider the expediency of including the list of props needed for the day (and perhaps a photograph of the assembled items) and pictures of what each person's wardrobe will look like. This is an extra step, and this is information that will already be on your breakdown; however, in the world of indie and low-budget, "belts and braces" can be a lifesaving model.

The callsheet is something that will be shared with everyone on set. It is a somewhat pared down version of information that represents the least common denominator of logistics and of salient information.

It is also advisable to create a shared Google map with your locations, to prevent people from getting lost **(Figure 4.9)**.

In addition to the callsheet, there is also the on-set Bible, which includes ALL pertinent information by day and also should include some information from the callsheets (e.g. nearest restrooms and hospitals). This is NOT shared with everyone and is instead an above the line and departmental head resource. It should always be with you on set.

Figure 4.9 Example of callsheet from Season 5 of *Orange Juice in Bishop's Garden*

Orange Juice in Bishop's Garden   Season 5 Call Sheet
                                         Thursday, July 7, 2011

Call Time	Cast or Crew	People		Location
7:00 a.m.	Crew	Otessa Ashley Jorge Dylan	Crystal Lis Cheyenne Emily	▮▮▮▮▮
8:30 a.m.	Crew	Bim Drew	Connor	Awakening Sculpture
8:30 a.m.	Cast	Nick DeAndre	George	Awakening Sculpture
1:30 p.m.	Cast	Ellen	Rachel	41st & Belt
3:15 p.m.	Cast	Shawn Nick	Sam Otessa	Watermelon House

Location/shooting List
1. Awakening Sculpture- Ep. 10 Sc. 3
2. Car (on ride from Awakening Sculpture) - Ep. 10, Sc. 4
3. 41st & Belt- Ep. 9, Sc. 1
4. Comet Ping Pong- Ep. 11, Sc. 4
5. Watermelon House Alley- Ep. 9, Sc. 4
6. 20/20 Productions- Ep. 9, Sc. 6

Scene Information

Start Time	Episode/Scene	Description	Cast
8:30 am	Ep. 10, Sc. 3 (2/8 pg)	Ryan & Drew wake Adrian up	Adrian, Ryan, Drew
10:00 am	Ep. 10, Sc. 4 (7/8 pg)	Ryan & Drew give Adrian "tough love" speech	Adrian, Ryan, Drew
1:30 pm	Ep. 9, Sc. 1	EST of girls sing & tell Chloe to dump Adrian	Sarah, Alex
1:30 p.m. (B-cam)	Ep. 11, Sc. 4	EST Comet Ping Pong	n/a
3:15 p.m.	Ep. 9, Sc. 4 (5/8 pg)	Sailor & Adrian pick up mystery power, accost Stranger	Adrian, Gordon, Stranger, Dealer
7:00 am	Ep. 9, Sc. 6 (1/8 pg)	Adrian bleeds w/ broken glass, fleas	Adrian

Orange Juice in Bishop's Garden   Season 5 Call Sheet
                                                    Thursday, July 7, 2011

Episode 10 Scene 3- Jeans on both, RYAN: brown stripe sweater w/ green grateful dead t-shirt. DREW: grey t-shirt w/ orange Orioles jersey. ADRIAN: white sailor hat, crackerjack uniform
Episode 10 Scene 4- Same as Scene 4
Episode 9 Scene 1- SARAH: green henley cardigan, ripped bellbottoms, hippypatchwork tanktop, converse (from pile of converses), ALEX: rio brazil shirt, tyedye slip dress, CASANDRA: pot shirt, blue cordoroy bellbottoms, converse
Episode 9 Scene 4- GORDON and ADRIAN: sailor uniforms and crackerjack hats, DEALER: orange corduroy high waters, blue work shirt, whatever shoes
Episode 9 Scene 6- ADRIAN: white sailor hat, crackerjack uniform

DIRECTIONS
20/20 Productions

Awakening Sculpture (149 Waterfront St., Oxon Hill, MD)
NH1 bus from Branch Ave. Metro Station
Some Parking available, mostly in garages.

Nearest Bathroom:
Fleet St. Garage, one block away (Fleet St. & American Way)

41st St. NW & Belt Rd. NW (Near Dancing Crab: 4615 Wisconsin Ave. NW)
From Tenleytown-AU Metro Station on the Red Line
Exit station, Wisconsin ave. is right behind the escalators
Turn right and walk up Wisconsin
41st & Belt is 2 blocks up on the right.

Nearest Bathroom:
Dancing Crab

Watermelon House (1108 Q St. NW)
From Shaw-Howard University Metro on the Green or Yellow Line
Exit station using 7TH ST NW & R ST NW exit
Walk a short distance S on 7th St NW
Turn right on Rhode Island Ave NW
Walk approx. 3 blocks SW on Rhode Island Ave NW
Turn right on Q St NW
Walk a short distance NW on Q St NW

Nearest Bathrooms:
Starbucks or Whole Foods on 15th & P

Orange Juice in Bishop's Garden

Season 5 Call Sheet
Thursday, July 7, 2011

On-set Phone: ███████████ UPM)

Additional Information
Breakfast: Ready to eat at call times indicated
Lunch: 2:30 pm- 3:15 pm
Day: 9 of 10
Weather: High 93 degrees. Low 72 degrees. Partial cloudiness early, with scattered showers & thunderstorms in the afternoon. A few storms may be severe. Winds light & variable. Chance of rain 50%.
wear sunscreen, dress appropriately for hot weather (light colors), wear comfortable, practical shoes
Sunrise: 5:50 a.m.
Sunset: 8:36 p.m.

Crew Directory

Title	Name	Phone	Email
Director/Producer	Ote█		
UPM/PC	Ash█		
1st AD/Sound	Jorg█		
2nd AD	Dyl█		
2nd AD	Crys█		
DP	Bim█		
1st AC	Dre█		
Gaffer/Key Grip	Con█		
Production Designer	Lis█		
Art Director	Che█		

Chapter Five
MONEY, BUDGET ALLOCATION, AND (CROWD) FUNDING

Congratulations! You've just been awarded $10,000 for reading this sentence. Umm, not quite — if only it were that easy. Although fundraising can be an arduous quest in and of itself, there are several avenues and opportunities you can explore, namely crowdfunding.

But before you even think about how to raise money, it's imperative that you figure out how much you really need. In other words, you need to establish your budget; ideally, you don't want to spend money you don't have. While some artists have successfully launched careers by maxing out their credit cards, many, many more have plummeted into irreversible debt. Consider that your first work, or works, may well be little more than a calling card, and what business card is worth several thousand dollars? Especially in the beginning when you are honing your craft, you are apt to make mistakes, so make the mistakes cheaply. And spend the big bucks when you feel confident that you have fully mastered your craft.

Don't Reinvent the Wheel

Use all the resources that you already have at your disposal and that are already in your wheelhouse. As mentioned in the Resources chapter, do some personal inventory. Your locations, equipment, software, cast, and crew may all be right around you, and free; you just don't realize it yet.

Be Realistic

When coming up with your budget, consider the following. Look at what your story is and determine its specific budgetary needs. The costs and needs of a period piece are going to be wildly divergent from a comedy.

Comedies are so much more performance driven that audiences tend to be forgiving if other elements are sloppy or somewhat gritty or even cheap. But a period piece will absolutely require a visually immersive and totally believable world. Similarly, a documentary will have markedly different needs from a sci-fi/fantasy piece. How much things cost and where the money goes, depend 100% on what type of story you have and what type of story you are trying to tell.

Think about your favorite films and shows. What do you love about them? Is it the genre, the locations, or the shooting style? Do you want to emulate *Ben Hur* or *My Dinner with Andre*? And what best serves the story? *My Dinner with Andre* would hardly benefit from 200+ extras. Now is the time to strategize and to decide.

Create a living budget that is changing at all times. It can be tempting to look at the budget numbers and want to raise them, but resist that temptation. You must first ask if your script is realistic. Can it work with the resources you have?

Don't Overlook

- Remember to think about food. In many cases, food can even be more important than equipment. Read over the Craft Services section in the Rounding Up Your Resources chapter for more information about planning and the costs involved with feeding your small army. Revisit your food budget if your shooting schedule changes over time. Keep in mind that the number of people on set will vary from one day to another and so will your food costs. On the days you are using specialized equipment, or doing more complicated scenes with many moving parts, you may need a full crew.

- Don't forget to include parking permits and insurance costs,

See more on that in "Planning and Scheduling" on page 73 ▶.

- How much equipment will you need? Props? Other resources? How much can you "beg or borrow" and how much will you need to rent? Be vigilant in doing you price-checks. Compare and contrast various

Money, Budget Allocation, and (Crowd) Funding

stores, websites, etc… to find the most budget-friendly solutions.

- What about your actors? Will they be volunteering their time or will you be paying them? And your crew? What are their rates? These decisions will greatly affect the budget.

- Continuously revisit your budget. For example, when scouting locations, decide if you can do more in that location than you expected. Don't lock the budget, but always stay realistic. Money can shift around to different areas. Also, some crew members might bring their own kits and materials— like a makeup artist might bring in makeup, but you still need to pay to replace things like that, which are going to be used up during the shoot. Also, talk to your crew about how to get good deals and the importance of them.

Don't Panic

- If you come out over your limit, consider ways to cut costs. Can you change the locations to more budget-friendly ones? Could you borrow your best friend's spare bedroom and use it as a set? Consider re-dressing sets to make a "new" room. This can be done multiple times with only small changes like changing the dressing on the walls. Re-purpose the spaces that are free and easy.

- Can you rent your most expensive equipment over the weekend when the rates are less and adjust your shooting schedule accordingly? Do you really need that steadicam? Can you edit the script to eliminate a scene and incorporate the ideas into another? Remember that locations, equipments, days, and pages all equal money. Your money.

- How will you be shooting and for how many days? Will you be filming one episode at a time or the whole series at once? It is almost always more budget-friendly to shoot in a non-linear, or discontinuous format. This is why feature films are shot that way. But doing one episode at a time may be what you can afford. You will have to compose your very own cost/benefit analysis, to determine what can stay and what can go.

> **OTESSA'S TALES FROM THE TRENCHES**
> **The Interminable Progression to Interior Kitchen Day**
>
> Last but not least, don't overdo it, but don't underwhelm it either. Beware of the "The Interminable Progression to Interior Kitchen Day". By which I mean, be careful not to minimize and cut back too far. Scripts have a tendency to start large and grandiose, a la —
>
> ```
> EXT. MAGIC HOUR — ON THE SURFACE OF MARS
> ```
>
> ...and the pressure of production and funding can easily turn this into —
>
> ```
> INT. DAY - KITCHEN.
> ```
>
> Just be careful that you don't downsize too much. Spend the money where it is needed. And make sure that as much of it as possible is "coming through the screen" - by which I mean it is appreciated as production value by your viewer.

Here is an example of a budget sheet (**Figure 5.1**). It may just be your new best friend. It "pays" to build a proper budget.

Exercise: Taking Cecil B. DeMille's *The Ten Commandments* as a reference point, reconsider the classic scene where Moses descends from the mountain with the tablets. How would you make this scene work on a shoestring budget? Remember, it still has to be powerful, visceral, and compelling. What elements can you focus on that would benefit the story, and yet transcend the budgetary limitations? Now, draft a preliminary budget for this scene.

Exercise: Take Season 5, Episode 1 of OJBG "Summer of '97" as a reference point. WATCH HERE. This scene was filmed with a five person cast and crew over three hours, mostly using a cheap HD FlipCam. How would you re-work this mermaid scene to accommodate for a much larger budget? Justify each cost increase and then build a budget sheet to reflect these changes.

Budget Sheet

Date:		
Title:		
Est. No. of Days:		

Acct. No.	Category	Total
1	Script	$0.00
2	Producers	$0.00
3	Direction	$0.00
4	Cast	$0.00
5		
	Total Above-the-Line	$0.00
6	Production Staff	$0.00
7	Production Design	$0.00
8	Wardrobe	$0.00
9	Hair/Make-Up	$0.00
10	Set Operations	$0.00
11	Electrical	$0.00
12	Camera	$0.00
13	Sound	$0.00
14	Transportation	$0.00
15	Location Expenses	$0.00
16	Craft services	$0.00
	Total Production	$0.00
17	Editing	$0.00
18	Music	$0.00
19	Post Sound	$0.00
20	Titles/Graphics	$0.00
	Total Post Production	$0.00
21	Insurance	$0.00
22	Permits	$0.00
23	General/Administration	$0.00
	Total Other	$0.00
	Contingency: 10%	$0.00
	Grand Total	$0.00

Figure 5.1   Sample budget sheet

Now that you have a better idea on how to organize a budget, you're able to compose a better picture of how much money you're going to need to raise. And because money doesn't grow on trees, a good fundraising option to consider is crowdfunding, or collaborative funding online. The beauty of crowdfunding is in its simplicity. Almost anyone can raise a few bucks online, but, nonetheless, there are some best practices to follow, if you really want to bring home the bacon.

> **OTESSA'S TALES FROM THE TRENCHES**
> **Losing a Location**
>
> When filming Season 5 of *OJBG*, we lost "the Barn", a location that was planned for multiple episodes and was integral to many storylines. The original space had an amazing, decrepit boat—that was especially perfect for a scene in the episode "Trial Expired". Unfortunately, when the barn went, the boat went.
>
> I loved the idea of the characters being cast adrift, literally, and yet, stymied and stuck, literally. What I told my AD (Jorge) and production designer (my mother, Lis) was: "I don't care where we film this now, just please GET ME A BOAT! Jorge, bless him, donated the use of his home. Then, he collected and borrowed a kayak from his childhood friend and then-roommate. My mom sourced/borrowed/bartered some life preservers and floaties, and... The scene was saved.
>
> You don't have to throw money at problems to make them go away. You can find inexpensive solutions to problems. And you can even like the solution! It doesn't have to be a horrible "sloppy second". It can be an inspired choice made during a time of hardship. Things fall apart. Don't lose your head: use your head. You will need it to problem solve.

CROWDFUNDING

The two biggest platforms for crowdfunding right now are Indiegogo and Kickstarter. The great thing about Indiegogo is, if you don't meet your fundraising goal, you still get some money back, which is always nice! Kickstarter, on the other hand, requires you to fulfill your fundraising goal in order for you to receive any money. They each have their advantages and disadvantages, though, so do your research in deciding which one is best for you!

Next up: how much money should you ask for? What's a realistic amount? You do see people making hundreds of thousands of dollars using crowdfunding, and they make it look easy. But don't be fooled! It's a lot of work! Keep your goal reasonable. You can make a web series for well under $10,000. If you keep your goal within the few thousand range, people will probably be more attracted to actually invest in your project because they think that you can actually get all the funding you need. In the end, the goal with crowdfunding isn't necessarily about raising a lot of money as much as it is about building the awareness for your project and about gaining lots of backers who are invested in it. If you build the awareness, then the money will come.

Case Study: StarForge

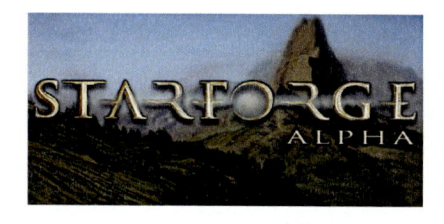

CodeHatch was started in 2012, in Edmonton, Canada, as a small start-up company, with the goal of creating gamer-friendly and gamer-centric content. Their first title, StarForge, was their maiden voyage video game product.

Combining elements from popular games like Halo and Minecraft, StarForge was a runaway success. It almost doubled its fundraising goal. It raised *awareness*, with ripples being felt throughout the gaming community. And their campaign built an army of nearly 5,000 eager alpha and beta testers![1] (Image Source: www.starforge.com)

Watch StarForge's campaign video: http://youtu.be/OSmlrPcXumc

---

1   "Indiegogo's Top 12 Campaigns of 2012," Indiegogo, http://blog.indiegogo.com/2012/12/top12.html

> **CASE STUDY: KAREN - THE BUS MONITOR - H KLEIN**
>
> After a video of Karen, a bus monitor in Greece, NY, being bullied by students went viral, a man who had never even met Karen rallied the support of tens of thousands of people around the world to support her. With $703,123 contributed, they didn't just raise enough for a vacation — but also for a great retirement.[1]
>
> A true mark of success is about more than just the money: it's also about the backers. This campaign garnered 32,251 backers—it wasn't just one person throwing a giant chunk of change their way. This is the beauty of working with crowdfunding services: you are building a caring, concerned community. This, in the end, can be more valuable than just having one giant company backing you.
>
> **View the campaign page:** http://igg.me/p/124322
>
> ---
>
> [1] "Indiegogo's Top 12 Campaigns of 2012," IndieGoGo, http://blog.indiegogo.com/2012/12/top12.html

The best way to make this work would be to have a teaser—something to serve as an example to the public about what you have in mind for your project. This could be a pilot, a trailer, a PowerPoint presentation, or even a personalized video from you, describing your passion and your goal. But it's not enough to just post it. You need to make it personal. You need to tell people *why* it's important to you. If you want more insight into good practices or tactics, consult the platform. Indiegogo has a blog and Kickstarter has a "school" that give you tips on how to build a successful campaign on their platforms. However, remember that these crowdfunding platforms for all types of projects. But don't worry; here are some tips for you, as a digital artist and filmmaker, specifically. For, say, a web series, you need to make your campaign fun or interesting. Make it something that reaches out directly to your audience and conveys why your project needs to be made and where their money will go.

How long should you have your crowdfunding campaign last? A month or two at most. Make a good outreach plan so that you're not annoying people, but are instead consistently messaging them to give them updates on the project and its progress toward reaching your fundraising goal. And, for some more tips, read on!

Without further ado, here are some crowdfunding suggestions. And if you crave some more help, do check out the primary sources of Indiegogo's blog[1] and Kickstarter's "school"[2].

Getting Started

- Choose the host site on which you're going to launch your campaign. Some good ones: Kickstarter, Indiegogo, RocketHub, Quirky
- In addition to how much you want to raise, you also need to know your campaign's time frame, before you launch it.
- Do you want to go the fixed or flexible funding route? If you're fine with collecting any amount, choose flexible because then if you raise more, terrific, you get it all. But, if you're relying on a set amount, opt for fixed.

Tell Your Story

- When things are personal, people feel more invested. And make sure to include a video.
- Be relatable in your video; do NOT beg or be a downer.
- Bring on some team members to widen your audience.

Include Perks

- Make them personal to spice up your campaign.
- Set a time frame or limit the quantity to up their demand.
- Don't be afraid to offer perks set at low dollar amounts.
- Follow through with your perks and actually send them.

Share Your Campaign

- Even before you launch it, you can start spreading the word.

---

1 Indiegogo Blog, Indiegogo Inc., http://blog.indiegogo.com/
2 "Kickstarter School," Kickstarter, Inc., http://www.kickstarter.com/help/school

- Don't neglect your inner circle.
- Make sure to keep people updated; give progress reports; include pictures and special images.

After the Campaign

- Thank your contributors.
- Consider continuing to keep your contributors in the loop with your project.
- Launch a follow-up campaign.

Overall, a good crowdfunding campaign will create an EXPERIENCE for its viewers through continual personal engagement. Make it something that a dentist would want to be a part of; make it something that seems cool; make it something people want to talk about at cocktail parties — that is what will make people more inclined to give you money.

If you're going to be seeking money outside of crowdfunding, consider that you can find potential funders and pique their interests through various social media platforms. But to do this, remember that you need a bang-up electronic press kit, or EPK.

For more information about EPKs, see "Best Practices for Your EPK and The Literary Pitch" on page 297 ▶

So there you have it, folks — our two cents on everything related to the scary dollar sign.

Chapter Six
READY, SET, GO

Getting Set-Ready and the On-Set Experience

You've done all the advance prep, and that's great — but in the high-pressure environment on on-set, you can quickly lose your grip on your project, despite all the best laid plans. The on-set pressure cooker can tear your team apart, or it can bring you all together most gloriously. Read through; learn to rally; and take heart.

TIPS, TRICKS, AND TOOLS OF THE TRADE

1. Always have your "On Set Kit" on hand. The kit should include copies of all the key papers and forms you will need with you.

    Find examples in "Important Documents" on pag321 ▶

2. It is important that people sign their paperwork and releases and, if they have not, make it mandatory. Make the paperwork a prerequisite before they can start their scenes or work with their departments.

3. Callsheets: they are a requisite, not a suggestion. Make sure they are clear, concise, and up-to-date. Make sure your AD (or whoever ends up creating them) knows exactly what s/he is doing. The callsheet ensures that everyone makes it to the right place at the right time — every time. A sloppy callsheet leads to catastrophe. It means you lose time, money, and opportunity. A bad callsheet can torpedo all your careful pre-production planning. Simply put, don't screw the pooch.

    For a refresher, see "The Callsheet" on page 90 ▶

4. Print out copies of the daily callsheet to have on hand on set. Even in this day and age of smart phones and data plans, you never know when these might fail you. So include the call sheets with the contact lists, etc., so people know whom to call in the event of an emergency and have the who/where/why/how information at their fingertips.

5. Consider having information on hand that is not necessarily on the callsheet — say, including contacts for vendors, food, locations, et cetera. Not everyone who receives the callsheet should have or need all those peoples' personal information, but you should still have that additional information at your fingertips. (E.g. Don't give out the location owner's personal cell phone to the entire cast and crew... However, in the event of need, make sure it is readily available for those in a bind.)

6. Getting there and away — determine and discuss transportation, to prevent onset issues. Figure out carpooling if necessary and include information on public transportation. Make sure to consider start-time and end-time for your day — will public transportation be open at those hours? If not, then find a plan B for those reliant on it. Also, (especially if you have minors), consider that walking alone at night can be an unnecessary risk. Make sure you have a system in place that is safe.

TALES FROM THE TRENCHES

On *OJBG* Season 1, there were several night shoots. Many of which were in parks, which while lovely and bucolic during the day, were sparsely-lit and somewhat scary at night. During such night shoots, adult crew-members would walk the minors (or anyone else) to their cars or to their subway station. It is never advisable to have your team members feel unsafe or ill at ease. Your working environment should be a sacred space. Walking people in a buddy system or en masse from a darkened park to their transportation instilled a sense of safety, and it also made people know that they and their well-being were valued.

From a logical standpoint, it's necessary to consider transportation. It may seem like the finer details of transport for your cast and crew are not your problem, but they will be your problem if someone shows up to set late. Losing time affects your entire day of shooting — and as such it should be stringently avoided and prevented. Transportation and time snafus can bury your whole project, and you must consider that someone being 15 minutes late is not merely a loss of 15 minutes. Take that 15 minutes and multiply it by the total number of your crew — that is how much time you just lost. Every minute matters, so get involved. Assist in coordinating ride-shares, if necessary; distribute maps; be sure that all of your occupants and gear can successfully fit in the number of cars that you have, and so on.

7. It is important to make good use of rehearsals and also to use cast downtime on set to continue rehearsing and running lines.

> **OTESSA'S TALES FROM THE TRENCHES**
> **Acting Excercises**
>
> My favorite, fun exercise is the "Private Moment." It has ties to Stanislavski, Strasberg, and Meisner, but remains useful to actors across the board. The exercise hangs around a simple idea: what does your character do when s/he is alone in his or her room? The private moment exercise should be something private, something not shared, and something that if another person were to walk in upon, you would immediately and unthinkingly stop doing.
>
> I love this exercise because it allows a character to become something with a life outside the screen — to become a fully fleshed out being who literally bleeds past the page and past the screen. It can also unlock moments and opportunities between your other actors and can act as an icebreaker for those who may not have worked together prior. In particular, it is important to remember that acting is not talking. And while knowing one's lines is great, running lines to death can create a stilted scene where actors are merely talking at each other by rote, instead of listening and interacting in the moment. The "Private Moment" exercise helps keep that misfortune at bay. It is a way to think about the scene, the character, the world, without running it into the ground.

See **"Forms, Paperwork, and Important Documents" on page 321 for more examples of acting exercises** ▶

8. And, also, use the rare crew downtime as a chance to prep for future scenes, to organize props, and to tackle/practice difficult and upcoming technical or production moves.

TALES FROM THE TRENCHES
Utilizing Down-Time

Set designing for the rave scenes in *OJBG* was challenging, but the results were worth it. The second rave scene (from Season 3, Episode 4) was shot in the same small, white room, but with totally different dressing. Because we were borrowing the space, we could not mar the walls. This room was also scheduled to be used first as Davis's TV room, so we had a miniscule turn-around time. Because the ceiling would not be visible in the "TV room" shots, we installed the ceiling's wire grid (upon which we hung the umbrellas) beforehand, using picture frame wire and brads nailed into the top of the window frames. We temporarily installed half a dozen umbrellas to see if the framework would hold (which it did) and then removed them until the other scenes were shot, leaving the grid in place.

Building, testing, and installing the grid is something we were able to do on set, but in advance of the scenes, during some down-time. It kept us focused and meant that we were better prepared when the time came.

Basically, just keep in mind that all time can be productive. Especially under grueling circumstances, it can be good to keep people's minds off, say, how hot it is, how rainy it is, or how uncomfortable they may be. You can and should use this principle to prevent people's minds from fixating on immediate problems or discomfort. This is basically what summer camp counselors do, but hey, it works.

9. Make people feel appreciated part one. Keep track of your cast and crew members' birthdays. If any birthdays fall during your shoot, celebrate! It keeps up morale and makes people feel special, which they should on "their day."

10. Make people feel appreciated part two. Allow people to be and to feel involved with the social media and marketing. Make people feel special and inspire them to help and contribute. Also, consider that if you guide them and encourage them in these practices, you are also helping to control the publicity and image of your own work, which is perhaps better than trusting the Facebook gods and letting your cast and crew go rogue.

> #### How to Do Social Media On-Set
>
> During your shoot, it will be important to get the word out about your series and to update your fans about what is going on on set. Using social media is a fun way to engage viewers and to promote what you're working on.

Come up with your preferred hashtags. Give people examples of language that is good to use to describe the production, their roles, etc. Give them calls to action and to engage their own followers. Actors, in particular, are social creatures, who are comfortable being in the spotlight — asking and engaging them in this way plays to their strengths, promotes your work, and promotes them as talent. And, during any downtime they have, when they may be feeling neglected or having lead-actor envy, this allows them to be center stage in a new and different arena.

Here are a few things to keep in mind:

Twitter: Have cast and crew always attach the hashtags and mention your show's Twitter handle in their tweets. Let your followers know when you are on set, where you are, and what you are doing. If something funny happens, tweet it! Try to set a hashtag trending in your area that draw attention to your production.

Facebook: Do mobile uploads! Take and post pictures of the shoot! Make status updates and tag your show's Facebook page.

Foursquare/Facebook Check-ins: Check-in to all shoot locations and tag who's with you! If you are in the office, check-in to there, too; and, if you use foursquare, have a fight to see who wins mayor.

Instagram: Assign an awesome hashtag for your project! Encourage everyone to use it whilst taking pictures on set or when doing prep work. Not only does this make the content easy to find and access, it also ensures a strong creative identity. You and your team can also check into set locations and share pictures and videos cross-platform. And, last but not least, make sure people tag your project's social media sites, you, and other cast/members. It creates a ripple of interest across every degree of separation.

11. Behind-the-Scenes and Bonus Content. This relates to #10 above, but also exists on a larger plane of influence. Grab behind-the-scenes and bonus content either in, before, or during your production. It will serve you for your real-time social media and marketing efforts. In addition, it will fill out your arsenal of tools when it comes time to release your work. And remember…

12. Even if you have to "kill your darlings" while on set, whatever is sacrificed or altered may make for awesome additional content, bonus content, or behind-the-scenes extras. For example, if something you were in love with simply does not work or must be scrapped or altered, don't consider it a lost cause. Your artistic "darling" may have a re-birth as something unexpected or extra.

13. The **RULE OF ATTRITION**: With low-budget and indie productions, things will not always go as planned. Be prepared to lose people or to have to let them go. We would always over-hire our team by a factor of 33 percent to 50 percent. Yes, that is right; we would always expect to end a shoot with a crew that was about a third to a half of the size of what we started with. Sometimes people lose focus or have little experience with being on set, or they come with romantic ideas of film being sexy and glamorous, of which it is neither. Loving movies is not the same thing as loving making them. These people will drop like flies. Also, sometimes, people will need to be let go, and you will need to have the resources and physical numbers to make those tough calls. As a corollary, just because someone starts out in one department does not mean that he or she should stay there. Reward competency. If someone is keen to climb and to be relied upon, allow him or her to be. A powerhouse PA could very well end up being one of the best costumers you have ever had.

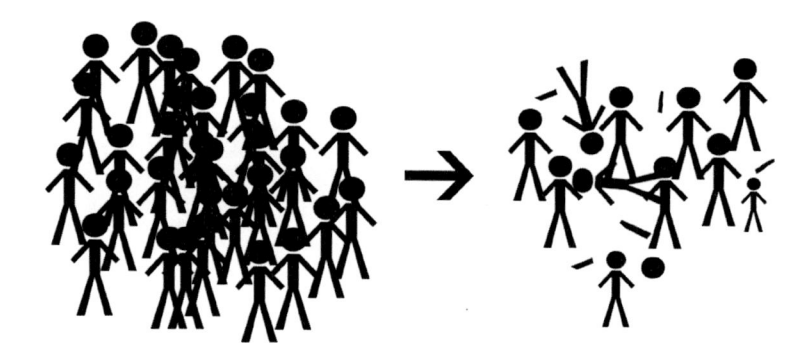

14. Putting down a camera can sometimes seem like an open invitation to trouble. While random strangers are probably unlikely to photobomb your beautiful still image photography, for whatever reason people (often the exact same people) have no qualms about walking into your shot and dropping a "Hi, Mom!" There seems to be no other term suited to describe it other than the "Jackass Factor," and apparently the moving image attracts it. So, a few pointers: lock down your set to the absolute best of your abilities. Make certain that only the proper personnel are on site. Make sure to have permits so

that you have rights over your space — these are rights that allow you to protect, reserve, and block access to certain areas and keep interlopers out.

> #### Tales From the Trenches
> #### Interlopers
>
> While shooting a scene from *OJBG* near a public parking lot located in a residential area, we were bombarded by a disgruntled woman who insisted we were breaking the law by trespassing on her property. She yelled at the crew, drove her car through the set, and completely disrupted productivity. Luckily, we had a copy of our permit for that location and were able to ease the disgruntled woman's concern enough to get through the scene. She still threatened to report us to the authorities, but having our permits handy meant her threats were meaningless and we were able to prevent the set from being shut down for an extended time.

> #### Otessa's Tales From the Trenches
>
> Other examples of interlopers — we had a FLASHER on set — it was a super late exterior night, what you might call the witching hour, and all but the skeleton crew was left. And… a flasher rolled up and, well, flashed us. Sound extreme? Unfortunately, this kind of stuff may well happen to you. And, as such, I would like to say this is how you deal with flashers (and others of this sort). People like this are keen to make others feel uncomfortable, to make them cringe, to feel powerless and speechless. SO turn the tables on them. Make a scene. I started yelling at the top of my lungs, asking all the adult neighbors to wake up, open their windows — and asking if, please, did people recognize this guy because they should make sure they keep their kids and others away from him and make sure they can pick him out of a line-up. Everyone woke up, looked out at the street, and this aggressor instead became a guy who was quite literally caught with his pants down. …Caught by his neighbors, because it turned out he actually lived on that street. Anywho, he zipped up, and made a quick escape through his front door. And we made a report to the police.

15. Strategize where you put your food and your equipment. Corralling people is going to be difficult, so make sure that you are not at cross purposes. Don't put craft service too close to where you will be filming (duh, because it might get loud). And don't stage your equipment too far away (duh, because it's heavy), and don't put your food and your equipment in intersecting "flight paths" because it just creates unnecessary traffic jams and confusion.

    Also, think about protection and containment. If you're outside and you need to stage equipment for use for the next shot or for the turnaround, make certain the equipment is SAFE. It should be locked up or guarded. And, if you have it guarded, make sure whoever watches over the gear actually has the means to protect it.

> **TALES FROM THE TRENCHES**
>
> On set of *OJBG* season 1, someone who was most likely under the influence of hard drugs approached our staging area. We had our gear for the next scene there, and (in theory) a few people were watching over it and prepping for the next scene. Unfortunately, all but one of the watchers developed a hankering for chips at the exact same moment, leaving just one person all by his lonesome with the gear. Yes, that's right, it was night, outside on the street, and there was some expensive gear watched over by only one person. Meanwhile, there was an interloper who had been lurking on the edges of the scene. The interloper had very carefully picked his moment to make a run on the gear. Fortunately, myself and another PA saw this person approaching, and we were able to call over several people to bulk up and protect our little pile of gear. The interloper suddenly stopped his run on the gear, pretended he suddenly had something to do in another area, and left. We then called the police because, quite frankly, the guy was trouble with a capital T.

16. Not only do you need to guard your gear/belongings/wardrobe/props/etc. from outsiders, you also should guard them from any internal issues. Make certain that the people who have access to elements are those who should; keep access restricted according to need, specialty, department, and knowledge. It's difficult to keep track

of things, and items can easily become lost, misplaced, or even stolen. Yes, stolen. Sometimes people have sticky fingers and may simply be too tempted if a five-finger discount is too easy. Don't tempt people. Keep it organized. This will be easier, or more logistically possible, with some elements than it will with others. Equipment can generally be more safely sequestered by department. There really is no need for outside departments or extraneous people to handle the gear. However, other things, like wardrobe and props, can be more difficult to manage (as they are inherently handled by more than just the Production & Costume Department from which they hail). Therefor, mark, label, bag, and tag your wardrobe (and props, etc.) carefully. To mitigate these issues, consider bagging and tagging by character, by scene, and by shoot day. Don't simply lump all the wardrobe and props together according to scene, episode, or character. Let your breakdown and schedule guide your efforts and use them as your informational backbone for bagging and tagging. This way you can grab your bins/bags/garment racks accordingly, without being bogged down by extraneous elements, and without having to sort and organize on set. As an example, you can physically hand actors a bag with the various components of their wardrobe and ask them to get changed for their scene. Perhaps their wardrobe for a scene consists of multiple different garments/pieces: you can write the number of items and descriptive information on the bag, include a checklist within, or keep a separate list. Either way, when they change out of their wardrobe and hand back their bags, you can run through the checklist to make certain that all elements are present and accounted for.

17. Also, where is your make-up/wardrobe room? You don't want noise pollution from this place, either. And you probably want a babysitter for that area. People can get distracted very easily, and having a babysitter can help make sure they are doing social media or running those lines.

Be certain you have a system in place so that people are brought to set on time from these places. Otherwise they will not leave the wardrobe room or will not remember to stop eating chips, and thus won't be on time when their scene is up. The second AD is specifically in charge of making sure the cast and extras are where they need to be. If you don't have a second AD, you could even have a trustworthy key PA do this. The first AD corrals the CREW. Just FYI they corral different people on set.

18. A note on staying safe: Having insurance is only part of it. You also need to follow through with your actions on set. Tape down cords. Be careful with equipment and hot lights. Make certain that the crew who touch such specialized gear are equipped with the knowledge to do so. Give your team enough time to set up gear and break things down carefully. You don't want to be rushing around, as it can be dangerous and lead to accidents. Realize that members of your cast and crew will need to start at different times according to the needs of the specific day, to the needs of the project, and to the needs of each person's specific role.

19. Walkie Talkies: you will need a system of communication, and this is a good one. Keep a walkie talkie sign-out sheet because, otherwise, you will quickly lose all your walkies.

    Find a sample of this form in "Forms, Paperwork, and Important Documents" on page 321 ▶

20. A note on power: you may not always have electrical access on set. Some of those beautiful, remote exteriors can be tricky to make work, as nature doesn't come with power outlets. You can always rent a generator, or "genny" for short; however, is this a truly necessary cost and production element for you? Whatever you decide be completely prepared accordingly. Your craft service and meal plan can work "off the grid" if need be. And what about your equipment? Does your shooting plan align with the realities of your location? If you plan on having lights, are they wired to power or can they be mounted on board to the camera? And what about your monitor? Is it power outlet reliant or is it a field monitor? Will you need to rent a field monitor for specific days?

    One last tip on the subject: it is well worth investing in an AC adapter for your car. It's inexpensive, and, with it, you can run a charging station for batteries, or a light, or a monitor, or a coffee maker off your car's battery.

21. Murphy's Law is in full effect: anything that can go wrong will go wrong. There are some things you can't plan for, like tornados and malfunctioning equipment. So plan for the unexpected by having alternative dates and considering pick-ups (getting certain shots later that you couldn't get on the day they were scheduled) or re-shoots (re-shooting problematic footage). Allow yourself (and schedule in) an extra day or two for pick-ups and re-shoots.

    For further reading, see "Planning and Scheduling" on page 73▶

22. FOOD: perhaps the single most important element of your production. It might even be more important than your camera because hungry people can halt your production in just the same way as an equipment failure.

    Two things to keep in mind: An army travels on its stomach. And hunger led to the French Revolution. Be warned.

    Don't cut costs through food. Having enough food, having healthy food, having delicious food: these are gifts that keep on giving.

    Be aware of *and keep a list* of people's food allergies and dietary concerns, to prevent any discomfort or mishaps.

    Remember the importance of variety in your meals and avoid having pizza more than once in a shoot. Lunch cannot always be sandwiches and cold-cuts. Try to serve one hot meal (unless the temperature is in the eighties or above) in a full day's shoot, preferably at dinner.

    Hydration is also a key detail that cannot be overlooked. It sounds silly, but in the heat of summer (or even if it's not summer — professional lights put off incredible amounts of heat and energy), stay hydrated. Make sure others are staying hydrated. This is a concern with serious consequences if ignored.

Doing all of this on a shoestring budget is difficult but not impossible, and it is well worth the effort.

CRAFT SERVICES

("Wait...what? I have to feed these people?")

This section may not be one of the most critical in the book, but it is important. An army travels on its stomach, and you and your cast and crew are an army. Hungry people do not work efficiently, and efficiency is critical for a successful film production. Not only that, but also a case of food poisoning can bring a production to a most unpleasant halt. So read on.

The food that you provide your cast and crew during the course of a film shoot usually falls under the craft services department. Craft service people are part of the crew. On large-scale productions, there may be a caterer who provides full meals, but for small scale productions, think of craft services as your cafeteria. Depending on your shooting schedule, you may be able to film with a minimum amount of food. Say that you are a point-and-shoot sort of filmmaker and will be filming just two or three hours each day. Well then, you can probably make do with a tray of snacks and beverages and order pizza. You can skim through this chapter. But more often, productions require more than a few hours of filming each day. Merely setting up a scene can take hours, and, with multiple takes, you can be on set for a long time. Your cast and crew need to eat a proper meal *every six hours*, and the maximum day length is a twelve hour day, so plan food accordingly. A meal should comprise a 30 minute time-out for your cast and crew. Although, in practice, since people have to go through "the line" as it were, this usually takes 45 minutes (so that the last people through still have their 30 minutes). And, never forget: the crew eats first.

You do not need much equipment to set up an organized craft services station. Purchasing a folding table is a great investment. If you use it on set every day, you will establish an eating area safely away from your expensive cameras and lights and out of earshot of your recording equipment. Plus, you can take the table with you when you shoot on location and make it your portable dining room. A few large coolers are essential, along with reusable cold packs to put inside. Add a large thermos for hot beverages and a water dispenser, and you are good to go.

Just as you need a schedule for filming, you need a meal plan for craft services. Set a budget and keep to it. Plan your meals for the entire shoot, week by week, but keep in mind that you may need to shift one day's menu for another's. The director cannot control the weather and, if it rains all day, Tuesday's outdoor shoot may need to move to Wednesday. Remember that a few of your cast or crew may be vegetarians, so be certain that your meals have a variety of balanced choices. And while you are making that menu, look online to locate the nearest food stores to each of your shooting locations; you never know when you may need to buy another bottle of ketchup to replace the one you left behind on your kitchen counter or to pick up a meal if filming runs later than expected. Purchase canned, frozen, and non-refrigerated food ahead of time and in bulk. Perishables can be purchased a couple days in advance. And, if possible, find someone to run craft services during the shoot because, let's face it, you will be far too busy to do it yourself.

Unlike casting a role in your epic, you can cast a larger net to find someone to take charge of craft services. Look outside of your film network. Think about your friends and family. Ask around. Believe it or not, many non-film people enjoy being on a film production. You don't need a gourmet chef, just someone who can cook, is well organized, has good people skills, and can pitch in as a nurse if necessary. Yes, a nurse. Film production often takes place in extreme conditions, like on days of 95 degree temperature and 80 percent humidity. Sometimes your cast or crew will be so busy that they neglect to stay hydrated or even to eat; someone needs to keep tabs on that. Who better than the person in charge of all that tasty food and beverage? If you find that golden someone, hand him or her this chapter.

Food safety is paramount and trumps both presentation and taste. You know the adage: "When in doubt, throw it out." Serve food that will not easily spoil. Keep hot food hot and cold food cold. Be certain that you have an ample supply of freezer packs inside your coolers. It possible, maintain two coolers: one for items that should be kept cold (such as meat, dairy, and egg-based products), and the other for items you want to keep cool (like beverages). This will limit the number of times that the cold food cooler needs to be opened. If your craft service table is outside, use plastic wrap (even better, use waxed paper) to ensure that flies and other vermin do not partake of your buffet. Discretely set a bottle of hand sanitizer near the paper plates. Food handling and mealtimes are some of the most prevalent opportunities for sickness to spread. And you simply cannot afford to lose the time and person-power that sickness causes.

Remember to ask about food allergies or dietary restrictions. Is anyone a vegetarian or allergic to glutens, tomatoes, or peanuts? Sometimes people are reluctant to bring up these subjects, so include them in the preliminary information sheet you send out to both cast and crew. If you discuss the issue ahead of time, you can work out a manageable solution. During one season on *OJBG*, our gaffer had a severe allergy to gluten. He actually brought his own gluten-free bread to set, and we made an effort to tone down the wheat-based food on the menu so that he always had options.

Time to talk trash. Be forewarned: food services produces a vast quantity of refuse, so keep several rolls of trash bags handy. Even if you are ecologically oriented, your cast and crew may not be. Place trash cans in an obvious location and label one for recyclable items. Put a couple of permanent markers on the craft services table and ask everyone to write his or her name on a disposable cup at the beginning of each day to cut back on the number of cups everyone uses. When out on location, ask people to help "sweep" up at the end of the day so that you leave an area as clean, if not cleaner, than when you arrived.

Now a few suggestions about actual meals. Have the craft service table ready fifteen minutes before call time to give the crew a chance to eat before they begin work. Breakfast is the most important meal of the day, so provide carbohydrates for long-lasting energy. When tidying up after breakfast, leave out some of the less perishable items for mid-morning snacks. Think like a hobbit: second breakfast, elevensies, and afternoon tea… food, treats, and healthy snacks should always be available. If the location or the season prevents the serving of a hot meal, make the other meals hearty and the food plentiful. Even so, offer a balance of filling meals versus lighter fare. Your crew will be doing heavy, manual labor and will need to replenish that caloric energy, whereas you cast may be spending time quietly rehearsing and not want to pile on the calories. Aim for a pleasing color palette for the meals. Borrow a concept from the stylists and add a pop of color: carrots, oranges, or sweet potatoes; tomatoes or red peppers. No one really wants to eat a plate of beige food no matter how tasty and nutritious it may be.

Prepackaged food or homemade? What about a blend of the two? Fast food and prepared foods can have amazingly high sodium levels, but do you really have the time to clean, chop, mix, or cook everything? If you do, then perhaps you might want to consider switching careers. Remember: time is money. Washing and tearing up a head of iceberg lettuce takes little time but preparing a lasagna takes far longer, so it may be better to buy the head of lettuce and the packaged, frozen lasagna. Budget your time as you would budget your money because you may have very little of either to squander.

Speaking of time, a twelve hour day may not necessarily mean three meals. If you begin the day with a 30 minute breakfast, you can then shoot for six hours, call a 45 minute lunch, and have four hours left for work, so legally no dinner would be required. Alternately, if you start straight off with a six hour shoot, have a 45 minute lunch, and then work for five hours work, no breakfast or dinner would be required. If that is your schedule, your craft service table had better be well stocked and the food exceptional, if you want to avoid a mutiny. Do not be a slave to your menu plan — you are the leader, not the dictator. For night shoots you may want to start or end with a meal, even though your cast and crew may have eaten earlier. They will be working hard and will need those calories. Mealtimes may not correspond to when people are accustomed to eating, but well fed people work better.

You may not have thought of yourself as a "restaurateur" when you decided to make a film, but, congratulations, you are! Keep in mind the derivation of the term and put the emphasis on the restorative nature of food. You are asking so much from your cast and crew: the long hours, the hard work, and the dedication to your dream. It is your "thank you" as well as your obligation to keep them healthy and well-fed.

Here is a meal plan and recipe to get you started.

Figure 6.1   Example of a meal plan for one week of shooting

FILM SHOOT MEAL PLAN: WEEK ONE

Day	Breakfast	Lunch	Dinner
Day One	Sliced bread, dry cereal, instant oatmeal. Peanut butter, jam, butter. Fresh fruit. If electricity available, bring toaster and electric kettle.	Sandwiches: sliced bread, cold cuts (allow 3 oz/person), sliced tomatoes, cheese, lettuce, mayonnaise, mustard, ketchup. Carrot sticks, pretzels, potato chips.	Store-bought roasted chickens, cut into pieces. Microwave-baked sweet potatoes, halved. Salad with rice vinegar dressing. Assorted cookies.
	Coffee, tea, milk, sweeteners.	Kool-Aid.	Decaffeinated coffee, tea.
Memo	Leave bread and peanut butter for snack.	Leave carrots, pretzels, and potato chips for snack.	Leave cookies for snack. Return freezer packs into freezer.
Day Two	Bagels, dry cereal, instant oatmeal. Peanut butter, cream cheese, jam, butter. Fresh fruit. If electricity available, bring toaster and electric kettle.	The Wizard's own Fiesta Bean Salad. Iceberg lettuce. Sliced baguette-style bread. Sliced pound cake.	Spaghetti with tomato sauce, grated Parmesan cheese. Garlic bread (using baguette bread). Mixed greens salad. Popsicles.

Day	Breakfast	Lunch	Dinner
	Coffee, tea, milk, sweeteners.	Iced tea, sodas.	Decaffeinated coffee, tea.
Memo	Leave granola bars for snack.	Remainder of Day One cookies for snack.	Fresh fruit for snack. Return freezer packs into freezer.
Day Three	Croissants, dry cereal, instant oatmeal. Peanut butter, jam, butter. Fresh fruit. If electricity available, bring toaster and electric kettle.	Tacos with guacamole, sour cream, refried beans, and onions. Corn chips. Sliced watermelon.	Tuna fish salad with iceberg lettuce, sliced bread, and sliced cheese. Assorted cookies.
	Coffee, tea, milk, sweeteners.	Iced tea, sodas.	Decaffeinated coffee, tea.
Memo	Leave croissants with jam for snack.	Corn chips and pretzels for snack.	Leave cookies for snack.
Day Four	Hard boiled eggs. Dry cereal, instant oatmeal, sliced bread. Peanut butter, jam, butter. Fresh fruit. If electricity available, bring toaster and electric kettle.	Sandwiches: sliced bread, cold cuts (allow 3 oz/person), sliced tomatoes, cheese, lettuce, mayonnaise, mustard, ketchup. Carrot sticks and cole slaw.	Cooked-from-frozen lasagna. Mixed greens salad with rice vinegar dressing. Bread sticks. Brownies.
	Coffee, tea, milk, sweeteners.	Iced tea, Kool-Aid.	Decaffeinated coffee, tea.
Memo	Leave bread and peanut butter for snack.	Granola bars and carrots for snack.	Leave brownies for snack. Return freezer packs to freezer.

Day	Breakfast	Lunch	Dinner
Day Five	Bagels, dry cereal, instant oatmeal. Peanut butter, cream cheese, jam, butter. Fresh fruit. If electricity available, bring toaster and electric kettle.	Chicken salad and potato salad with quartered tomatoes and lettuce. Potato chips, pretzels and corn chips.	Cheese (vegetarian) and pepperoni pizzas! Green salad with ranch dressing. Cupcakes.
	Coffee, tea, milk, sweeteners.	Iced tea, sodas.	Decaffeinated coffee, tea.
Memo	Leave bagels and cream cheese.	Leave carrots, pretzels, and potato chips for snack.	Leave cupcakes and fruit for snack. Return freezer packs to freezer.

Figure 6.2   Example of a meal plan for one week of shooting

THE WIZARD'S FIESTA SALAD
(from Lis de Tuerk Ghadar, Production Designer)

3 32 oz. cans of cooked kidney beans, rinsed
3 Granny Smith apples, cored, chopped, and sprinkled with 3 tablespoons of lime juice
1 15 oz. can of sweet corn (vacuum packed if possible), drained
1 red onion, diced
1 red or yellow pepper, seeded and diced
3 - 4 tablespoons of rice vinegar
4 -5 tablespoons of sesame seed oil or vegetable oil
4 -5 tablespoons of dried, crushed herbs (choose either: tarragon, dill, or basil)

Add salt and pepper to taste

Combine first five ingredients. Add last three ingredients and mix gently. Add salt and pepper as needed. Chill. Serves 12. Serve with iceberg lettuce, iced tea, and popsicles for dessert.

Chapter Seven
POST-PRODUCTION

And now for a history lesson. Yes, this is a book about the future and the rapidly changing face of art in the digital age, but it's important to understand the post-production lineage, in order to appreciate its simplicity today. So bear with this section for a bit because it promises some valuable information that's grounded in present-day post production, too.

In the past few decades, post production has become one of the most streamlined processes, thanks to advancements in technology, mostly due to the emergence of nonlinear editing platforms. Before the digital days, post production was a very labor intensive and often costly process. If one was shooting on film, he or she would have to pay for film stock, pay to have it developed, and take the time to sync audio tape if recorded separately — all before actual post production began. Following all that pre-editing work, editors would then have to physically cut and splice together strips of film until a cut was complete. Then a master print would have to be made, along with any other copies — and more film stock means more money. And that was the professional route; if you needed an alternative, a couple of tape decks and a bunch of play/record button presses were involved. The good part about all of this is that many of these hurdles editors had to jump through are no longer an issue in the digital age, but it is important to know from whence the medium has come. Thanks to digital nonlinear editing systems, one is able to go from shooting to editing in a matter of minutes. Though, while you could conceivably drop your footage into an editing program of your choice, cut something together really quick, export it and be done, there are a few more steps to take into consideration, which we'll go over.

First things first, keep in mind that your camera choice can affect your post-production workflow, and can necessitate the use of specific programs. As an example, DSLR cameras capture stunning image quality; however, you will need to sync audio in post. Meanwhile, the workflow for, say, the Sony EX-1 or the RED camera will necessitate specific software. These are just tips of the iceberg, which will be expanded upon later in the chapter. But do keep in mind that post-production hinges upon choices made at various steps along the way.

After you've shot all your footage, the first obvious step will be bringing it into your hard drive, so you can begin to edit. For your sake and for anyone who works on the project, make sure to keep your files located and organized in a logical manner. Next, you'll want to pull in your footage to your editing software, as well as any other audio or graphics you may need; again, organization is key here, as it will save you numerous headaches. If you recorded audio with a standalone microphone, as opposed to your camera's microphone, the next thing you'll want to do is sync all your audio because it's a lot easier to do now than when everything is cut together. Audio syncing itself can seem like a daunting task. But there are various programs — such as one called Pluraleyes — which automate the syncing process, so editors don't have to manually match up clips and audio themselves. Once all that is set up, you're ready to start cutting together your project, which will obviously take up most of your time.

During this process, remember to keep in mind the **Keystone Method**. While editing, you don't want to accidentally bury your inciting incident. Your editing should always work with and support your story and shots. And, just as the principles of the **Keystone Method** can elucidate the story and shots, it can also lead you to build a meaningful final cut that fully actualizes your creative vision. Another thing to keep in mind is that depending on whether you're editing a project for a client or for a collaborator, you may want to first assemble a rough cut, which doesn't have to be perfect, just get your idea across. Then, you can submit it for feedback and fine tuning from there. Your goal is to get to "picture lock," where on a basic visual sense, all your cuts and edits are good, everyone agrees that's how the project is going to look, and you can move on to the next couple of steps.

See more in "Structuring Story for the New Format" on page 21 and "Revisiting the Keystone Method" on page 30 ▶

From here on out, most of these steps are "as needed," due to these steps being dependent on what kind of video and audio you were able to record. Once you've achieved picture lock, you'll want to fine tune your project just prior to export. This is the time where you'll want to fix your audio levels, add music, sound effects, etc. Audio is one of those things that can generally be saved for last. From the visual side of things, you'll want to add any graphics needed, such as title cards, lower thirds for interviews, or any other photos. Finally, take your footage through a round of color correction. No matter how high quality your camera is, more often than not, your footage could look better. Given how long it could take to render, this is ideally your last step before export. Basic color correction tools are a standard feature set of any editing software, but there are other third party programs, such as Magic Bullet, which offer many visually distinct presents (that remain customizable), for those who are looking for a specific tone and feel to their footage.

Once you're picture locked, your audio levels are good, you've added any additional graphics, and you've color corrected, all that's left to do is export, and you're done.

A final note, you may come across two editing terms: "Offline" and "Online," which refer to the two major stages of editing. Offline editing encompasses everything from import of your footage to editing it down into a picture locked cut. On the other hand, online editing is everything past picture lock to exporting your project; in other terms, online editing is basically fine-tuning your project for release.

NEED TO KNOW: SOFTWARE FOR THE NEW FRONTIER

Post-Production Software

The major decision to be made when entering post-production is what programs to use for editing. Currently, there are three major companies making post-production tools: Apple, Adobe, and Avid. The catch is that Avid is, by comparison, incredibly expensive and is therefore mainly used as a professional editing program for "big-time" feature films, TV shows, and commercials. It does not target itself toward the new media or web video markets. Thus, new media creators are mainly split between Apple and Adobe products. Picking one of these companies and sticking to it can be advantageous because each company has a creative suite of programs that work best in conjunction with each other. Apple's software in the Final Cut Studio suite (like Final Cut Pro, Motion, and Soundtrack Pro) are designed to work in tandem with each other, and Adobe's Creative Suite lets you quickly share files amongst all its programs. In reality, though, it is not impossible to flip-flop, picking the programs you like the most from any companies and coaxing them to work in harmony, with only a couple small features and a little ease of use lost. That is why it is best to break down the possible programs in each step.

Importing Footage

Editing has almost entirely turned into a digital workflow, meaning editors are presented with hundred of digital files instead of tapes or reels. These digital files from the camera should be saved in at least two places at all times so that there is always a backup.

Both Adobe and Apple offer programs to log, capture, rename, tag, or sub-clip your video files before editing (Adobe Prelude or Log and Capture within FCP), but you could also drop the raw footage into your editing program and fire away (not recommended). Also note that some video files require conversion before they can be processed and used for editing.

Editing Footage

Then comes the most important step: the bare bones editing. Both Apple's Final Cut Pro 7 and Adobe Premiere are great editing programs that can be both simple or extremely complex, depending on how deep you want to get into them. Final Cut Pro (FCP) has been around for a longer time than Adobe Premiere, and thus much of the Adobe workflow is FCP inspired, making them fairly similar. Premiere is constantly being updated and improved, whereas FCP 7 has not been updated in years and users worry that it may never be again. Apple released FCP X, but many users found it to be a major step back and have likened it more to iMovie than a professional editing program. So the choice will likely come down to personal preference.

> ### A Note on the DSLR Revolution... And a Tip
>
> For Apple users, editing with the DSLR RAW files is a bit complex. Final Cut Pro 7 can edit the raw footage, but a powerful computer is needed and incessant, inexorable rendering will be required. The better path is to convert the footage to ProRes, for extremely high quality files, or Apple Intermediate Codec, for video that will look great online but might suffer a bit, if projected onto a large screen. Compressor is the default tool for these changes, but the free program **MPEG Streamclip** can do the job easier and faster. Just open up **MPEG Streamclip**, fetch a batch list going with all the files, and the rest will be self explanatory. Keep copies of the original camera files, but these new converted files will be what is imported into Final Cut Pro 7.
>
> Adobe users have it a bit easier here. Premiere Pro can easily process and edit files from the new DLSR's. This does require a decently powerful computer, but that is a requirement for any video editing. The footage can also be brought through Adobe Prelude first if logging, renaming, tagging, or sub-clipping is necessary, but most users should simply open up Premiere, import the raw files that have been copied from the camera, and start editing. No conversion needed.

Visual Effects

After doing basic editing and piecing everything together, it might be necessary to do some visual effects to either improve what is already there through processes like camera stabilization or to add new elements to a work, like explosions, car crashes, or 3D titles. The two key programs with which to do this are Apple's Motion or Adobe After Effects. Both can accomplish similar things, but, if given the choice, After Effects has some advantages that may make it your favored option. For one, its constant updates (versus Motion's infrequent ones) are extremely useful in the field of visual effects, where staying current is key. After Effects has also been in existence for significantly longer, and has thus had time to establish itself in the field as an industry standard. As a corollary, the most common way to learn new techniques in these programs is through online guides and tutorials, of which a greater abundance has amassed over time for the older After Effects than for the young Motion. Both programs can be effective for almost all visual effects needs, but Adobe does seem to have the lead in this field.

Audio Editing

Final Cut Pro and Premiere can likely accomplish much of the audio editing needed for Internet or prosumer projects, but if audio needs special work or wants to be brought to the next level, Apple's Soundtrack Pro or Adobe's Audition can do that. The contention between these two is similar to the editing program debate. Neither has any killer features that make one far superior to the other. Soundtrack Pro is the "old stand by" program currently, and thus has more online tutorials and potential teachers, but, the future is of course unwritten. Overall, it is advisable to pair them with their respective editing programs because that will make transferring audio files much easier. If using Final Cut Pro, Soundtrack Pro is best. With Premiere, use Audition.

Color Correction

The final step in the editing process will likely be color correction. This is one area especially where most needs can be met inside the editing program, as the 3-Way Color Corrector in both Final Cut Pro 7 and Adobe Premiere is an extremely powerful tool. For more complex needs, including different color grading in a single shot, you can move the footage to a different program. Apple's program Color and Adobe's Speed Grade both have a high learning curve but can yield professional level results, if given the time and effort. Again, the programs are fairly similar in their abilities, so it is best to stick with whichever corresponds with the editing software used. An extra option is Magic Bullet by Red Giant. Compatible with Final Cut Pro and Premiere, Magic Bullet provides a nice middle ground in color correction and gives a lot of complex correction presets that can either be tweaked or left as is. The results are a step-up from most corrections without requiring the enormity of time or the expertise required of Color or Speed Grade. Some say the software is a shortcut or a cheater's way out, creating dynamic appearances with a click of the mouse as opposed to creating one's own looks, but the results can be stunning, and everything the software does is customizable. For obtaining a relatively-painless, yet dynamic, engaging, and even non-traditional look, Magic Bullet is certainly something to check out.

Editing Basics for Digital Days
Some Baby Steps

Technical Aspect of Editing

The following steps are specific to FCP 7, however the same principles apply for other programs.

Organizing & Backing Up Video & Project Files

Before creating any new editing project, it's important to first create a single folder where all the files created during the editing process (such as render files) can go. For the sake of organization, it is best to keep this one folder for all your various projects, as a program like Final Cut Pro 7 will automatically separate project X's render files from project Y's into their own folder.

Setting Sequence Settings (Autosave Vault, Render Files, etc.)

When opening Final Cut Pro 7, the first thing you'll want to do is set the system settings for your new project. From the top menu, go to Final Cut Pro > System Settings. From here, you'll want to set the Scratch Disk, Waveform Cache, Thumbnail Cache, and Autosave Vault to the previously mentioned folder. Then, from the same Final Cut Pro menu, under user preferences, it's always a good idea to set the Autosave Vault to save a copy of your project every five minutes or so — that way, progress will periodically be saved, as program crashes aren't exactly unheard of.

Once editing is done, a vast majority of exporting can be done in Final Cut Pro or Premiere, with Apple's program Compressor available for more complex export jobs. Upload your work to the Internet; burn it to a DVD with Apple DVD Studio Pro, iDVD, Adobe Encore, or freeware Burn; or simply let the file sit on a computer. The post-production software has done its job for you.

Exporting: You've Edited a Masterpiece, Now What?

Since film schools generally gloss over, or do not cover at all, exporting techniques, it seems well worth the effort of covering here. In particular, when exporting video for the web, here is some information to keep in mind.

Export options

Under the "Options" menu, you will be given numerous options on how you would like your video to be encoded. For exporting your video, the easiest way is to go to File > Export > Quicktime Conversion. This dropdown menu option gives you greater customization, than the "Quicktime Mov" option does.

Keep in mind that you can export still images, image sequences, audio files, and more. You have a plethora of options. Make use of them according to your needs.

Frame Rate

You'll want to make sure your export's frame rate matches your editing sequence's frame rate. A safe bet is usually "current," but if you're editing footage from different types of cameras, you'll want to make sure to set your frame rate accordingly. Generally, 24 frames-per-second and "progressive" (as opposed to "interlaced") are the rule of thumb for a cinematic look, so make certain that your on-set and post-production plans take frame rate, etc., into consideration.

Video Codec

Under Video Settings, "H.264" is a good bet, as it has become an industry standard for online video codecs and is accepted by most, if not all, video platforms. "It is currently one of the most commonly used formats for the recording, compression, and distribution of HD video."[1]

H264 manages high quality video in relatively low bitrates. "You can think it as the "successor" of the existing formats (MPEG2, MPEG-4, DivX, XviD, etc.) as it aims in offering similar video quality in half the size of the formats mentioned before."[2]

Converter Options: Diffused, Soft focus

Under the Video Settings button, you can add a filter, such as a soft focus, to your final export, but it is best to void those in general.

Size (e.g. 1280x720 vs 1280x720 16:9)

In video size, you'll want to make sure you keep your project's native aspect ratio, unless specifically required to do otherwise. Most cameras all shoot in HD, which means they'll be in a widescreen 16:9 aspect ratio. Make sure to select either 1980x1080 (1080p) or 1280x720 (720p) as your size setting. Two things to note: higher resolution will mean higher file size, and if you shot in native 720p, it's generally a poor idea to upscale the footage to 1080p.

The Difference Between PCM and ACC for Audio

So what do these even mean? AAC stands for Advanced Audio Coding. AAC is a compressed, or "lossy" audio compression format, which is the industry standard for all Apple Products and the iTunes platform. AAC is also based around the MPEG2 and MPEG4 standard.[3]

Since AAC is compressed, some information will be lost in the format,

1   "H.264/MPEG-4 AVC ," Wikipedia, http://en.wikipedia.org/wiki/H.264/MPEG-4_AVC
2   "What is H.264 format ," Digiarty Software, Inc , http://www.winxdvd.com/resource/h264.htm
3   "Audio file format," Wikipedia, http://en.wikipedia.org/wiki/Audio_file_format

A Note on Target Bit Rate and Compression

Virtually all video content that we shoot or watch has been compressed. Video files, in particular, are huge, lumbering beasts of files, and this makes them difficult to work with, difficult to port, and difficult to send. It is for precisely this reason that it is so incredibly important to find ways to make them smaller and more user-friendly, without losing too much quality.

In fact, this is where the cute moniker for "codec" comes from: (COmpressor/DECompressor).[1] A codec denotes a highly specific set of information, which determines how a file is to be reduced or compressed, and then also how to decompress or to bring it back to full quality playback.

Much higher compression ratios are at the cost of a decrease in quality.

Higher compression rates also mean your file is easier for others to access; even if the end-user has low-bandwidth or is using a cell phone, he or she should still be able to access your content.

Simply put, think of it like this: you can't watch a Blu-Ray on your cell phone.

These are recommended settings for putting your work online:

Format:
Quicktime .MOV or .MP4
H264 Compression
Resolution: Native Resolution

Bit-Rate, SD:
Video Rate: > 2.5 Mbits/s
Audio Rate: >256 kbits/s
Audio Format: AAC

Bit-Rate, HD - 720P:
Video Rate: >5.5 Mbits/s
Audio Rate: >256 kbits/s
Audio Format: AAC

Bit-Rate, HD -1080P:
Video Rate: >10 Mbits/s
Audio Rate: >256 kbits/s
Audio Format: AAC

---

1   "Choosing the Best Video Codec ," Edit Smarter with Larry Jordan, Larry Jordan & Associates, Inc., http://www.larryjordan.biz/technique-choosing-the-best-videocodec/

hence the term "lossy". So AAC, while lossy, does provide a smaller and more user-friendly file size. It also helps that it has become the Apple industry standard and that it is attuned to the MPEG format. All of this means that it works well cross-platform. Generally, for web, AAC is a solid choice.

PCM stands for Pulse Code Modulation and is also known as Linear PCM. PCM is an uncompressed and lossless format for audio. Incidentally, it is also the standard audio format for CDs.

Do note that PCM, as it is uncompressed, will increase your file size. Also, consider that the quality of your file's audio is just one part of the equation. What is the expected end-user experience of your work? Will people be experiencing your creation on their laptop? Their cell phone? As excellent as your audio may be, keep in mind this adage: you can't get Dolby on your iPhone. So the end-user experience may curtail and prevent your best efforts to provide the best possible audio.

Target Bitrate

As for the target bitrate, it determines the overall quality of the audio. Final Cut will default to 128 kbps, but if you want your audio to be a touch cleaner, a good level is 256 kbps. Anything below 128 kbps is usually not advised.

Image Files: JPEG, PNG, TIFF

When exporting a still image, PNG and TIFF formats are best for maintaining both high quality and transparency. TIFF files are suitable for print and image manipulation purposes. These files have the ability to store image data in a lossless format, can be edited and re-saved without losing image quality, and support layers. PNG files support lossless compression but are not suitable for professional quality print graphics. PNG has its purposes for the web, most notably when maintaining transparency information in the image is important, or when you need something high-resolution. As a rule of thumb, PNGs make for much larger files than JPEG. If you just need a flattened image, or small file size is a must, you can export a JPEG. JPEG is a lossy format, however for the web this can be a pro because the substantially compressed files make for faster loading and viewing.

AIFF, WAV, and MP3

AIFF and WAV are lossless, uncompressed audio files, derived from PCM, or pulse-code-modulation, which was touched upon before. AIFF is to Apple as WAV is to Windows PC's. That said, both operating systems will recognize both file types.

MP3 is a lossy audio file format. Slow bandwidth or limited hard drive space can make this a go-to; however, keep in mind that information and quality are lost with the MP3 file format.

How MP3 Cornered the Marketplace
A Classic Case of VHS vs BETA

If those lossy MP3's lag significantly in audio quality compared to their lossless brethren AIFF and WAV...why did the MP3 become the go-to format? In a word: Napster. The file-sharing service not only revolutionized how we access and listen to to music, it also revolutionized how those files were wrapped. MP3 were light and flexible — undeterred by even dial-up bandwidth and small enough to fit on those 90s era hard-drives. [1]

---

1 "Which Audio File Format is Right For You?," Free Stock Music, http://www.freestockmusic.com/audio-formats/

The Future of Frame Rate
Case Study: The Hobbit

It's the classic tale of adventure and risk taking, but perhaps a bit too much risk was taken by Peter Jackson when he decided to give many theaters versions of *The Hobbit* with 48fps prints. As a filmmaker of tremendous talent, in addition to a champion of new technology, Jackson's aim was to make the cinematic experience more "immersive" (to use his own wording).

(...The Future of Frame Rate continued)

The thought was that for 2D and 3D viewing, in particular, it would improve the feel of the traditional 24fps — which, for decades, has been the standard frame rate for film. Without getting too deep into the science of it, 24fps was able to register at just the right speed at which the human eyes and brain can process visuals. Thanks to this "persistence of vision," we see a string of still images as a constant and seamless flow of information. And, over time, this frame rate has become the norm and is thus associated with the cinematic look. But, with the introduction of digital video, 30fps has become increasingly common, and with further technological advancements, higher frame rates (i.e. 60fps, 120fps, etc.) have become the goal for many. In fact, James Cameron plans to make a 128fps film.

Nonetheless, audience and critical response to *The Hobbit's* 48fpfs was mixed and interesting. In particular for 3D viewing, many viewers found the 48fps much easier on the eye, as it made for smoother, less flickery 3D viewing. However, the 48fps high frame rate also granted the viewer much more visual information. As a result, much of the artifice of the movie was exposed — the fact that rain was only falling on a set area of the mise-en-scene made one aware of a rain machine. And every costume, makeup job, set piece, and visual effect element was so extremely clear and present that it ruined the fantasy. The viewer was able to see that they were actors wearing make-up, which made it hard to believe in the hobbits and dwarves. The costumes were sometimes made out of cheap materials. The eagles had velveteen footpads, etc... Another common complaint was that even though it remained divisible by the sacred number of 24, the increase in movement and visual information actually prevented some of that movie magic we have grown to love.

Where the future of frame rates in the industry goes is up to debate. Perhaps, the real future of the higher-frame-rate process is not in the fantasy narrative realm, but in the hyper real. Documentaries, sports coverage, news, concerts, non-narrative, docu-dramas, etc... the advantage of feeling completely THERE would be granted to these, without any risk of exposing the "artifice" of movie magic.

Key Programs

Outside of the typical wheelhouse of your main editing suite, there are also some key programs to keep in mind for your workflow. Many of these will not only make the process easy, but many of these are also free.

- Magic Lantern

- PluralEyes (especially useful if a DSLR was used, as the audio is not synced in-camera).

- XDCAM Clip Browser and XDCAM Transfer (specific to the Sony EX1 camera)

- REDCINE-X PRO (specific to handling RED camera footage)

- Magic Bullet

- Mpegstreamclip

- Burn

Programs to make grabbing footage and pictures off of phones easier (as handling large and bulk files through traditional methods can cause freeze-ups and failures):

- Android:

  - Android File Transfer for Mac
    You don't need extra software to transfer files from an Android device to a Windows PC, but AirDroid offers extra features like wireless transfers and the ability to see through the lens of your Android's front and back camera from your computer.

  - AirDroid

- iPhone:

  - Image Capture (an application preinstalled on Macs)

- PhoneTrans (also available for Windows)

And for creative how-to's and solutions to common problems, visit one-stop resource Creative Cow: http://www.creativecow.com

EDITING TIPS, TRICKS, TALES FROM THE TRENCHES

1. Don't be afraid to get weird. This is the medium to do so.

Figure 7.1 Characters from *Orange Juice in Bishop's Garden* experiencing the effects of drug LSD

The web is a largely un-inscribed place for nontraditional storied and non-traditional storytellers.

Figure 7.2 *Orange Juice in Bishop's Garden* has a cast of characters with diverse backgrounds, and features a lesbian relationship

Don't just emulate features and TV shows and shorts — this is its OWN THING. Find that identity and run with it. Also, in the event that you find you don't have enough footage or your video is corrupted, etc., getting weird can provide a solution for your lack of coverage.

> **OTESSA'S TALES FROM THE TRENCHES**
> **Editing "The Winter of Our Discontent"**
>
> Season 5, Episode 7 of *OJBG*, "The Winter of Our Discontent" was an episode that was plagued by some issues... namely it was 120 degrees on set, when it was filmed and, at those temperatures, people are at risk of heat stroke. Dan Curl was guest directing this episode, and he shot the episode quickly, with limited takes, for the sake of the crew and cast. This was a kindness to be certain.
>
> However, when we got into the editing room, Connor (Key Editor) and I found ourselves craving MORE material... more footage... more takes... just more. More is something a lot of editors wish for, but without a genie, your wish is not a command. So, we decided to think outside of the box. I really love some of the 70s and early 80s cinematography and editing styles. So many of these are things that have gone COMPLETELY OUT OF STYLE. And I don't care because I love them. Namely: Ending on freeze frames, overlays, soft focus cross dissolves (hello, *Tom Jones*), breaking into picture-in-picture a la tiling (*Thomas Crown Affair*), zooms (*Parallax View*)
>
> But in particular, at this time, I was completely and utterly obsessed with this movie *HAUSU* or *HOUSE*. It is a JAPANESE HORROR-COMEDY, set to a psych-surf soundtrack, FROM 1977 AND IT IS AMAZING. They do overlays into close-ups, laying them over master wide shots. Oh, and did I mention that they set them to a soundtrack that's like a psychedelic pop wonderland, like Japanese-style Beach Boys? And it is so jarring and so unsettling. I was inspired. And so, here you have the out-of-the-box solution to our quandary.

2. Circling back to the Keystone Method: It is important to underscore shot choices with the editing. Build up to and around major moments with your editing. Make sure your editing is creating a conflu-

ence with your shots. They should not be fighting against each other.

3. Sometimes you will have to "Kill Your Darlings" — it just happens. Your "darlings" are those ideas, images, artistry, or lines of dialogue that you just fell in love with: you feel married to them, but because of some misfortune, they just aren't working according to plan. If you do have to scrap them, it's OKAY. Just let it go. In the film world, there is a saying that every project is made three times: there is the film that is written, the film that is shot, and the film that is edited. They are all different films. This is why: sometimes things just don't work. Sometimes bad things happen. Sometimes you have to kill your darlings. You might not be able to use what you have the way that you wanted. But it is okay. JUST CONSIDER THIS: how are the broken pieces you've been given secretly the components to make something even better? And who know, maybe those darlings will have new life in a new form.

   If that absolutely doesn't work, consider you might have to do re-shoots. But try to avoid them because they are expensive.

4. Consider your backlog of footage and unused content as potential b-roll or bonus content for the future. (And, hey, maybe you can resurrect your darlings here.) Never close the door on your work. Your are building a library and a collection, whether you realize it or not.

5. People love bonus content. Bloopers, deleted scenes, wallpaper images for desktops, and behind-the-scenes content — you name it, they'll love it. Even if you don't use your content immediately, or in the initially intended way, it can still have a meaningful existence in the bonus arena.

6. Consider that your end-user experience will be on the small-screen, so the impact of scale alters.

   See "Shot Choices" on page 30 and "Shot Lists" on page 41 for more on re-imagining scale ▶

7. Consider not including credits in your video export for online; instead, consider including them in your textual description box.

Most people stop watching as soon as the credits roll, so instead of rolling credits, immediately start the next episode auto-playing ASAP. They're tremendously more likely to *keep watching*. Get your viewers hooked, and that's how you make fans.

8. Instead, consider including your social media links, your website, and a call to action.

   See "Social Media" on page 152 for an in-depth review ▶

9. Some sites, like Youtube, will desaturate your film, so be prepared to compensate. Meanwhile, a site like Vimeo will offer a lusher viewing experience, which is more like what you saw on your original timeline, with your editing software. The advantage of YouTube is the more active social environment, while Vimeo is more like a collective of filmmakers. You may find you need both. That said, because the viewing experience is not quite the same on each one (again, desaturation, etc…), you may want to consider doing separate exports for each one, so that your work always looks its best.

10. For serialized content, consider the importance of including "previously on's" or recaps at the beginning of piece of programming. It's all about ease of viewing and ease of use. And making the viewing experience as user-friendly and accessible will only help you.

11. Cold open or beginning with title sequence? Two schools of thought here: #1, do you want to start with your episode's first scene and then interrupt your episode play with your opening sequence. Or #2, do you want to start with your opening sequence right off the bat? Cold opens can work tremendously well in TV. Reason for this: TV advertising placement is standardized and keyed to the final episode edit. And, each advertising break presents a challenge: it's a time when you can get bored and potentially change the channel. Hence all those cliff-hangers in TV shows right before the commercial break… anything that gets you hooked and invested means you're less likely to change that channel. And a cold open is just such a neat little ploy — t gets you hooked right off the bat. However, in web, you are not so beholden to advertising breaks. So, if you can get #1 to work, great.

But if not, that's fine, too. Think about what's right for your project and choose what enriches the viewing experience.

Task: Acclimate yourself with the free programs listed earlier in the chapter, in **Post-Production Software**, and with any additional editing software that you can get your hands on.

Task: Film a very simple scene (you can even use your phone) and then string it together according to the steps that we listed, using the Keystone Method. Practice logging and capturing. Try giving it some different visual looks through color correction.

Task: Using the following *OJBG* script pages, shoot the scene yourself (again this can be simple). Try editing the piece a few different ways. Try cutting with the audio and soundtrack elements front-and-center to your thought process. Next try stringing your work together, using color and visuals as your main reference point. Third, cut according to performance exclusively. Last, try cutting your scene to a specific music track, using that track as the scene's backbone. What have you noticed between each of these different cuts? What choices did you make that were specific to one, or shared by many? How do these choices and inferences inform how you would make a final, locked cut?

Figure 7.3 Excerpt from the Season 5, Episode 1 script of *Orange Juice in Bishop's Garden*

```
Tamsin= still asleep. DREW, flirtatiously, takes a blade of
grass-- tickles the end of Tamsin's nose with it. She wakes
up & sneezes.
                    TAMSIN
          What the hell Drew?  Ugh I want
          coffee.
DREW--very much INTO Tamsin. She doesn't reciprocate.
                    DREW
          I'll go get it for you.
Tamsin USES HIM LIKE A PUPPY DOG-- pats his head. Drew goes
to rush off.

Ryan side-steps Drew --
```

```
                    RYAN
          Look, I know you like her, but
          don't mug yourself.

                    DREW
          Don't mug myself? Wha?!
                (beat)
          Is it that obvious--

                    RYAN
          Don't let her treat you like a pet.
          If she doesn't respect you, she'll
          never be into you. I'm just saying
          from personal experience.

Bri eavesdrops--

                    DREW
          But maybe it's different with
          Tamsin.

                    RYAN
          Don't reward her when she dismisses
          you. If you do, it'll just bring
          out the worst in everyone,
          including Tamsin.

                    DREW
          I'm going for coffee. "Don't mug
          yourself." You must think you
          smooth.

PAN OFF of DREW, Back to the lawn--

                    SARAH
          So I've been thinking about
          expanding "my act" from the whole
          solo singer songwriter thing... I
          want a band. A full band.

Everyone is excited... they want to be in the band. --Ryan
especially.
```

POST-PRODUCTION MUSIC

When choosing a song to set your project to, you can't just put up any music track you want online. This comes down to copyright, royalty, and monetization issues. Artists who create music do so out of love for music hopefully, but they also do so as a career. Ripping them off is both unkind and also illegal. If you upload a video to, say, YouTube that has Rihanna's latest and greatest chart-topper, you can expect an email sitting in your inbox in the very near future. What does this email say? Further ruminations into a crystal ball, and just plain common sense will dictate that. This is a song that requires a licensing agreement: a sync agreement, a master agreement, and royalties. Do you have this? If so, prove it. If not, you have violated copyright. YouTube will open a case file for the issue. They will remove monetization options and ad revenue on your video. And as a last resort, they will pull down the video entirely. This also constitutes a mark on your "permanent record" and if too many of these instances occur, they will forcibly de-activate your account. Sound scary? It is.

What your videos will need if you want to put them up online, is music — totally legal music. And here, you have some options. You can secure the sync and master rights to a song by contacting the rights' holders. Alternately, you can find royalty-free music. Or, if you're talented, you can create your own original composition.

Royalty-free music tracks are audio music tracks that have had the copyright owner give their consent for them to be widely used by anyone, without paying royalties or licensing fees per use. If you upload a video with one of these songs to YouTube, you should be free and clear. Royalty-free music can be found in various websites and databases, both for free and paid licenses (in the way of a flat one-time fee). Some of these resources are listed below.

Just remember that you also need to check the *public copyright license*, which the artist has attributed to their work. There are many different types of public copyright licenses. Just because a song is royalty-free and listed on one of these sites does not necessarily mean that you have commercial rights. If you want to monetize by way of pre-roll advertising on YouTube, that can be considered commercial use and you could find yourself in the wrong. When in doubt, contact the artists directly, and explain yourself. It may be that they have no problem with you putting your work up on YouTube in this way, and that they were mainly concerned with becoming the next soundtrack for FIFA on PS3 without receiving a little income for their next rent check.

As explained by Wikipedia: "The CC licenses all grant the "baseline rights", such as the right to distribute the copyrighted work worldwide, without changes, at no charge. The details of each of these licenses depends on the version, and comprises a selection of four conditions"[4]

Icon	Right	Description
	Attribution (BY)	Licensees may copy, distribute, display and perform the work and make derivative works based on it only if they give the author or licensor the credits in the manner specified by these.
	Share-alike (SA)	Licensees may distribute derivative works only under a license identical to the license that governs the original work. (See also copyleft.)
	Non-commercial (NC)	Licensees may copy, distribute, display, and perform the work and make derivative works based on it only for noncommercial purposes.
	No Derivative Works (ND)	Licensees may copy, distribute, display and perform only verbatim copies of the work, not derivative works based on it.

Figure 7.4 Source: Wikipedia

Five combinations of these attributes are valid and used Creative Commons licenses.

Icon	Description	Acronym
	Attribution alone	BY
	Attribution + NoDerivatives	BY-ND
	Attribution + ShareAlike	BY-SA
	Attribution + Noncommercial	BY-NC
	Attribution + Noncommercial + NoDerivatives	BY-NC-ND
	Attribution + Noncommercial + ShareAlike	BY-NC-SA

Figure 7.5 Source: Wikipedia

---

4   "Creative Commons license," Wikipedia, http://en.wikipedia.org/wiki/Creative_Commons_license

Alternatively, you can buy a flat-fee license to a music archive or collection. These sort of archives can usually be found advertised online or in trade magazines. Either way, if you want your upload process to be as hassle free as possible, you're going to need to make sure that you're not in violation of any copyright laws first.

FREE MUSIC SOURCES

Music for your clips is essential, but sometimes it can be difficult to find music that doesn't violate copyright laws or royalty agreements. If you don't want your videos to be automatically taken down because of music-related blunders, trying hunting and pecking through the following:

Sources:

http://freemusicarchive.org   http://freeplaymusic.com

http://incompetech.com   http://royaltyfreemusic.com

http://freesoundtrackmusic.com   http:// audiosocket.com

http://mobygratis.com   http://www.smartsound.com

http://ccmixter.org

However, let's say that none of the royalty free routes suit you and composing your own composition is out of the question. How do you secure the rights to that must-have song?

Here is a step-by-step guide:

1. "That Song You Love" —It is your new favorite obsession and you now need it for your artistic work to be complete. Do a search in the online ASCAP and BMI music libraries to determine who owns the publishing rights to the work. Once you have that name…

2. Do a Google/Facebook/phone book/Twitter/et cetera search for that person's name — this is to find a means to reach out to them. If the rights holder is a mega-corporation or label, the contact information

is easy to find, so just navigate accordingly and email the appropriate parties.

3. Reach out to a representative. (NB. In the event that the rights holder is a mega-corp, it certainly does you no harm to reach out to the artist directly and plead your case. If the artist feels strongly about your work, or responds to your passion, you may well be able to negotiate a better deal or lower fee when dealing with the mega-corp.) There will be questions and perhaps even a form to fill out, in either case you should know the following...

4. Do you want that precise recording of "That Song You Love" ? Or would you be willing to settle for the rights to make your own cover of "That Song You Love". If it's the precise recording of said song, then you will need both the Sync and Master rights to "That Song You Love". If you are willing to consider making your own cover — then you only need the Sync (which is generally cheaper).

5. Consider what rights you need, how many seconds of screen time you need for the song — all of these considerations can make the rights more or less expensive and you should specify this to whoever you are trying to obtain the song from.

6. There is always bargaining to this process. If you cannot afford what you are quoted — come back with a counter offer. Consider if you have anything you could offer to make yourself more interesting to the artist/publisher/record company. This can be especially helpful if you are dealing with an artist who hasn't fully "arrived yet". Perhaps are you a power-blogger? You could offer some set services. There are ways that you can scratch each others' backs and forgo money altogether. Think about it.

7. Get it in writing. You need your Sync and/or Master Rights Agreements in writing in case there is any dispute about the legality of your music use. It is insurance against any future bogus copyright claims.

8. Sign it. File it. Stick a fork in it: you're done.

Chapter Eight
SOCIAL MEDIA

So, do you already have an agent or manager?

If the answer is no, then, guess what, you'll be functioning in those capacities yourself, and social media is the forum to do so. Even if you do already have representation, your use of social media can still either make or break your career.

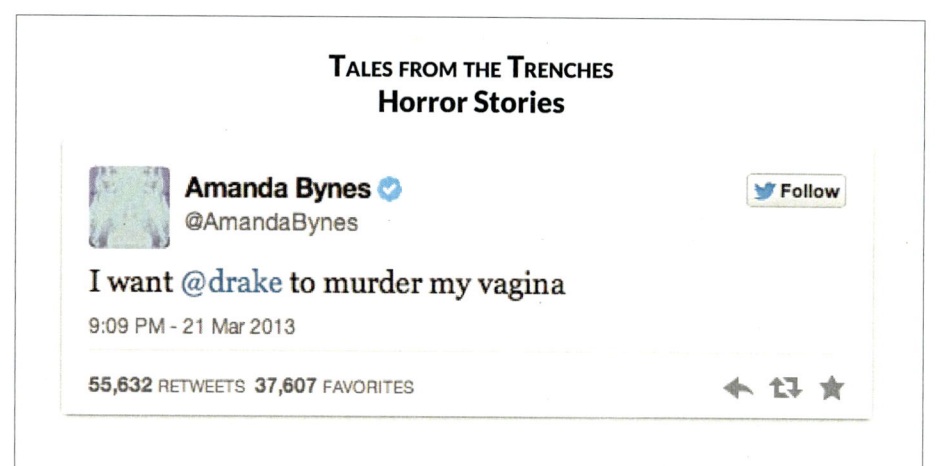

> **TALES FROM THE TRENCHES**
> **Horror Stories**
>
> **Amanda Bynes** ✓   Follow
> @AmandaBynes
>
> I want @drake to murder my vagina
>
> 9:09 PM - 21 Mar 2013
>
> 55,632 RETWEETS   37,607 FAVORITES
>
> Actress Amanda Bynes single-handedly delivered a sabotaging blow to her own career via Twitter by posting bizarre and unusual tweets and controversial selfies (a hand-held self portrait photo). Democratic U.S. Congressman Anthony Weiner's actions prompted the term "Weinergate" to trend on Twitter, when he accidentally publicly tweeted an incriminating photo of himself intended to be a secret sext (sexual text message). He tried to cover it up by saying he was hacked, but he later admitted to sending the photo. He resigned from Congress a month later. Lesson learned: use social media wisely!

Unfortunately, sometimes mistakes are unavoidable. So, when they do happen, it would be nice to be able to recover from them without having careers sabotaged or having to resign. Fortunately, this is totally possible — take a tip from actress Alison Pill, who accidentally tweeted a photo of herself topless.

> **TALES FROM THE TRENCHES**
> **Snatching Victory from the Jaws of Defeat**
>
> Pill quickly deleted the tweet, but was kind enough to confirm that, yes, she did in fact post a naked photo of herself to Twitter. She tweeted a cute apology:
>
> **Alison Pill** ✓
> @msalisonpill
>
> Yep. That picture happened. Ugh. My tech issues have now reached new heights, apparently. How a deletion turned into a tweet... Apologies.
>
> ← Reply ↻ Retweet ★ Favorite
>
> Instead of sabotaging her career and enraging the citizenry, the acknowledgment of her own mistake (rather than blaming it on a random hack) actually made her endearing to the public, and her career was left secure and intact.

Now, consider how you first learn about new movies and television shows. You hear a certain director is in "talks" about making a certain picture or a network's new TV show. You later see previews of the film or show, watch trailers of it, read reviews and interviews about it, then you finally watch it. But social media changes this formula for independent creators. You now have the opportunity to captivate your audience before you even have a product to reveal — and for pocket change or even for free! With the immediacy of social media, you can generate interest in your project through real-time updates regarding the unfinished elements of your work. You can invite people to provide feedback on your process, to get involved and to pay attention to your story. This on-the-ground, behind-the-scenes sharing creates a personal, intimate relationship that mass media and traditional marketing does not. This is social media's comparative advantage: it invites viewers to become more than just passive spectators, but people active and involved in a project. Readers can become commenters and authors. Viewers can become creators. And artists can actually be approached.

In a sense, social media becomes your guerilla warfare arsenal against the established, entrenched mainstream media moguls. Because of their largesse and standardization, their set to distribution process can be lumbering and sometimes anticlimactic. Having largely free reign and not being weighed down by the constraints of procedure or of advertisers, you have the flexibility to promote your material at any time and by almost any medium throughout your production process. Social media is an equalizer of content. Given promoted posts or special ads aren't bought, your posts will still be on as equal a footing as any other media mogul. You also have the advantage of establishing real interactions and relationships with others, which most large media companies don't invest in cultivating. So, while you may not have ads on TV or in theaters, your content can be widely viewable everywhere online.

Most importantly, new media is intrinsically *personal* while being social. When done right, social media has a way of revealing the human behind the technology. It becomes an extended story, a public journal of whom you are, of what you're doing, of your tastes, of your inspirations, and of your aspirations. This includes sharing the obstacles you come across, unexpected challenges, and triumphs. Sharing these inherently personal aspects with the extended social sphere gives a chance for anyone with a similar interest to develop a personal connection to you and to your story. The attention your audience invests in your story and the connections you build by sharing yours can be key to how your content is seen and supported.

Justin Bieber, teen pop star sensation, made his fame through his strategic and genuine use of social media. He's been sharing his story and broadcasting his thoughts continually — from his inception as a young YouTube "nobody" to the global sensation he is today. Many people have talent; yet, sadly, talent does not necessarily guarantee success. So how did social media grease the wheels for this epic journey? "JBiebz" reached out in an average person way, not as a mega-idol. He threw in his lot with us, with the people. And people love him for it; he has the most loyal and committed "beliebers".

> ### Tales from the Trenches
> ### Success Stories
>
> Klout, a social media indexing site of the most influential contributing users online, consistently ranks Justin Bieber at the top as the most influential user, often above the likes of President Barack Obama and the Dalai Lama. Actor Bill Murray jokingly tweeted that Justin Bieber gets 40,000 retweets by tweeting "thanks" and tried to surpass JB's number of retweets (and succeeded!).
>
> **Bill Murray** @BillMurray
>
> Justin Bieber gets 40,000 retweets when he says "thanks" so here is my attempt.
>
> Thanks.
>
> Reply   Retweeted   Favorite   More
>
> 42,428 RETWEETS   3,054 FAVORITES
>
> 6:56 PM - 17 May 13
>
> Essentially, JB can tweet the most mundane thoughts, and they will still go viral. Over 107,000 retweets for tweeting this ":)" shows the magnitude of his social media impact. This is not to say that you can be mundane and become influential. You still have to be interesting and be offering something worthwhile. And, if you do invest in sharing your story on social media, it could end up being a large payoff.

In between getting your cast together, trying to make funds meet, and filming, you may think you don't have any time to spend posting on Twitter or updating your friends on Facebook. You may even think posting photos on Instagram is just a waste of time. Many of the relatively younger web series creators out there, however, can attest to the crucial role social media can provide to boosting any of their efforts. Each platform has its purpose, its strength and weakness, its own organic structure and mode of use. Using the following principles of social media as a guide will help you efficiently and effectively promote your content across various platforms and across various audiences. If you avoid the pitfalls of carelessness that led to Weinergate and refrain from going all Amanda Bynes, you should do just fine!

> **TALES FROM THE TRENCHES**
> **Looking Forward to Look Back**
>
> Augusto Pinochet held Chile under oppressive rule for years. In 1988, at worldwide pressure, a plebiscite was called whereby the Chileans would vote "Yes" or "No" to keep Pinochet in power for another eight years or to end his regime. It was considered by many to be a lost cause. Many citizens thought the ballot would most likely be rigged and that those who worked for the "No" side would be harassed or fall into danger, as "disappearances" were common during Pinochet's dictatorship. Thus, the advertising and language of the "No" campaign had to make the choice of "No" feel safe — to feel like freedom, like joy. To do so, they used imagery that looked like it came right out of a Coca Cola commercial. They had a catchy jingle. There were mimes! And picnics! And dancing! Even humor! Their logo? It was a *rainbow*. It was a fiesta for the eyes and ears — and made for an opponent that the "Yes" opposition had no idea what to do with. "Yes" looked bitter and stodgy, and had no immediate grounds for vilifying "No" because what could they do, persecute the "No" for looking like a Coca Cola ad? For not being serious enough? For looking cooler? "No" was a deceptively-sugar-coated, self-aware, guerilla tactic. Simply put — in today's parlance — "No" went *viral*.

That said, take these principles and try to use them positively. Remember, as a general principle of advertising, people are drawn to joy. Don't fear monger on the past. Don't beg. Don't moan. Sell the beautiful future of what can be. What are the strengths of your work? Of your idea? Sell others on that experience, on that promise, on that future. Make them want what you have. Make it seem like your work is something that will enrich their experience. Give them tidbits that they can drop in conversation, that make them look interesting, and that make your work look meaningful.

Key Terms

Avi: Often referenced on Twitter as #avi, the term refers to the graphic image, or avatar, for a user's Twitter account.

Call to Action: A specific mass request to all social media followers for an attempt to achieve a common goal.

Direct Message (DM): A personal, private message sent between people who follow each other on Twitter.

Facebook (FB): An abbreviated way to refer to Facebook on Twitter and other social media, usually used in order to save space by using fewer characters.

Facebook stalker: A person who frequents other people's accounts, continually checking up on users' activity. An unfavorable term, people can also sometimes get called one, if they "friend" others whom they don't know well.

Friend/De-Friend (as a verb): To add or erase someone as a friend or contact on a social media platform, generally Facebook.

Favorite/Favoriting: A way of acknowledging or bookmarking content you find enjoyable, often other users can view another's likes and favorites.

Flashback Friday: Similar to #TBT, #flashbackfriday or #fbf is when social media users reference events or memories that happened in the past. Often accompanied by a picture, these posts typically appear on Instagram,

Twitter, Tumblr obviously on Fridays.

Follow Friday (#FF): Usually seen on Twitter, users will tweet the hashtag #FF followed by a sequence of users whom they wish to recommend their followers follow.

H/T (Hat Tip): Way to direct users to where just mentioned information came from, hat tipping to the source website.

Handle: The user name used by individuals on social media sites.

Hashtag: A word or phrase that follows a # symbol, which allows the term to become search-able, to trend, and to go viral within social media networks. Hashtags are sometimes referred to simply as tags.

In Case You Missed It (ICYMI): An alert to followers to point them in a direction to specific content they may have missed earlier in the day.

Incentivizing: When users give their followers or other social media users a reason to share or like their content — many times this is done by promising the same in return, by holding a contest, or by offering free or exclusive content.

In Real Life (IRL): IRL functions as an abbreviated reference to *offline* life and friends.

Like/Liking: A way of acknowledging or bookmarking content you find enjoyable, often other users can view another's likes and favorites.

Microblogging: A type of blogging service that offers up brief, to the point content pieces of text, video, or images, rather than full text posts.

Modified Tweet (MT): Similar to a retweet, but slightly editing it to save space or to get to the point.

News Feed: A streaming compilation of all content posted by the users and pages an individual follows.

Original Poster (OP): The user who creates an original tweet or post on social media, which is later shared or modified by others.

Reblogging: On Tumblr, re-posting another user's post, with added thoughts, much like a retweet.

Retweet (RT): On Twitter, copying another user's Tweet and reposting it to your own followers.

Short Message Service (SMS): Synonymous with text messaging, SMS allows the exchange of brief messages between devices and across communication platforms.

Spam-bot: A term used to reference fake accounts created with the intention to spam other social media users with unwanted information..

Throwback Thursday (#TBT): Flashback to the definition for Flashback Friday, as the two are essentially the same. On Thursdays, social media users will post a reference — often with a picture attached — to a past occurrence and tag it with #TBT.

Troll/Trolling: Internet slang term for someone who purposefully or accidentally makes situations unpleasant or disruptive, often so that s/he can provoke a response from other users. The Internet troll was born in the online message board community, but nowadays the term "troll" reflects a wider online context.

Widget: A small application embedded on a (frequently personal) website. Though widgets can be used to track page views or show the time, they are often used to link to the user's other social media accounts.

Some Cross-Platform Basics

1. Update profiles. Identify keywords and tags. Add buttons and widgets. Search for "your people" and audience.

2. Don't hard sell. Be a person, not a robot. Provide content that genuinely reflects who you and your brand are. Encourage interaction and engagement.

3. Identify your top influencers. Do some research. Who are the top names in your niche? And who are your biggest fans? Converse with

them; acknowledge them; and reward them.

4. Respond quickly — especially to complaints. Encourage open dialogue and recommendations. Make changes on the fly if need be. Learn from your mistakes.

5. Study up on your competition. Identify your competition or niche-companions and watch and learn from their successes and failures.

6. Access your analytics. Study your traffic. Set goals. Test hypotheses. Your analytics are a source of power: harness this power and let it guide you.

7. Be aware of your privacy and location settings. Some platforms will allow you to add your location to a post; you don't want to unknowingly broadcast your home address.

DEMOGRAPHICS

According to recent Pew Research Center studies published early in 2013, over 70% of USA adults online currently engage in social media networking sites. This marks a huge growth from the reported 8% when the study was first conducted in 2005. Yet, the term adult is broad, as it covers a range of age, education level, gender, ethnicity and more — and as someone using social media as a way to market oneself and one's brand, it's important to know who exactly is on which platform. With results from three Pew studies — an August 5, 2013 update called "72% of Online Adults are Social Networking Site Users," a Feb. 2013 report covering ages 18 to 65+ called "The Demographics of Social Media Users — 2012," and a May 21, 2013 youth report called "Teen, Social Media, and Privacy" — what type of people are on which platforms can be somewhat ascertained. While this data is relatively recent, it is important to note the digital landscape and its trends are constantly changing and evolving — enough so that the Pew Research Center found an update for 2013 necessary. What seems to remain consistent, though, is that the core group of people using social media is between the ages of 18-29. Surprisingly, though, the most recent growth in social media use can be seen in people over the age of 65, according to the Aug. 5th report. [1][2][3]

Worthy of consideration is how Pew collected its data. Notably, adults and minors were not studied together; instead they were divided and studied separately according to different parameters. For the Aug. 5 adult report update, 41,291 landlines and 24,698 cellular lines were dialed, with a 10% response rate for landline and a 13% response rate for cellular. The Feb. 2013 adult report had a 11.4% response rate for the 33,785 landlines dialed and a 12.6% response rate for the 19,800 cellular lines dialed. The youth study, however, was not conducted using phones. Rather, with the help of the Berkman Center for Internet & Society at Harvard, in person interviews were conducted on 156 participants ranging in age from 11 to 19. Additionally, Pew Internet Project held two online focus groups totaling 20 people ranging in age from 12 to 17.

Though certainly a massive undertaking with some illuminating findings, there are some quirky elements to these studies. Such a heavy reliance on landline data is odd. Could landline owners generally be older or perhaps more rural, or late-adopters to tech trends? And is landline ownership dropping? Could this choice potentially skew the scientific sampling pool? Even the size of the sampling pools is wildly divergent. As well, if we are to inspect the most current *trends* in how the Internet and social media are being used — does it make sense to separate the youth, those whom have grown up digitally fluent? Won't the youth of today determine how we use the Internet in the future? If so, why exclude those under 18 from the from the adult study?

Nonetheless, this dialogue is merely meant to engage deeper thought

---

1   Brenner, Joanna and Aaron Smith. 72% of Online Adults are Social Networking Site Users. Pew Internet & American Life Project, Aug. 5, 2013, http://pewInternet.org/Reports/2013/social-networking-sites.aspx
2   Brenner, Joanna and Maeve Duggan. The Demographics of Social Media Users — 2012. Pew Internet & American Life Project, Feb. 14, 2013, http://www.pewInternet.org/Reports/2013/Social-media-users.aspx
3   Beaton, Meredith, Sandra Cortesi, Maeve Duggan, Urs Gasser, Amanda Lenhart, Mary Madden and Aaron Smith. Teens, Social Media, and Privacy. Pew Internet & American Life Project, May 21, 2013, http://www.pewInternet.org/Reports/2013/Teens-Social-Media-And-Privacy.aspx

about online use, rather than to disparage the Pew's herculean effort, which seems to be the most reliable source of information on the nature of the Internet landscape and its inhabitants. This information points to trends in demographics; it must be considered that there is no foolproof method of collecting specific information about every visitor to a website or user of an app. Statistics on demographics should be taken with a grain of salt, but can help you to determine a general sense of how each platform caters to your target audience. Check out the following charts to see Pew's findings. Chart 1 is the August 5th update:

Who uses Twitter
% of internet users who use Twitter

All internet users (n=1,895)	18%
a	Men (n=874)	18
b	Women (n=1,021)	17
Race/ethnicity	
a	White, Non-Hispanic (n=1,331)	14
b	Black, Non-Hispanic (n=207)	27[a]
c	Hispanic (n=196)	28[a]
Age	
a	18-29 (n=395)	30[bcd]
b	30-49 (n=542)	17[d]
c	50-64 (n=553)	13[d]
d	65+ (n=356)	5
Education attainment	
a	Less than high school (n=99)	16
b	High school grad (n=473)	15
c	Some College (n=517)	20[b]
d	College + (n=790)	19
Household income	
a	Less than $30,000/yr (n=417)	15
b	$30,000-$49,999 (n=320)	16
c	$50,000-$74,999 (n=279)	20
d	$75,000+ (n=559)	22[a]
Urbanity	
a	Urban (n=649)	21[c]
b	Suburban (n=893)	18[c]
c	Rural (n=351)	11

Figure 8.1

Source: Pew Research Center's Internet & American Life Project Spring Tracking Survey, April 17 – May 19, 2013. N=1,895 adult internet users ages 18+. Interviews were conducted in English and Spanish and on landline and cell phones. The margin of error for results based on all

From the February 2013 Report:

The Landscape of Social Media Users — Figure 8.2

	% of internet users who....	The service is especially appealing to ...
Use Any Social Networking Site	**67%**	**Adults ages 18-29, women**
Use Facebook	67	Women, adults ages 18-29
Use Twitter	16	Adults ages 18-29, African-Americans, urban residents
Use Pinterest	15	Women, adults under 50, whites, those with some college education
Use Instagram	13	Adults ages 18-29, African-Americans, Latinos, women, urban residents
Use Tumblr	6	Adults ages 18-29

Facebook
% of internet users who use Facebook

		Use Facebook
	All internet users (n=860)	**67%**
a	Men (n=418)	62
b	Women (n=442)	72[a]
Age		
a	18-29 (n=164)	86[bcd]
b	30-49 (n=254)	73[cd]
c	50-64 (n=231)	57[d]
d	65+ (n=183)	35
Education attainment		
a	Less than high school/high school grad (n=261)	60
b	Some College (n=250)	73[a]
c	College + (n=345)	68
Household income		
a	Less than $30,000/yr (n=223)	68
b	$30,000-$49,999 (n=152)	62
c	$50,000-$74,999 (n=127)	69
d	$75,000+ (n=248)	73
Urbanity		
a	Urban (n=261)	72
b	Suburban (n=442)	65
c	Rural (n=157)	63

Instagram
% of internet users who use Instagram

		Use Instagram
All internet users (n=1,802)		**13%**
a	Men (n=846)	10
b	Women (n=956)	16[a]
Race/ethnicity		
a	White, Non-Hispanic (n=1,332)	11
b	Black, Non-Hispanic (n=178)	23[a]
c	Hispanic (n=154)	18[a]
Age		
a	18-29 (n=318)	28[bcd]
b	30-49 (n=532)	14[cd]
c	50-64 (n=551)	3
d	65+ (n=368)	2
Education attainment		
a	Less than high school/high school grad (n=549)	12
b	Some College (n=519)	15
c	College + (n=721)	12
Household income		
a	Less than $30,000/yr (n=409)	15
b	$30,000-$49,999 (n=330)	14
c	$50,000-$74,999 (n=283)	12
d	$75,000+ (n=504)	12
Urbanity		
a	Urban (n=561)	17[bc]
b	Suburban (n=905)	11
c	Rural (n=336)	11

Pinterest
% of internet users who use Pinterest

		Use Pinterest
All internet users (n=1,802)		**15%**
a	Men (n=846)	5
b	Women (n=956)	25[a]
Race/ethnicity		
a	White, Non-Hispanic (n=1,332)	18[bc]
b	Black, Non-Hispanic (n=178)	8
c	Hispanic (n=154)	10
Age		
a	18-29 (n=318)	19[cd]
b	30-49 (n=532)	19[cd]
c	50-64 (n=551)	12[d]
d	65+ (n=368)	4
Education attainment		
a	Less than high school/high school grad (n=549)	11
b	Some College (n=519)	16[a]
c	College + (n=721)	20[a]
Household income		
a	Less than $30,000/yr (n=409)	10
b	$30,000-$49,999 (n=330)	15
c	$50,000-$74,999 (n=283)	23[ab]
d	$75,000+ (n=504)	18[a]
Urbanity		
a	Urban (n=561)	13
b	Suburban (n=905)	16
c	Rural (n=336)	18

Source: Pew Research Center's Internet & American Life Project Post-Election Survey, November 14 – December 09, 2012. N=1,802 internet users. Interviews were conducted in English and Spanish and on landline and cell phones. Margin of error is +/- 2.6 percentage points for results based on internet users.

Note: Percentages marked with a superscript letter (e.g., [a]) indicate a statistically significant difference between that row and the row designated by that superscript letter, among categories of each demographic characteristic (e.g. age).

Social Media

From the Youth Report:

Figure 8.3

Which social media profiles or accounts teens use most often
% of teen social media users who use the following sites most often ...

	2012
Facebook	81
Twitter	7
Instagram	3
YouTube	1
Tumblr	1
Google Plus	1
Yahoo (unspecified)	*
myYearbook	*
Pinterest	*
Gmail	*
MySpace	0
Meet Me	0
Other	1
Use all my social network profiles/accounts equally	2
Don't Know/Don't have own profile	1

Where teens have social media profiles or accounts
% of teen social media users who use the following sites ...

	2011	2012
Facebook	93%	94%
Twitter	12	26
Instagram	n/a	11
MySpace	24	7
YouTube	6	7
Tumblr	2	5
Google Plus	n/a	3
Yahoo (unspecified)	7	2
myYearbook	2	*
Pinterest	n/a	1
Gmail	n/a	1
Meet Me	n/a	1
Other	8	6
Don't know / Don't have own profile	2	1

Source: The Pew Research Center's Internet & American Life Teen-Parent survey, July 26-September 30, 2012. n=802 for teens 12-17 and parents, including oversample of minority families. Interviews were conducted in English and Spanish. The margin of error for teen social media users is +/- 5.1 percentage points.

Note: This chart is based on an open-ended question that asks: "On which social networking site or sites do you have a profile or account?" and was asked of anyone who had answered yes to one or both of two previous questions "Do you ever use an online social networking site like MySpace or Facebook?" and "Do you ever use Twitter?" Sites listed for comparison were those that were reported in 2012 by at least one respondent.

Asterisks (*) indicate that less than 1% of respondents gave the corresponding answer.

SOCIAL NETWORKING WEBSITES AND APPS

Facebook

Facebook is the social media standard for those of the post-Internet generations. Facebook, out of all of the major current social media platforms, is the oldest, longest-running, and most relied upon. It provides a mashup of images, texts, posts, and integrated apps, all of which reflect your life and simultaneously create an Internet avatar existence. Facebook can be said to measure your online footprint, the extent of your reach, and the level of your engagement.

Though people change their relationship statuses, post inappropriate party pics, live-blog their meltdowns via Facebook statuses, etc. on their personal accounts, it's important to keep in mind that on your own official artist page, you should remain professional albeit engaging. Even reality shows, like *Real Housewives* and *Keeping Up With the Kardashians*, which are full of tears, name-calling, and even the occasional brawl, keep it mellow on their official pages.

In terms of social media platforms, Facebook is hardly the first of its kind. In fact, it is more of a successful revamp of Myspace, which itself was a re-vamp of the original Friendster platform. The reason why Facebook was initially able to surpass the others is because Facebook was exclusive. Facebook, in its inception, only allowed membership to Harvard students. This was then expanded to the Ivy League, Boston area universities, and Stanford. Over time, Facebook opened up to a slew of other universities, and then high schools, before finally settling into its current policy of "anyone over the age of 13 can join". But back to this notion of exclusivity. Registering on Facebook once required a university e-mail address as proof of identity.

Myspace and Friendster had no such limitations — there was no "velvet rope". On Myspace and Friendster, you could create fake accounts or multiple accounts. You could lie about your identity. But none of these behaviors instill feelings of trust and safety. Hence Facebook's *exclusivity* led to its success. People were interested in social networking, but they wanted to interact with real people within their academic and social spheres as opposed to strangers.

What does this mean for you as a professional? It means that because Facebook is intrinsically tied to your own social sphere — because in order to create a company or artist fan page, you must have a personal Facebook account — gathering the attention of strangers and unknown quantities can be more difficult. Though it is certainly possible that a stranger may "like" your artist or company page, it is much more easy to connect with people who you are friends with on your personal account. Actively engaging strangers (even if said strangers share similar interests) through your personal account is unusual and may be misconstrued, or even considered a faux pas. (Hence the term "Facebook stalker".) Although this limited accessibility might seem like a detriment, keep in mind that these qualities allow for Facebook to be a lot more personal than other social media platforms. Because of this, your community or audience is already naturally more supportive and thus probably more willing to share with their respective audiences about your new endeavours. So, don't underestimate Facebook's potential at helping to launch your company, vision, or project.

Mode of Use and Interactions

When using Facebook, you have some options — do you want to create a personal account for yourself? Or would you prefer an entity page like a fan or company page for your work or business? Or how about an entity page in the way of a group page where a small community can network? Perhaps you would like an event page for an upcoming bash, screening, reading, or premier? Each of these options comes with the same abilities to post, share, and comment upon a mash-up of images/video/text/et cetera. Determine which page type is most beneficial to your specific needs. You have many choices! ...And yet in one way you do not: you cannot create an entity page, unless you yourself have a personal page. This, in effect, makes the entity page like a shell account for YOU. Facebook, as a social networking platform, is unusual in its insistence on this fact. And do keep in mind that this personal/professional link may work both for or against you.

So what to do with this account? **You create a digital avatar.** You project yourself, your essence, onto the screen. You create and populate a Facebook page with content about you that reflects your life, your interests, and your sur-le-vif existence. You then connect with other avatars, by way of friends, fans, and invitees. You communicate and share content with each other in the virtual arena. The content you share can run an extra-large gamut — from text, links, images, videos, polls, and games. From your personal account you may join common-interest communities and hubs, all arranged by page. You may also arrange your own friends into sub-groups and categories delineated by parameters of your own choosing (eg "Work Friends" "Family" "People You Don't Actually Like But Felt You *Had* to Accept as Friends"). All of these sub-groups have customizable privacy options whereby you can determine how much access you would like each to have to your personal page and how much you want to share per group. You are, in effect, writing the rules and curfews and behavioral traits for your avatar's interactions with other avatars. The notion of the avatar is, at its simplest, one of a digital representation of self. However it is also intrinsically tied to the notion of *construct* in that people *construct* their digital identities and *choose* their representations. These are not perfect reflections of self — they are edited and imperfect. And yet... if this is so, why didn't Facebook go the way of the dodo bird, or of Friendster? *Why does Facebook work?* Recall that so much of Facebook's success and draw is because its virtual world and the avatars who populate it are drawn from and paralleled by your actual world and the real people who populate it. There is, at the center of its core processing-servers...something akin to a heart.

Facebook's primary application and advantage is to interest and inform people who are already *connected* (in some way) and would like to know more. You may use your personal account to attract and to stabilize consistent interaction through intimate engagement from your actual social circle — almost like using your personal account to piggyback off your entity account. Benefit from Facebook's insistence on the personal avatar, by using your personal page to bolster your other pages, and vice versa.

It's unfortunately necessary to monitor your Facebook account in the professional working world because the FB avatar is so transparent! In using your personal account as a shell for your business or company, you should be vigorously maintaining the image you desire best for your company. Online activity, whether yours or a Facebook-friends, can negatively affect your image. Be aware and vigilant when it comes to content (comments, photos, etc.) in which you are tagged, in addition to that which you yourself post. This is especially so in the pursuit of employment or universities, or even just to refrain from horrifying your dear, sweet, elderly auntie, should you have one on FB. In an article by ABC, posted in May of 2011, Facebook was being used as a personality test by companies and businesses. " 'It turns out you can get to within 10% of a person's personality score by looking at Facebook,' said Jennifer Golbeck, a computer science professor who has become an expert at social media studies." So, keep your personal life personal; Facebook is a place where people can "Facebook-stalk" other people, and it is not good to reveal too much personal information about yourself to the public.

A Note on Toggling Between Accounts

The pro of having the entity page linked to your personal account is that it is easy to toggle between your personal account and entity account. The con is that it is easy to toggle between your personal account and entity account. (This is not a typo). Although being able to switch accounts easily is convenient, it is also important to be careful when using Facebook so that you don't accidentally post something unintentional or inappropriate to your business page.

Another thing to keep in mind is that Facebook interactions can go on for hours or even days because of the unique algorithm Facebook uses to display updates on people's news feeds. Therefore, content writing doesn't rely on time for effectiveness. You need not worry about posts being buried by chronology on a news feed. Facebook utilizes its EdgeRank algorithm, which shows users the posts that are the most relevant to them. EdgeRank determines relevancy by assessing the number of likes and comments a post receives. While Facebook's EdgeRank algorithm is considered largely proprietary, it is safe to say that what can and will bury your content is a lack of interest. What this means for you is that to be seen by as many people as possible, you'll need to post the most engaging, useful, relevant information for your target audience. On the bright side, interesting and engaging content will be buoyed up despite the passage of time.

A final note on mode of use, the ability to segment content based on topic (aka hashtagging) is a feature Facebook has historically not offered. It's also a reason why certain people gravitated toward other platforms. But the social media landscape is continually changing, and Facebook has introduced a hashtag feature to its network. Facebook is integrating clickable hashtag phrases and words in status updates. Clicking on hashtags will prompt a pop out feed that aggregates others posts that have been tagged with the same phrase. Essentially, this makes it easier to see what other people are talking about on related topics. According to Facebook, hashtags have become a vital part of popular culture, and since people had been using them on Facebook organically (although they failed to aggregate or link to anything), Facebook has decided to implement hashtags into its network. However, initially, what comes up during a hashtag search will be limited by privacy settings.

> As a final note, remember this: Facebook is constantly updating its interface, revamping its platform, and reworking its modes of use — all without releasing much information on the new changes. Because of this and its "locked books", users generally do not know exactly what the ramifications of these updates are — making it even more difficult to track how effective your work is with Facebook marketing. It does serve you well to look into the specifics of each update and to thoroughly inspect your privacy settings after each change.
>
> Here are some resources for the down low on the nitty gritty details of current Facebook use:
>
> https://www.facebook.com/help/
> https://newsroom.fb.com/
> http://allfacebook.com/
> http://mashable.com/search/?t=stories&q=facebook

Best Practices

Be responsive. Interacting on a regular basis with Facebook friends and fans is vital for continued growth and success. You can interact with people who are already following the page by posting new content. Content can run the gamut from photos, video, text, polls, and more — simply put, it is anything you post or share. Keep track of the comments to your posts. When others comment, their comments will appear immediately below your content, and a notification will also appear in the top corner of your page. All of your content is meant to engage people. So respond to comments, ask questions, and like comments (and content) added by fellow users. Comments responding to questions should be helpful and polite. If a user has a more complicated issue that will require a lengthy explanation, it is good to offer the user an email address to write to.

When you post new content, you are interacting with everyone who likes your Facebook page. Psychologically, this means that individuals may or may not pay close attention to what is posted because it is meant for a wider audience. This is one of the reasons why it is important to keep your content brief and to include an image in order to engage your audience more. Liking certain people's comments is a good way to quickly show you are paying attention to what is posted on your Facebook feed. This is more personal than posting new content because you are giving something or someone individual praise. Likes require minimal effort, so they are more like a pat on the back than a hug. It is unnecessary and redundant, however, to like your own posts from your business account. It is better to like the content from your personal account, if you must do so, in order to follow the Facebook etiquette of not liking your own posts.

Demographics

Though Facebook initially began as a site exclusively for the college age population, its demographic has increasingly opened up to include an older group of people. According to to the Feb. 2013 Pew report, 35% of people 65 and older use Facebook. Nonetheless, its target audience currently remains at the 18 to 29 age group, with about 67% of Internet users having an account. Additionally, according to the same study, more women use Facebook than men do, and Facebook's users are predominantly wealthy and urban, with some college education. According to Pew's 2013 youth report, youth have saturated Facebook more than any other social media platform.

When considering the demographics of Facebook, it is important to consider the audience that you are trying to reach, or the audience that you have, rather than the audience that Facebook reaches as a social media platform. You can try to force square pegs into round holes, but perhaps it would be better to find something that fits. For example, posit two types of online shows: one is a web series about college dorm-life and its wild parties. The other series is a serious study about life as an octogenarian. These shows have different core audiences, and one audience's presence on Facebook is different than the other's. Even though, according to Pew, the 65+ age group is growing on Facebook, you may still find it difficult to secure traction and develop a huge audience. Meanwhile, the college dorm show just might be more in its element on Facebook. You will benefit from monitoring your Facebook presence to check. It is important to reap what you sow with your social media efforts. You want as much return on your investment as possible. Put your efforts into Facebook to the extent that it makes sense for you. However, if another platform brings you a higher rate of return and a higher rate of engagement, then consider making that your primary focus.

Layout

Having a clear, high quality cover photo and a visually interesting profile picture is important **(Figure 8.4)**.

Your Facebook page should also provide an "About" section, which should summarize your work, your art, web series, or production company in one sentence. Providing "Basic Information," such as the location, founding year, mission statement, plot outline, company overview, and contact information, is highly recommended. As for your "Wall", posts run the gamut in terms of content type and as a general rule the posts run chronologically. However, despite this, you can still carve out a place for your posts by accessing the privacy settings on a case by case basis and also by "hiding" or "highlighting" posts. "Highlighting" posts in your timeline puts them front and center: it is a way of making important information and media standout.

Figure 8.4 **Cover photo on** *Orange Juice in Bishop's Garden* **Facebook page**

A note on apps.

There are a variety of Facebook add-on apps, tabs and services that give their users an opportunity to go beyond the Facebook Page elements and greatly expand the platform's functionality and capabilities. These apps allow you to integrate custom marketing and communications tools that are not natively available on Facebook. For example, there are several installable apps that add the ability to include custom tabs to your Page, where you can insert your own HTML and other Web code. This would allow you to embed images, video, text, and other media in any layout your imagination and web design skills can cook up. You can also use similar apps to create a landing or welcome page that describes your work in detail and encourages visitors to "Like" your Page. There are apps to sell products directly from Facebook, create polls to get feedback from your fans, display YouTube videos, insert a contact form, integrate your Twitter account — and the list goes on and on. If you want to be truly unique, Facebook provides tools for new developers to get started with building apps. Basic website building skills are needed, or you can even search the Jobs or Developers for Hire section of Facebook's Developer Forum to hire a programmer to work on one for you. *Please see the chapter on WEB DESIGN for a more in depth look.

Last Looks and Helpful Tips to Avoid Common Mistakes

1. When using Facebook as a company, you should focus on talking to your audience instead of talking at them. Asking your audience questions about its opinion is a good way to make sure your conversations on Facebook are not one-sided.

2. Most people will not pay attention if there is too much text on your Facebook page. Make sure to keep your posts brief and break up the text by adding a photo, video, etc.

3. Sharing content from other networking sites (such as Instagram, Youtube, Vimeo, Wordpess, Blogspot, etc…) is acceptable and can add some extra value and diversity to your feed. However…

4. Refrain from sharing content from Twitter. It is highly recommended that you do not have your Twitter automatically upload content to Facebook because Twitter is much more fast-paced in terms of the number of acceptable times to post a day. Auto-linking your Twitter could easily make for dozens of additional posts, which could inundate and annoy your Facebook audience. Keep in mind that Facebook is a personal social networking site, and people go to the site to network with their friends and family. It is important to post sparingly on Facebook in order to maintain your Facebook likeability: posting three or four times a day is sufficient **. Also, the posts you write will show up on other people's feeds depending on their Facebook preferences. Overposting leads to news feed spam, and some users might "hide" your posts as a result. If so, you will still have the same number of "likers" or friends, but your reach will be crippled.

   The 3 to 4 times a day is not a rule written in stone. Your analytics will help you glean just what is the best mode, method, and times of use for you.

   Consult your analytics, which we will tell you how to install and to analyze in "Analytics" on page 177 ▶

5. When posting, you should keep in mind that the majority of people who have liked your page are already interested in what you are post-

ing. You should focus on sharing additional information about your work that you would like the fans to be aware of, such as new photos, videos, or blog posts.

6. Consider incentivizing content by making extra content Facebook-exclusive. For example, if people want access to deleted scenes, perhaps they can access them only by liking your Facebook page.

> **CASE STUDY**
> **The Atlantic Asks: Is Facebook Making Us Lonely**
>
> In the article "Is Facebook making us lonely? published in The Atlantic, author Stephen Marche presents numerous theories on whether Facebook is contributing to a loneliness pandemic plaguing the United States and the world, at large. According to the article, about 20% of Americans reported feelings of unhappiness because of loneliness, a psychological and not a physical state. "Similarly, in 1985, only 10% of Americans said they had no one with whom to discuss important matters, and 15% said they had only one such good friend. By 2004, 25% had nobody to talk to, and 20% had only one confidant." But is the evolution of Facebook and the Internet, in general, responsible for this trend? Some have argued that because the world has become increasingly more virtual, there are fewer opportunities for people to build worthwhile relationships that lead to potential confidants. And, though loneliness is hard to define, some studies have reported links between loneliness and Facebook use, especially in terms of feeling isolated from one's family. Yet, Moira Burke — who organized a study of users' Facebook activity — found that whether one is lonely depends largely on how a user engages with Facebook. Namely, if a user is engaging in it passively, s/he will tend to find himself or herself with residual loneliness, after viewing Facebook. This is largely because people who sit on Facebook and merely scan their news feed often feel like an entire world is going on without them. Yet, if someone uses Facebook to actively communicate with his or her social network, he or she may experience feelings of happiness, especially if that activity leads to social engagement outside of the virtual community. Overall, Burke's research found that people who experience loneliness through Facebook are already lonely; Facebook might just exasperate those feelings.

> *(... The Atlantic Asks: Is Facebook Making Us Lonely continued)*
>
> Additionally, studies have found that people who tend to be active on Facebook are those who are narcissistic because they enjoy how Facebook gives them a podium to broadcast about themselves, and narcissism and loneliness often go hand-in-hand. Moreover, because of the nature of Facebook, it nearly demands constant interaction from its viewers, both those who are using its passively and actively. This, in turn, ultimately "denies us a pleasure whose profundity we had underestimated: the chance to forget about ourselves for a while, the chance to disconnect."
>
> So, in general, what should you, as a digital creative, take away from these findings? There are a couple things to consider. Firstly, because a large number of people on Facebook are reportedly lonely and possibly narcissistic, it is important to engage them when posting. For example, instead of merely posting a photo with a quick explanatory caption, perhaps ask your audience a question to encourage a dialogue. Secondly, inspire positive interactions within the Facebook community. So, say someone starts a private conversation in a public forum, try to reopen the conversation so that it applies to everyone. In particular, keep an eye out for people who try to carve out individual conversations with you on your own business fan pages. Make sure you are responsible for piloting the conversations back to the entire group; this can be done by asking the whole group for their thoughts on the "private" conversation. This action, in turn, will make people feel included and valued![1]
>
> ---
> 1   "Marhe, Is Facebook Making Us Lonely? ," The Atlantic, http://www.theatlantic.com/magazine/archive/2012/05/is-facebook-making-us-lonely/308930/

Twitter

Twitter's logo is fittingly a swift and chatty bird. It's flock-friendly and reliant on the support from its surrounding network. With the contributing tweets of millions of users every day, and conversations and interactions across all topics, Twitter gathers the scoop and the news from our near and distant neighbors. Compared to Facebook, it is more about hearing and seeing rather than about showing and telling. But Twitter's not just about peacocking. As a platform, it is driven by conversing and community-building. There's only room to grow for the chattiest birds with the most engaging songs, best listening skills, and good posting etiquette. Yet, keep in mind, while on Facebook unfriending your buddies is a massive faux-pas, the same is not so for Twitter. There's less shame with Twitter's unfollow, so you better be interesting! But more on this later.

Figure 8.5 Twitter profile bio for *Orange Juice in Bishop's Garden*

Twitter gives you powerful context to connect your message to what's happening in your industry in real time. It means your tweets can influence conversations in a way that can help build your project, expand your recognition as a tastemaker, make yourself someone worth following and supporting. The beauty of Twitter is that there's no need to be overly formal. In fact, the less business/ad speak, the better. Twitter puts every user on a level playing field. Joe Shmoe from the coffee shop's opinion is just as accessible as the leading film critic's. As long as you have something relevant, valid, or interesting to say, people will listen to and engage with you. It's less about who you are and more about the content of your tweet (that is, unless you're Justin Bieber).

Mode of Use and Interactions

As a social networking website, Twitter is a microblogging service that allows users to post and to read text-based messages, or "tweets," of up to 140 characters. It's basically the SMS dialogue of the Internet. It's the real-time conversation of what's happening in the world, the pulse on what's on people's lips (or fingertips). People join Twitter to bring them closer to the things they care about, whether it's cool digital photography, what's going on in the Middle East, or what new flavor the gelato shop down the block is offering. It's the platform for the infovore; people on Twitter want to be in the know.

While most Facebook connections are founded in offline relationships, such connections aren't as necessary on Twitter. Interactions on Twitter are more based on shared interests and are less reliant on IRL acquaintanceship. There's no limit to whom and how many people you can follow, tweet at, retweet, or mention. This makes Twitter a place rich with diversity in people and in content. There are economic development experts, geriatric oncologists, presidents, web series creators, and teen Tumblr addicts — and they're all given equal space to project and connect on Twitter.

Despite not needing any credentials to have an opinion, Twitter is actually a surprisingly legitimate and trustworthy source — so much so that major news outlets now employ their own social media news-gathering departments. Sure, trusted press sources have been hacked, but on the whole, if you want to know what's happening in real time from the source, you don't go looking for a newspaper or online article, you go to Twitter.

However, when hackings happen, mass hysteria can ensue...

Social Media

> **TALES FROM THE TRENCHES**
> **Horror Stories**
>
> ---
>
> **AP** **The Associated Press** ✓   [Follow]
> @AP
>
> Breaking: Two Explosions in the White House and Barack Obama is injured
>
> ← Reply ⟲ Retweet ★ Favorite ••• More
>
> **483** RETWEETS   **17** FAVORITES
>
> 10:07 AM - 23 Apr 13
>
> ---
>
> The Associated Press's Twitter account was hacked in April 2013. Within seconds of a false tweet reporting that the White House had been bombed and President Barack Obama injured, panic erupted on the U.S. stock market and the Dow Jones Industrial Average immediately fell by 150 points. The AP quickly deleted the fake tweet, but however brief the panic it caused, the hack demonstrated how tightly intertwined Twitter has become in our culture and economy.[1]
>
> ---
>
> 1   Wang, Kisling, Lam, "Fake Post Erasing $136 Billion Shows Markets Need Humans," http://www.bloomberg.com/news/2013-04-23/fake-report-erasing-136-billion-shows-market-s-fragility.html

Those exaples just go to show how many of the interactions on Twitter are between complete strangers and how this works to Twitter users' advantage. Interestingly, this hasn't made Twitter a creepy medium. While people regularly "Facebook stalk" one another, and the term has become a common phrase in our culture's lexicon, there's no equivalent reference to Twitter. The alarm of stranger danger is absent from Twitter.

Twitter is an ideal venue for the content-focused user for several reasons. First, the amount of information you share about yourself is decidedly less. All you need is a valid email, a username, and a password to set up Twitter. There's no prying into your gender, your location, your education, your work, website, political affiliation, or religion. Twitter doesn't care who your mother is, what siblings you have, what your favorite music, books, or movies are. Your profile picture need not even feature you. It's easy to join and to participate on Twitter anonymously with your Twitter handle alone — no name is even necessary.

Second, Twitter doesn't aggregate all tweets and mentions of yourself in one public arena like a Facebook profile does. Instead, Twitter gives you a profile page that consists of your list of tweets. You can even protect your tweets by making them private, which means that requests to follow must be approved or denied by you first. Tweets consist of your text, with additional photos and videos if you chose to post them. Users can search for every mention of your specific Twitter handle, or user name; however, these are just mentions of say @YourName) and not a multi-medium aggregate of photos, quotes, check-ins, places/things you like, etc. This means that it is more difficult for people to stalk you. This relative anonymity on Twitter creates comfort of use and a platform for people to openly share their opinions, thoughts, and interests.

Adding to the appeal of anonymity and interacting with strangers, Twitter takes the awkwardness and fear out of following and unfollowing users. As touched upon in the Introduction, if someone follows you on Twitter, you're not automatically obligated to follow him or her back. As a platform that is not as tied to your real-life social sphere, you are freed from certain restrictive etiquettes. It is considerably more acceptable to stop following people on Twitter. After all, your followers are not necessarily your everyday acquaintances. And if you unfollow a user, it's not as personally affecting as when you unfriend someone on Facebook because a Twitter user will still be able to freely view your tweets. But because of the seamless ability of users to follow and unfollow, you must be interesting or people will not follow you. This creates a Darwinian survival of the wittiest. People come to Twitter to be informed, entertained, amused, or directed to a place where they can be. And if you're not, you won't gain any interest or following.

With an extended social sphere, you're not expected to share intimate personal content on Twitter. If you end up sharing too many mundane things about yourself that aren't of interest to other people, watch your number of followers begin to slip! Facebook is the appropriate show-and-tell platform, where you have photo albums of yourself and your friends. That is the medium to post, boast, and brag about your life — not Twitter. Your followers won't appreciate if you "blow up" their Twitter feeds with your moment-to-moment ramblings about how hungry you are or how the bus is late (unless you're funny about it). And they definitely won't appreciate countless plugs and self-promotion tweets for your content. Just be you. This gives you room to be creative, to have some fun with wordplay, and to share the interesting things going on with you or with your projects. Just remember it's a conversation. Your tweets are thrown into a milieu of pre-existing dialogue, so always try your best to be value-added.

The ability to hashtag, or segment content based on topic, is a feature Twitter has always offered — it's part of the socio-gravitational pull of Twitter. Twitter allows users to take advantage of hashtags, trending topics, and saved searches, giving Twitter users a large circle of influence. Essentially, this makes it easier to see what other people are talking about on related topics. It creates cataloguing and search options for what would otherwise be just a massive information dump.

There is also a great culture of attribution etiquette on Twitter. Attribution is provided on other forms of social media, but Twitter attribution is clear and unmistakable. Simply by clicking the retweet (RT) button, the original poster's tweet is tweeted to your followers unchanged, in the original words and with the OP's avatar. The key is that you are giving credit and maintaining the original language. Other times, if a tweet can't fit in under 140 characters, users can post a MT, modified tweet, where they modify the language, while maintaining its essence and still crediting the original poster. Additionally, on Twitter you don't necessarily have to agree with a tweet that you're sharing. It's commonly stated on Twitter that RTs are not endorsements, and in most cases, this is treated as a given. Compare this to Facebook, in which a lot more interaction is required to share an item. You cannot share with just one click: it is a multi-step process, with an emphasis on you writing your own tagline to describe the shared content. This restricts the number of times a post is shared on Facebook and attests to the virality of tweets and rapidity at which people follow new users on Twitter.

Figure 8.6   An example of the ease with which one can join and participate in discussions on Twitter vs sharing a link on Facebook

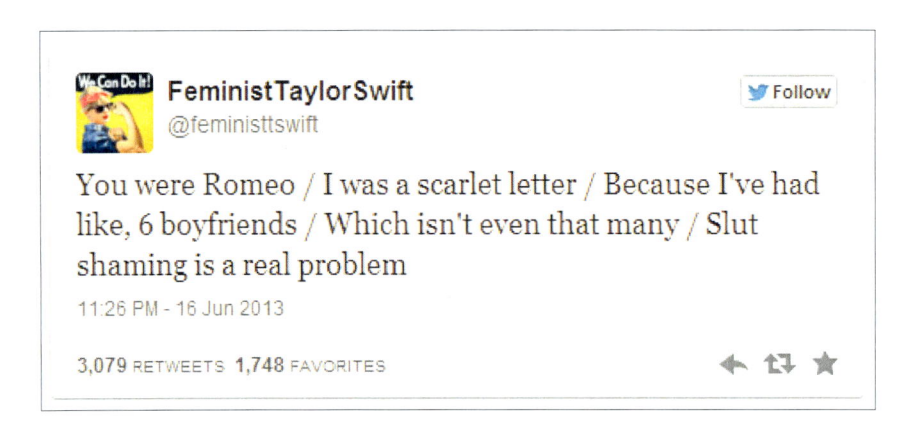

> **FeministTaylorSwift**
> @feministtswift
>
> You were Romeo / I was a scarlet letter / Because I've had like, 6 boyfriends / Which isn't even that many / Slut shaming is a real problem
>
> 11:26 PM - 16 Jun 2013
>
> 3,079 RETWEETS 1,748 FAVORITES

Clara Beyer, better known as @FeministTSwift, hilariously takes pop-star Taylor Swift lyrics and gives them a feminist slant to address issues like sexism, gender roles, and female empowerment. FeministTSwift's account amassed more than 75,000 followers in just under a week. Consider, however, if she had created a FeministTSwift Facebook page first. The ease of following, the RT, and instantaneous "shareability" of tweets allows traction to catch on faster on Twitter compared to other social media platforms. With the push of a single button, a tweet can be shared with thousands of users.

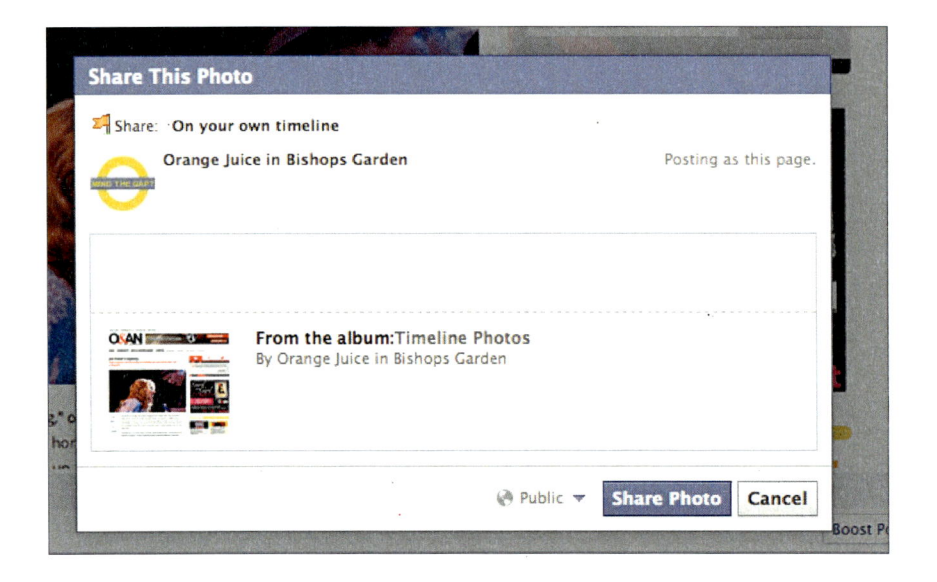

Share This Photo

Share: On your own timeline

Orange Juice in Bishops Garden   Posting as this page.

From the album: Timeline Photos
By Orange Juice in Bishops Garden

Public ▼   **Share Photo**   Cancel

Best Practices

The following are a few best practices to keep in mind when you begin your Tweeting:

Be Interesting and Informative

What you say, how you say it, and how often you respond all have a tremendous impact on the relationships you build on Twitter. Your tweets should reflect your individuality and the essence of your project. Write a Tweet like you're having a conversation with a friend and strive for a genuine, approachable communication style. However, the digital world is crowded and you've only got 140 characters at a time to get your message across, so keep your tweets interesting. The more cunning and interesting your tweet, the more memorable you are and the more rewarding you are to follow.

Additionally, be informative. If you just released a new video, blog post, or photo, share it online with a brief description and a link. Also, tweet tips or relevant breaking news even if it's not directly related to your content. Is there a new web fest taking submissions? If you have a technique or favorite camera to use, tell people about it! Tweet about topics other than your specific production or web series-related stories. You can tweet just about anything if it's interesting and representative of the image you want to portray. Keep in mind that the most retweeted content on Twitter tends to contain links, pictures, videos or quotes.

Also, highlight positive press stories and news about your work, industry or community that your followers will find interesting. Always remember to tweet your press in a way that rewards those who mentioned you! Include the @username of the reporter and media outlet when you tweet your press to provide clear attribution. Highlight the people in your production by tweeting photos of them hard at work on set, or having fun at the editing station is also a great reminder that there are actually humans behind accounts. Having cast members tweet in character can also provide this human element. It provides another way for users to feel connected with you and can also be a great way to make your project look appealing to possible funders.

Sharing is Caring

Users come to Twitter to get and share the latest insights, so give it to them! Share unique information about your work that can't be found elsewhere, like a glimpse of developing projects and events by sharing behind-the-scenes photos of filming or live tweet of events with teasers. Now with the Vine app, you can even share short video clips directly from your Twitter account. Alternatively, you can ask your followers for advice or input for certain decisions relate to your production. Twitter is filled with people wanting to share their opinions, so give them an opportunity to do so! This also shows your followers that they're important to you and that you listen to their comments. Doing a group post including a "call to action" or question that includes all the other people in the post is also a way to extends social media recognition joy to others.

Another way to provide users an incentive to follow you is to tweet updates about special offers, discounts and time-sensitive deals related to your work. For example, launch special Twitter-only promotions to your followers, such as giveaways, sneak peeks, etc. Just be aware, however, that your tweets show up in other people's news feed. Having several tweets in immediate succession about the same thing to various users will annoy your Twitter followers. And once you give a user a reason to stop following you, it's difficult to get them back!

Also, make it easy for your followers to retweet you. Be conscious of the 140 character restriction when writing your Tweet and allow enough character space for users to fit RT + @yourusername. This means that your original post shouldn't be more than 80 or 90 characters. While this may limit how much you can say, you will be rewarded with many more retweets as a result.

Be Involved

Because Twitter is like a conversation, best practices recommend that you regularly monitor the comments about your content and reply in real time. Favorite and retweet positive messages about you and thank those who praise you for your work. Also promptly address critical tweets about your content in a helpful manner to show you appreciate follower feedback. This can be as a public tweet or sent as a direct message, which is private. However, in order to send a direct message to a user, they must be a follower of yours.

> **20/20 Productions DC** @OJBishopsGarden   3 Jun
> Part of our inspiration for ou r#CapPride13 Tapestry project for is learning @NeilGGiuliano's story. It's incredible! bit.ly/15ngckp
> Expand
>
> **Neil G Giuliano** @NeilGGiuliano   1h
> @OJBishopsGarden Thx for the shout out! Keep up all your gr8 work!
> ● Hide conversation ← Reply ↻ Retweet ★ Favorite ••• More

Figure 8.7   Positive Twitter interaction that elicited a reply

As a general rule, because Twitter is an informal avenue for communication, don't be afraid take risks and branch out! If you have a question about submitting to a festival, or want to reach out to a Hulu executive. Many of them are available on Twitter and willing to interact. Also sending tweets to reporters and editors, actors and directors, media outlets and organizations, politicians, about your content or special events is a great way to bring attention to your content. Calls to action are also well responded to if you're a Twitter user with whom people are familiar and enjoy following.

Calls to action are also well responded to, if you're a Twitter user with whom people are familiar and enjoy following. For example, 20/20 Productions released a call-to-action video that featured the Washington, D.C. Mayor Vincent Gray's impassioned plea for marriage equality. When tweeting about the video, the tweet came with the video-link and mentioned the mayor's Twitter handle in addition to other organizations with similar lines of interest. The tweet was subsequently retweeted by the mayor and other users. The mayor then followed the 20/20 Productions account and sent a direct message with an email contact for follow up opportunities. Additionally, other related organizations offered their support in response and a continuing dialogue outside of social media emerged. In this way, Twitter became more than just a social media platform: it became a springboard for joint interests that led to further business opportunities.

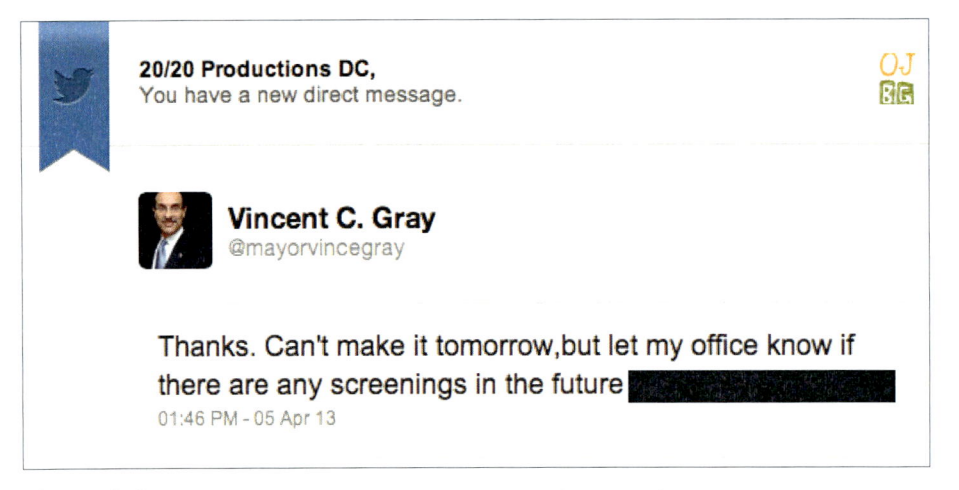

> **20/20 Productions DC,**
> You have a new direct message.
>
> **Vincent C. Gray**
> @mayorvincegray
>
> Thanks. Can't make it tomorrow, but let my office know if there are any screenings in the future
> 01:46 PM - 05 Apr 13

Figure 8.8   Twitter outreach to Mayor Gray led to a direct message

Make use of Twitter Apps

There's a plethora of applications that serve to simplify Twitter. There are apps that allow you to schedule tweets so that if you've created content you want people to see, you can schedule the same tweet to post multiple times throughout the day or week. Because of Twitter's real-time communication, it is important to post content several times per day. This helps reach as many users as possible because you have a better chance of posting while they are reading. But, bear in mind that unfortunately, when scheduling tweets, Twitter's Tweetdeck does not allow you to include photographs in scheduled tweets. This is just another example of how Twitter is more words-driven than visually-stimulating. There are also analytical apps that can tell you when the best time of day or day of the week for you to tweet is, and when you get the most retweets or new followers. All this information will be specific to you, your followers, your location, among other factors, and there are many analytics programs that help you find your tweetspot — for example: TwitSprout, Twitonomy, Hashtracking, TweetReach, Mentionmapp, Follwerme, Tweet Archivist, Twitter Grader, Tweriod, FollowerWonk, TwentyFeet, Twtyland, Xefer, Twitalyzer, etc.

Demographics

While the image of a social media maniac is often viewed as someone from the younger generation, Twitter initially drew the attention of "adults who might not have used other social sites before Twitter," according to a New York Times article published in 2009.[4] As found by the same NY Times article, one of the main reasons teenagers were originally turned off by Twitter was because of its seemingly professional slant. Despite being intended to communicate with friends, like Facebook, Twitter attracted users who used it as a means to market themselves and to share ideas and ask questions. Now, however, the 18 to 29 group (the youngest adult demographic in the Pew Aug. 5 adult Internet update) composes the majority of Twitter users, followed by the 30 to 49 age range (**Figure 8.2**). Still, Twitter does not seem to be wildly popular with those under 18, as only 7% reported using it, according to the 2013 youth report by Pew.

Layout

Twitter is also unique in the sense that all tweets are presented chronologically (although you can pay for a promoted post in which Twitter advertises your tweets). Thus, nearly all the activity and engagements with your tweets happen within the first hour of their posting. Twitter users are worried about the immediate present. They use the network for real-time communication, often to find pertinent, time sensitive information. Outdated news will be skipped because thousands of other tweets will have appeared before you got around to posting anything.

Despite the focus on strict chronology, there are still customizable elements to your Twitter page and it always behooves you to create and curate your online identity. You can alter and create a custom background, to make it more engaging or specific to your work and audience. Your profile image and avi are also customizable. They need not display you, but may instead showcase people/places/things of relevance. Switching up these images creates visual interest and may even be a conversation starter within your community.

---

[4] http://www.nytimes.com/2009/08/26/technology/Internet/26twitter.html?_r=0

Additionally, you may choose to create public or private lists, which appear on your side-bar.

Helpful Tips to Avoid Common Mistakes

1. *Avoid starting tweets with usernames.* If you mention another user in a tweet, for example @OJBishopsGarden, at the very beginning of a tweet, only the users who follow your account AND @OJBishopsGarden will see the tweet in their timelines. If you would like for a tweet to been seen all your followers timelines try rewriting your tweet so it doesn't begin with a username, or place a period (".") at the beginning of the tweet.

2. *Tweet multiple related people at once.* Certain information can be sent to relevant groups. If you have video content that would be relevant to the lesbian, gay, bisexual, and transgender (LGBT) community, you can mention several LGBT usernames within a single tweet. If all relevant users you would like to reach cannot fit into one tweet, divide them up as evenly as possible. When you get new followers, you can also tweet them all together thanking them for following you.

3. *Use hashtags when appropriate.* Developing a hashtag specific to your content is useful in branding yourself and giving other users a way to mention your work, or things associated with it, in a concise way. For example. *Orange Juice in Bishop's Garden* (a lengthy name) developed the hashtag #OJBG, making it easier to include the show in tweets using fewer characters. Also, use hashtags for larger topics or any fun topics that are trending. Think of hashtags as the theme of your Tweet. Users can then click on a hashtag to see other similarly-themed tweets and find yours in search. Trends come and go on Twitter, but participating in conversations about trending hashtags can bring visibility to your account. There are also recurring trends that develop over time. For example #FF or "Follow Friday" is a great way to bring visibility to yourself by way of promoting other twitter users you enjoy following.

4. *Use the search function.* Twitter provides the unique ability to simultaneously see what other creators and people are tweeting about. The search function is a great tool to search industry keywords to quickly gather information and to use and inform your strategy. More useful, however, is searching for terms related to you and your content. Twitter allows you to save certain searches, so creating a search for your terms and variations of it will be helpful in finding people who are talking about your content without mentioning your username or hashtag. For example, searching for tweets related to *Orange Juice in Bishop's Garden*, appropriate searches would include the name with and without the apostrophe, *OJBG, OJinBG*. Also searching the creator's name or the name of cast members can help you find people talking about your content. And if ever beneficial or appropriate, it gives you the chance to reply to, mention, retweet, follow, and build a connection with anyone who has mentioned you.

5. *Create and subscribe to lists* **(Figure 8.9)**. Once you begin following users on Twitter, your timeline feed can become overwhelming and unproductive. As an instantaneous feed, everything is in real time. Creating lists of related users will allow you to see tweets surrounding a certain group or topic without having to sift through your constantly refreshing feed. Once you create a list, you have the choice of making it public or private. Meaning you have the option of allowing others to view your lists and subscribe to them if they're interested. It's another way of showing users you recognize them and provides users a way to know to whom you're paying attention. You can also add users whom you don't follow to a list. So adding people onto lists may be a good way to keep your following to follower ratio down. (It's recommended that you maintain a ratio whereby there are more people following you than people you actually follow.) Essentially, lists help reduce the information overload that can often accompany Twitter.

Figure 8.9   Example of a Twitter Lists

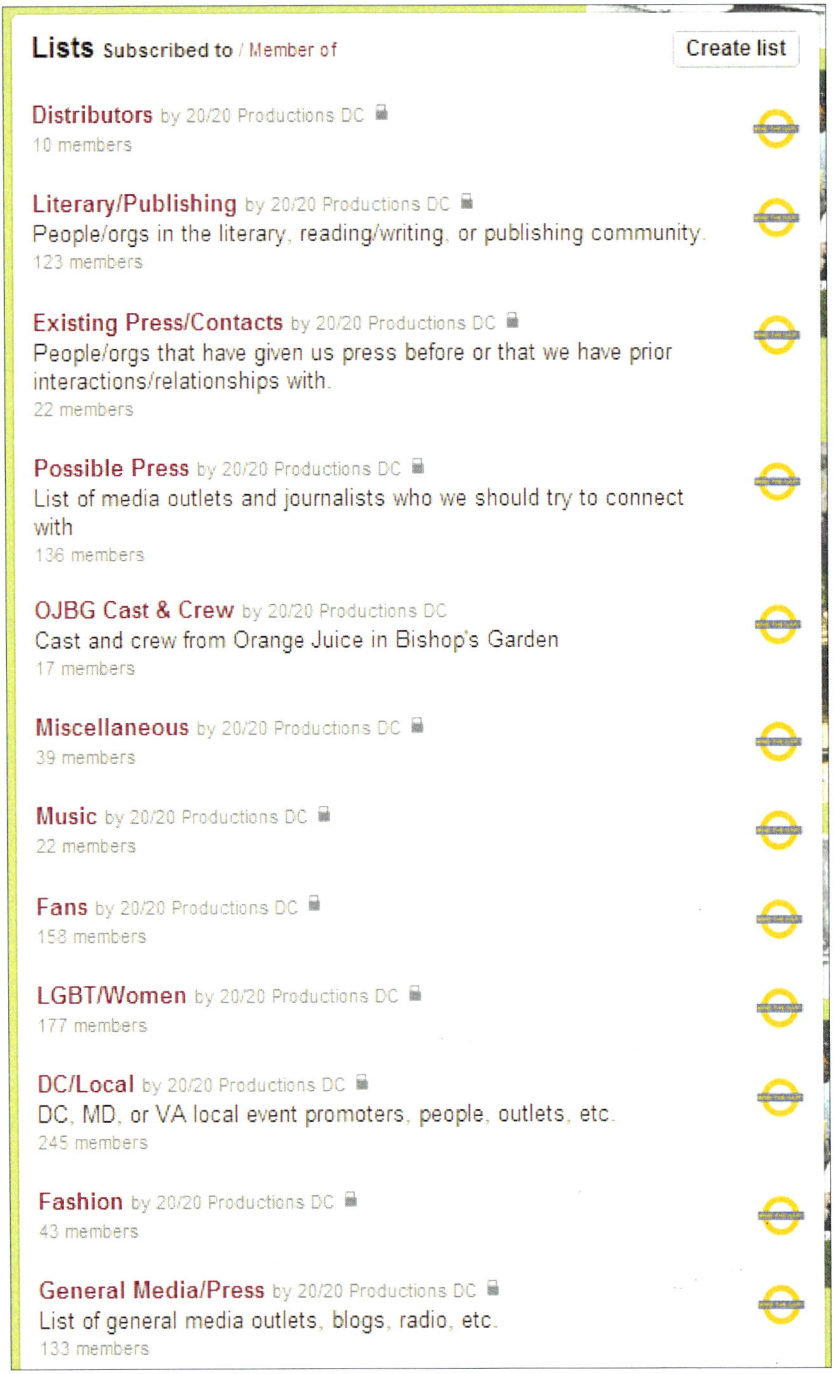

Lists Subscribed to / Member of — Create list

Distributors by 20/20 Productions DC
10 members

Literary/Publishing by 20/20 Productions DC
People/orgs in the literary, reading/writing, or publishing community.
123 members

Existing Press/Contacts by 20/20 Productions DC
People/orgs that have given us press before or that we have prior interactions/relationships with.
22 members

Possible Press by 20/20 Productions DC
List of media outlets and journalists who we should try to connect with
136 members

OJBG Cast & Crew by 20/20 Productions DC
Cast and crew from Orange Juice in Bishop's Garden
17 members

Miscellaneous by 20/20 Productions DC
39 members

Music by 20/20 Productions DC
22 members

Fans by 20/20 Productions DC
158 members

LGBT/Women by 20/20 Productions DC
177 members

DC/Local by 20/20 Productions DC
DC, MD, or VA local event promoters, people, outlets, etc.
245 members

Fashion by 20/20 Productions DC
43 members

General Media/Press by 20/20 Productions DC
List of general media outlets, blogs, radio, etc.
133 members

Pinterest

Remember those old school cork boards where you could tack on reminders, letters, pretty photos and basically anything else you wanted to include? Remember how much fun it used to be to buy one and tailor it so that it served as an inspiration board of sorts? Well, with the introduction of Pinterest in 2010, now all that fun has gone virtual. This aptly-named site allows users to pin photos onto as many boards they wish to create. Although Pinterest is often associated with crafty, artistically-inclined, suburban or rural women, this isn't the full picture. Pinterest can certainly be useful to you as a digital creator and curator. In fact, Pinterest has quickly become one of the biggest, well-known social media platforms.

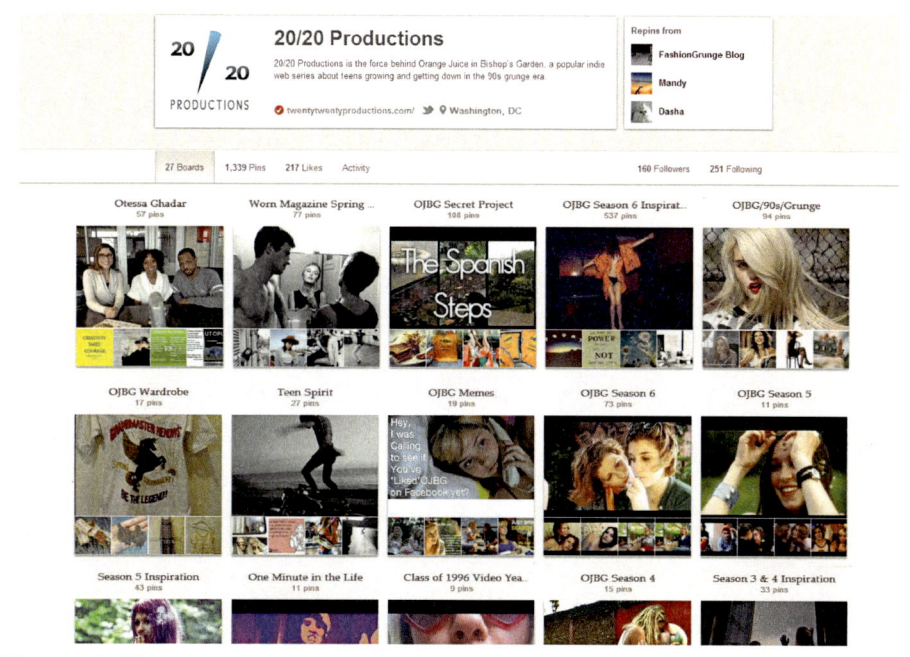

Figure 8.10   Example of Pinterest boards on 20/20 Productions page

One of Pinterest's comparative advantages is that it gives the public a sense of whom you are as a brand, by displaying what kinds of things you like, what interests you, and what inspires you. It's essentially a visual representation of the lifestyle of your brand, what you represent. It also sets you up as a tastemaker. If people enjoy your aesthetics, they'll follow and repin you. According to a recent survey, 43% of Pinterest members agree that they use Pinterest to associate with retailers or brands with which they identify, compared to just 24% of Facebook users. As a means of holistically connecting with the public, Pinterest can be key.

Additionally, of all the social media platforms, Pinterest is by far the one through which most users actually shop and pay for products. While Facebook users are mostly interested in interacting with friends, and Twitter users want engaging conversations and news, users on Pinterest focus on striking visuals and imagery. This can make Pinterest the perfect platform to share stills or promotional photos of your video content. Because pins can be linked to other web pages, if you put your most eye-catching content on Pinterest, you'll find an engaged and active community, ready to repin, like, and buy into your content.

Mode of Use and Interactions

Pinterest, like Twitter, is largely anonymous. On Pinterest, though, it's not what you say but rather what you share visually. Holly Housewife in the Middle-of-Nowhere, America can gain thousands of followers and repins, if her pins and boards are aesthetically pleasing to a broad range of people. Though Pinterest does allow users to include a caption, what people are drawn to aren't the words on the screen but the large, colorful images. Even more noteworthy — although you are able to gain followers and follow others — unlike Facebook and Twitter, Pinterest doesn't rely on its interactions. It's generally not a place where people actively engage in conversations. Instead, it's more about an individual's *interests*, which makes it even more important that your pins are visually striking.

With a Pinterest account, users are given the ability to create new boards, create new pins from uploaded images or images from the web, follow other users' boards, repin and like other users' pins, and share pins via Facebook or Google. If you so choose, you can also join Pinterest as a business, which allows you to verify your website so that other pinners know about your brand.

But what exactly are boards and pins? In order to understand the concept of a board, it is at first important to know that a pin is essentially any virtual image that someone has decided to upload onto Pinterest. It could be a recipe, a quote, a photo of a landscape or fashion model — it's up to you and to other users to decide! A pin is then hyperlinked so that when users click on it, their directed to either the original source or to another website. So, for example, say you pin a photograph of a scrumptious-looking loaf of banana bread; you could hyperlink it to bring users to your awesome culinary blog where you've written the recipe. Or are you a baker? You could link to your bakery's site. The same could be done for any entity. For example, on 20/20 Productions Pinterest account, we've often pinned *Orange Juice in Bishop's Garden* memes we've created and then linked them either to our YouTube account or to our website. In general, pins are a great way to direct to traffic to another source, hopefully generating more viewers for you, your work, and your brand!

So, now that you understand what a pin is, the concept of a board can be tackled. Basically, a board allows users to categorize their pins by topic. Because users must name each board, boards provide an easy way to market the brand (or interests) of a user. So, for example, on our 20/20 Productions account, we have boards for each of our shows, where we pin relevant clips linking to their respective YouTube accounts. But we also have other boards, such as "Teen Spirit" and "90s" & "Grunge", that fall in line with the image of *Orange Juice in Bishop's Garden*. What's additionally great about boards is that users can follow other users' boards, essentially establishing an audience for each new pin.

Additionally,—calling all shoppers and sellers!— Pinterest is often used as a portal for online shopping. In fact, according to Huffington Post's 2012 social media study, Pinterest post with prince tags boast 36% more (re)pins than those without them.[1] So, if you have items from your work that you can monetize and that you want to sell — such as the dead wardrobe from your web series — don't be afraid to post them on Pinterest!

Overall, Pinterest is a positive place focused on uplifting images and messages. There's a lot of snark and sass on Twitter and Facebook, but studies show that less than 1% of posts on Pinterest are negative in tone. So, at least for now, Pinterest is a happy place to be — an important fact to keep

[1] Honigman, "100 Fascinating Social Media Statistics and Figures From 2012," TheHuffingtonPost.com, Inc., http://www.huffingtonpost.com/brian-honigman/100-fascinating-social-me_b_2185281.html

in mind when you go about pinning items onto your boards.

Best Practices

Get creative with it. Create memes, post stills, wardrobe pics, sell items from the set, etc. Create boards that represent your entity but don't solely feature your work. Let your hair down a little bit; be a human and express your personality. Gather pins that are related and would have a similar audience. How does what you are sharing relate to your brand and to your image? Categorize your boards into what you believe in and think about the messages you want to portray. In addition to being creative with what you pin and what boards you create, don't forget to be savvy when it comes to crafting captions for your pins. Although you'll see many pins without a caption and even though the pin itself is more important than the caption, an engaging, informative caption can help to further build your audience. Plus, for photos that aren't fully self explanatory, captions can paint the complete picture. But be careful with the length of the caption. Though you don't want them to be uber short, remember you're not writing America's next greatest novel. Aim for a length akin to something you'd see printed alongside a photograph in a newspaper.

Pin video clips of your actual show. To do this, simply pin the item like you would any other pin from a website. If for some reason this doesn't work, you must go to the source website for the video and press the "pin it" button on the toolbar. For the captions of all video pins, be sure to include a description of the video, with the episode title and number. It's also helpful to add in the website of the original content just for clarity sake. To keep Pinterest users happy, it may also be wise to create a separate board exclusively for your video clips.

Know your audience. Like every other social media platform, it's vital that you know who you're targeting when adding pins and creating boards. Additionally, make sure to continually review analytics (which Pinterest offers itself) to ensure that you're actually reaching your target market.

Repin others. Although it's true that Pinterest isn't about holding conversations, you should still aim to build or target a community on it, and one of the best ways to do that is by repinning others. Whenever you pin someone else, s/he receives a notification with your avatar linked to it. And if s/he is a curious sort of folk, then perhaps s/he will check out your boards and will hopefully like what s/he sees! In addition to repinning other users, you should also follow other people's boards.

Act as a resource. Pinterest isn't about blatantly selling a product or service. Even though a bunch of business talk has been thrown out, it's important to bear in mind that people don't solely come to Pinterest to make a purchase. Much like Twitter, don't just pin items you sell or that are directly related to your content; pin things around the web you like and want to share, too. Often, Pinterest users are just there to feel inspired. So, make sure your account offers up some valuable information and content for your audience. That's the way to a Pinterest user's heart.

Promote your pins on other social media platforms. When you post a new image to a pinboard, you can also share a link to it on Twitter, Facebook, and other social networks, which is a great way to spread awareness.

Organize contests through Pinterest. If you're just starting out on Pinterest and you want to get some likes and followers quickly, then running a contest might be the perfect solution. To run a contest, there are many apps that you can, some favorites include Woobox and Votigo. But, make sure you read Pinterest's Terms of Service first, so you don't violate any rules or have your contest time period run out too soon.

Layout

Like Twitter, Pinterest displays pins chronologically. The difference is that because of Pinterest's boards feature, pins are also divided up onto a user's various boards. When looking at a user's account page, a small dashboard can be viewed with the user's account name and description. Obviously your account name is a given because you'll want it to reflect your brand, but get creative with the description. Choose colorful language that shows you have character! When looking at someone's account, you'll also have access to viewing that user's boards, pins, likes, followers, and who s/he follows. Through a user's account page, you can also have the option of following a board, multiple boards, or all of them. Cover photos for each board can also be selected to further market the concept of the individual board and of your brand as a whole. Because these photos are often the first thing people see when looking at a user's account, make sure they're intriguing. Also, keep in mind the notion of scale online. Landscapes do not work as well for cover images because they just look too teeny. Capture something that's either identifiable or something that's so abstract that people won't be constantly wondering what exactly they are looking at. Because cover photos are really the only customizable part of a Pinterest layout, make sure they really speak to your viewers!

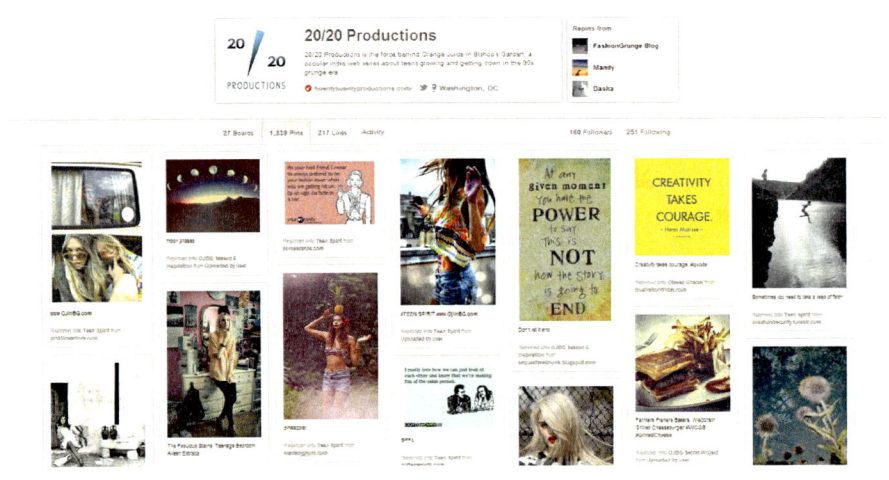

Figure 8.11   Example of Pinterest boards on 20/20 Productions page

Demographics

According to Pew studies published in Feb. 2013, the average Pinterest users are white, well-educated women. Both the 18-29 age group and the 30-49 age group each comprise 19% of interest users who use Pinterest. Most of the people using Pinterest reside in rural settings.

Interestingly, according to the dazeinfo.com 2013 study, 97% of the fans of Pinterest's Facebook page are women.[2]

One more interesting thing, as reported in the same article — 57% of

---

2   Shree, "Social Media Statistics 2013: Facebook, Twitter, Google+, Instagram, Pinterest And More!!!," Dazeinfo, Inc., http://www.dazeinfo.com/2013/01/10/social-media-statistics-2013-facts-figures-facebook-twitter/#ixzz2ePkhdIAM

Pinterest users interact with food-related content and its said to be the number one category of content.

Also interesting statistic that according to the Huffington Post's 2012 social media study, Pinterest posts with prices get 36% more (re)pins than posts that do not have them.[3]

Last Looks and Helpful Tips to Avoid Common Mistakes

1. Hashtags are no longer reserved for Twitter's domain. Use Relevant Keywords. For the SEO buffs, it's a no-brainer. You want your content to be search-able, so remember to include a description with relevant keywords for everything that you share. Pinterest has enabled a search function to categorize relevant topics. For example, if you manage a Superman fan site, many of your Pinterest shares should include the #Superman hashtag in the description. This will help other users easily find your content in their searches.

2. Make yourself "pinnable". If you want people to start pinning from your sites (which is an incredibly efficient way of spreading the word), then you have to make your website, blog, et cetera very visual. Add "Pin it" buttons and widgets across your various platforms to encourage in-depth engagement by others. Cross-platform optimization also improves your branding and ensures your efforts are supporting each other. PS Make certain the button or widget is installed in a clear and obvious place.

3. Attribution, attribution, attribution — pin from an original source when at all possible and make sure that credit and source links are provided. A nice touch is to mention the owner by name as well, when applicable. Not only is this excellent etiquette but it is also akin to backlinking: it helps boosts your efforts and boards too.

4. The now and later method – pin at all points of the creative process. Your boards make excellent inspiration sources while ideas are still in

---

[3] Honigman, "100 Fascinating Social Media Statistics and Figures From 2012 ," TheHuffingtonPost.com, Inc., http://www.huffingtonpost.com/brian-honigman/100-fascinating-social-me_b_2185281.html

infancy. Pinterest boards can even provide a visual outlet and resource for crowdfunding efforts. To boot, you can highlight your process while it's in full swing — or after when you are ready to release your brain child to the wild. The salient point is that at any point in the creative process you have something meaningful to share, which is particularly well serviced by the Pinterest platform.

5. When group thinking isn't "groupthink". Pinterest provides an excellent visual outlet for multi-person projects or departments. Themes, images, and expressions are readily accessible and the visual layout is excellent for hashing out ideas in the abstract, before wading into the deep-end. When used wisely, Pinterest boards can save crucial time and steps by deciding what works and what doesn't in the digital realm, before investing serious resources in the real physical realm.

Instagram

Instagram is a public scrapbook — but unlike physical scrapbooks of the past, Instagram is in real time. It is a representation of what is happening, instead of what has happened. It is a platform to post photos and short videos, with captions, and to see and comment on the image captures of others. Among such a vast collection of scrapbooks, you must stand out to succeed.

Why Instagram? It can open up your content to an entirely different group of viewers. This is the realm of the visual. As such, it denotes a different mode of viewing, of understanding, and of learning. Integrating with Instagram may not only link you to others you may otherwise have missed, you may also find that the visual method aligns more closely with your own mode of interpreting and interacting with the world.

In a way, Instagram combines the best features of Facebook and Twitter; it allows you to couple a photograph with text that can feature hashtags. Hashtags allow you to become a hit in one word— it links you to your people.

Mode of Use and Interactions

Instagram is a visual social networking platform for sharing photos and micro-videos (e.g. super short videos). Users apply "filters" to photographs and videos from their mobile phones, add relevant "tags" and comments, and share them with other users on Instagram, or elsewhere.

Content is catalogued via hashtags, and captions add additional spice and flavor. Bear in mind that hashtags and captions can be more than just descriptive. Clever, humorous, or ironic touches may make for viral content. Additional cataloguing is available via geo-locational settings. When your locations settings are activated, all images are posted to your "photo map" — a cartographic representation of what snaps you have taken where. You can choose to add (or not add) on a case by case basis with each upload. Geo-tagging is like checking-in to a location. You add or type in the location of an image, and the location is listed as a sub-heading. Geo-tagged content is not only added to your photo map — it is also publicly sortable. Shared images can be sorted and viewed by location based check-ins. As an example, all (non-private) geo-tagged content of, say, the Washington Monument is filed, sorted and catalogued. You can literally view thousands of other people's moments and snaps, via location.

You can interact with other users on Instagram by following other users, liking their photographs, tagging friends in your photos, and responding to comments left on your photographs. How to find your niche? Consider searching by tags. Which tags are specific to you, your work, or your company? Finding out who is posting images to your niche tags will help you find a relevant and welcoming community. Follow those users, and then extend it into another degree of separation. Determine who they are interacting and liking, you may also find those users of interest and importance to you.

Best Practices

Creating Traffic is tantamount to your Instagram success. First things first, it is recommended to upload high quality photographs, but ones that do not appear to be professionally taken. Professional photos aren't received well because they make you look like you're trying too hard. On Instagram, users appreciate an insider's view, as if they are getting a behind-the-scenes look at a world. There is an interest in the personal, as opposed to the exclusively professional. It is not a place to simply repeat and re-post professional images from one's website or reel. Successful accounts, whether they be for designers, companies, artists, or beyond, are notable for documenting the interesting life and its process — not just regurgitating promotional images.

So you have a thrilling photo and are ready to post a photostream masterpiece. What next?

Engaging images, which are properly labeled, are more likely to reach their target audience. This is why making use of tags is so important. Adding relevant tags to your photographs will create traffic to your Instagram account. Tagging your account with popular tags will bring more traffic than tagging with unpopular tags. Popular tags can be determined by visiting a site like webstagram, which lists the top current tags in order of popularity.

 If you are aware that your audience is likely to search for a particular tag, then it is important to use that tag when posting your photos. For example, college-aged users are likely to search for the tag #college or #freshman. Alternately, foodies are likely to use and search for #foodporn, #foodgasm, #nom, or #vegetarian. If your image is tagged thusly, then it will be a part of the tag timeline, and it may bring in new viewers. A note of caution though, over-tagging can garner you many likes and followers, but it doesn't necessarily connect you to a community. Instead you may find that you have many one-time likers who never return and that your tagging habits have instead caught the attention of spam-bots and fake accounts. Over-tagging can even be a turnoff to some Instagram users, who will view it as a desperate attempt to grab likes and attention, as opposed to building something organic over time. Find relevant tags, but don't go overboard by posting the 25 most popularly-used tags regardless of of whether they even relate to your content.

Additionally, Instagram is like a scrapbook in that captions (whether comments or hashtags) add a nice personal touch. When uploading photos, write an interesting, witty, or informative caption that tells people why what they're looking at is important. In keeping with the real-time, off the cuff feel, colloquial captions can be preferable. And remember, everyone gets a slice of cake at the end — i.e. a community of users will gravitate toward that picture of you at the #Trekkie convention last summer.

Demographics

For Instagram, which is a relative newcomer to the social media market, statistics age quickly. It has been stated that Instagram experienced 900% user growth in each of its first two years of life.[4] As reported by the Feb. 2013 Pew adult study, the majority of Instagram users are young adults in the 18-29 demographic, with a focus of interest in minority communities and in urban centers (**Figure 8.2)**.[5] Users are also more likely to be female than male. But, remember that this study excluded minors. Fortunately, another even more recent study conducted by Marketo, a company that builds marketing automation software, did include minors in their analysis. According to its research, women make up 55% of the 100 million Instagram users, with 45% being male. The largest user demographic is the group aged 18 to 24, consuming 34% of the proverbial pie; this is shortly followed by the 25 to 34 age group, which comprises 33% of users. Users aged 12 to 17 make up 20% of the total. Meanwhile 8% are 35 to 44, and 5% are 45 to 54.[6]

Layout

Instagram does not allow to alter or customize your layout. As a result of this, your Insta-feed will look just like everyone else's...except for the images themselves Thus, consider the quality of the images and captions. Also, it behooves and benefits you to focus on the flow of images from

[4] "Instagram Statistics," Teleportd, Ltd. , http://nitrogr.am/instagram-statistics/
[5] Duggan, Brenner, The Demographics of Social Media Users — 2012 , Pew Internet & American Life Project , http://pewInternet.org/Reports/2013/Social-media-users/Social-Networking-Site-Users.aspx?view=all
[6] "What Your Instagram Filter Says About You [Infographic] ," Marketo Blog, http://blog.marketo.com/blog/2013/03/what-your-instagram-filter-says-about-you-infographic.html

one to the next. In addition to having each photo be appealing, the overall montage, or catalog of view, should be enticing as well.

Last Looks and Helpful Tips to Avoid Common Mistakes

1. Keep it updated. Instagram accounts are more likely to be "un-followed," if they are not frequently updated.

2. Avoid the "feast or famine" situation. It's better to have a steady influx of photos, rather than vacillating wildy between all or nothing. In other words, don't lay off the Instagram for a week and then bounce back by posting 15 photos in rapid-fire succession.

3. Too much is #toomuch. Don't over-do it by over-tagging.

4. Make use of your own entities' hashtags and stick with them. Frequent use will make sure other users remember that these tags are yours. Encourage others to make use of your tags. It's DIY branding. And the tags are trackable! (Ex. #WildWestofFilm)

5. Keep a keen curatorial eye and create captivating images. Behind-the-scenes and personal snaps are best. Avoid sharing captures which are purely promotional, overly professional, or which are readily available other places. Your Instagram feed should be special and different — otherwise why have one? Because Instagram has a focus on *real-time* updates, try to focus on documenting your *process* or your *behind-the-scenes world*.

6. Be wary with selfies, your breakfast/lunch/etc, pet and/or baby pics. People can have violent reactions to an overload of the above. Feature these sparingly and make certain they are captivating, relevant, and/or have snappy tags and comments.

7. Post images of special offers and giveaways. It incentivizes others to frequently check-in and interact with your Instagram feed.

8. Save some mystique. Yes, you can document and share your entire life in real-time, from here to eternity. That doesn't mean you should.

Be a good editor. Avoid TMI (too much information) moments. And don't post anything that would endanger your job prospects or your security. Be particularly aware when selecting the geo-tagging option. Geo-tagged content is added to your photo map. This means that if you take a photo at home, you could be sharing your home address with strangers.

9. A note on smartphone-centric use: Instagram was intended as a platform to share snapshots taken in real time, via smartphones. Some Instagram users upload professional (non-smartphone) photos to their phones and then load them to their Instagram feeds; there is some controversy and backlash to this use.

10. Don't hard sell. Promoting yourself or your entity by following a bunch of irrelevant people or by promoting via comments on other people's photographs is not recommended, as it will irritate many Instagram users. It is better to sparingly promote by captioning your own photographs on your Instagram account. Be thoughtful and logical about your interactions and promotional efforts.

11. Desperation is embarrassing! Don't request that people follow you.

12. Don't be a robot. Interact and discuss. Follow relevant users and comment sincerely and engagingly. Encourage others to share their thoughts on your work.

13. Be wary with regramming. And — never steal someone else's image and then pass it off as your own. It's not just morally reprehensible, it's also a violation of someone's intellectual copyright. This is why you have to exercise such caution with regrams. A regram is a repost of another user's capture. Only post a regram if you are certain it is applicable and welcome. Here is the etiquette: give credit where credit is due, add the person's Instagram handle, and state that this is a #regram.

14. Try creating a meta-thread or meme. Consider encouraging others to take and share images that relate to your work, project, or brand. Then actively highlight their efforts.

> **TALES FROM THE TRENCHES**
> **One Day i December**
>
> December 17, 2012 heralded new Terms of Service for Facebook's then-recently-acquired Instagram platform. It was, simply put, an EPIC FAIL. Wired called it a "boneheaded." "PR disaster." Mashable called it "brazen." National Geographic was "very concerned"[1] What was all the fuss about? The new terms stated that Instagram claimed rights on all photos posted publicly from Jan 17, 2013 on. Any licensing or revenue was Instagrams. Your images could be sold or licensed without your knowledge or consent. And, bizarrely, if any legal problems arose from said use, you were liable. The Internet at large threw an intellectual copyright tantrum. A class action lawsuit materialized. Instagram quickly capitulated. And what about the users? They vacated the Insta-sphere. The app reportedly lost four million users as a result of that scandal, though Instagram denied that this was the case. [2]
>
> That said, Instagram has been steadily bouncing back ever since it dropped the offending language from its Terms of Service.
>
> ---
>
> 1   "Instagrab: The Story of the Instagram Rights-Grab Mess ," PhotoSecrets, http://photosecrets.com/instagrab
> 2   Loeb, "Get ready for ads on Instragram within the next year," Vator, Inc., http://vator.tv/news/2013-09-09-get-ready-for-ads-on-instragram-within-the-next-year#xBYEtiLI511KSuev.99

Tumblr

As a social networking website, Tumblr is a microblogging service that allows users to post rich and varied content — visuals, text, and beyond — with an attention to personalized layout. It is akin to a digital magazine in that you can create and curate content to reflect your tastes and interests. But it is also different in that it gives you the ability to interact and engage with others through reblogging and liking posts, and following other users.

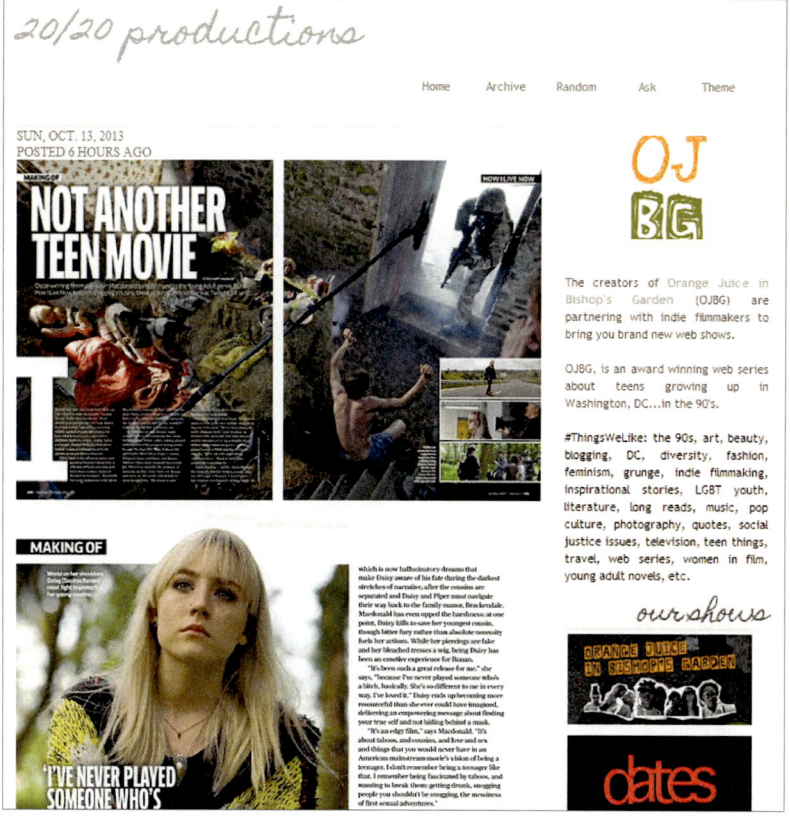

Figure 8.11 Example of Tumblr page

Of all social media platforms, Tumblr is the most like a traditional blog. However, one of the main differences is that it encourages brevity. Like Twitter, Tumblr utilizes hashtags to enable search-able trending and provides you with a chronological news feed of posts from the people you follow. These posts can vary from photos, texts, quotes, GIFs, videos, personal stories, articles, etc., as Tumblr was created to share many different forms of content. In contrast to Twitter, users on Tumblr typically spend much more time on one account, scrolling through that person's blog like they would flip through the pages of a magazine.

Mode of Use and Interactions

For the average Tumblr user, there is little desire or pressure to present a personal image or to interact with others in an intimate way. Tumblr users tend to build communities through shared interests expressed on their individual Tumblr blogs, and then they find support within those communities. For a digital creator, brand, or Internet aspirer, it is important to find the right community with whom to interact. Confused about how to find a community? Here is a very simple way to get you started. Communities may be found by searching particularly relevant hashtags. Observe what results ping back at you. There are certain users who will frequently post content in those particular tags. If their page relevant to you, "follow" them. Now, expand your breadth of focus by a degree of separation. E.G. which users frequently interact with your new favorite Tumblrs? Who do they reblog, and who reblogs them? These "second degree of separation" Tumblr users may have much to offer you, as well. Consider "following" them, too. Searching by tags and tracing interactions and reblogs will pinpoint your potential community. Hopefully, once you start following them, they'll check out your blog, like what you have to offer, and follow you back! Tumblr users are a dedicated, supportive crowd. Once you gain a follower, there's a good chance they'll come back to it.

Circling back to the theme of Tumblrs being both creators and curators… what's additionally unique about Tumblr is that it empowers users to also become authors and editors — instead of merely commentators. In reference to the magazine analogy, Tumblr allows you to write your own content (yay, you're an author), but it also encourages you to reblog other people's posts onto your own Tumblr blog through a simple click of a button (congrats, now you're an editor). Some may find that they're more comfortable including original content on Tumblr because it doesn't stand alone. Also, it's important to note that Tumblr retains authorship. When you reblog someone else's post — although you are given the opportunity to add your own commentary — the post can still be traced back to its original author.

Best Practices

Stay focused. Like a magazine, Tumblr accounts should keep their intended audience in mind, as the most successful accounts post content related to a specific topic. There is a bit more flexibility in terms of combining categories on Tumblr than there is in the magazine industry, but try to create limitations so that you're not just blogging about anything and everything. Remember you're trying to create and interact with a community on Tumblr. If you really want to be incredibly broad with your account, at least make sure you tie it together with a specific visual or literary style.

Add relevant "tags" to your posts. These tags should be consistent with the focused identity you are crafting through your Tumblr blog because then they will obviously draw in more of your intended audience. But you should also keep in mind which tags are often frequented by users to spike traffic to your blog in general. You can tell which tags are the most popular on Tumblr by searching or navigating to the tag and seeing how frequently content is posted in that particular timeline. This search feature also allows you to look at content that might be useful for reblogging purposes. When tags are too specific, they are less likely to be frequented.

INSERT TEXTBOX

TALES FROM THE TRENCHES: A closer look at tagging

For the purposes of 20/20 Productions and *OJBG*, tags such as #quotes, #indie films, #90s, #films, #fashion, and #grunge are some of the more popular tags with which we tag our content. These tags remain tied to our personal identity, but their also wildly popular on Tumblr. We still use specific, less popular tags, such as #women in film, in order to reach people who have specific interests. But we often make sure those tags are in addition to the more frequently searched for tags. Also, it is sometimes useful to add several variations of the same tag to a post, as people write things in different ways. In order to attract people who are interested in the 90s, we have tagged #1990s, #90s, #I love the 90s, and #90s flashback. And, of course, don't forget to brand yourself! Determine your own hashtag: use it and encourage others to do the same. (As an example, we went the route of brevity and chose *#OJBG*). In addition to tagging your own posts, it is important to regularly check on tags specific to your project or company, in order to interact with people who have expressed interest in what you are working on.

Mix reblogs with original content. Although it is perfectly acceptable and even recommended to "reblog" other Tumblr accounts, a company-owned Tumblr account should never solely reblog. As a company and artist, it is important to establish your own voice, no matter the social media platform, and you can't do that by simply reblogging others. Moreover, because you are a creator with a product — however fledging it may be — you still inherently have a voice! People will follow your account due to their interest in the topic of your content, so posting original content is an easy way to promote your project or company. One important thing to remember when posting original content is to be informational and interesting, as Tumblr users are not keen on heavy promoting.

Be consistent with your voice. Although Tumblr is a casual social media platform, it is up to the user to determine whether he or she wants to be colloquial or more formal. On Twitter and Facebook, people are often expected to be more informal and to include many emoticons or exclamation points, in order to lighten the mood, but this is not necessary on Tumblr. It is perfectly acceptable to be direct on Tumblr. Although brevity is often encouraged, you should not feel the need to over-simplify your message. Successful Tumblr accounts often contain a mixture of informal microblogging and long, more formal blogging — but they have one common thread: in both their microblogs and long forms, the voice remains the same. The magazine analogy works again here: if you teeter between conversational and formal voices, you'll only confuse your loyal readers. One thing to keep in mind, if you do decide to approach your account with a formal voice, don't be too robotic. Users like to know there's a human behind every account!

Engage with the community. Tumblr accounts owned by a company or an artist who would like to self promote should focus on interacting with other users by adding commentary to posts uploaded by other users. Additionally, make sure to promptly respond to all messages received.

Schedule your posts. Fortunately, on Tumblr, posts can be put on a "queue" you determine so that a certain number of posts are released during the day between a specific time. Think about when your target demographic is mostly likely to be online; then make extra certain to set your queue to align with those active hours. Additionally, make sure these posts are spaced out throughout the designated time period. Similar to Twitter and Facebook, an account will lose followers if the updates are infrequent or too frequent. It is recommended that users post approximately five to 10 times a day.

Demographics

Relatively speaking, Tumblr reaches a niche group. Unlike other social media platforms, few Internet users are active on Tumblr. According to Pew's Feb. 2013 Pew adult study, only 6% of Internet users surveyed engage on the site, and most of them are between the ages of 18 to 29 years old. A review of Pew's 2012 teen study reveals that only 5% of teen social media users have a Tumblr.[7] That being said, Tumblr shouldn't be neglected, because, as mentioned previously, the Tumblr community is incredibly supportive.

In addition to the age group remaining consistent with other platforms, Tumblr users also tend to skew toward both the urban and educated. Interestingly, however, Tumblr is equally divided between male and female users, which cannot be said about other social media platforms.

Layout

Although it is clear that content is incredibly important for a successful Tumblr account, because of the visual nature of Tumblr, an account's layout and theme is almost equally important. A Tumblr account won't sell if it's disorganized, cluttered, and aesthetically displeasing. Avoid using a busy background — a solid white or off-white background is recommended because it allows your posts to speak for themselves. Once your background is in play, think strategically about *how* your content is organized. Select a layout that highlights and ameliorates the type of content you have. Layout should work with, not against, the specificities of your posts. And, of course, remember that just because a layout looks lovely or cool, does not guarantee it will be the best fit for your needs. For a Tumblr account that is photographically driven, it may be beneficial to

---

[7] DeSilver, "5 facts about Tumblr," Pew Research Center's Internet & American Life Project, http://www.pewresearch.org/fact-tank/2013/05/20/5-facts-about-tumblr/

have a multi-column layout. A text or video driven Tumblr, however, may work best in a single-column layout. There are many themes available for Tumblr that are free to use, so long as the appropriate credit is given to their original creators. These themes can be customized by editing CSS and HTML to change the color scheme and other attributes, or by adding widgets and other third-party add-ons.

See **"Web Site Basics and Web Design" on page 307** **for more information on customization** ▶

Last Looks and Helpful Tips to Avoid Common Mistakes

1. In addition to picking a simple layout, you should make sure that "like," "reblog," and "follow" buttons are easily located. If these button are not immediately obvious, it is possible that users will give up and move on.

2. Avoid adding background music. Not only is it often seen as annoying or unsettling to those perusing your posts, but the music will also restart every time a new page is loaded. If you would like to feature audio, consider adding it to a specific post that can be played intentionally, at the user's discretion.

3. Another community building feature Tumblr offers that you should use is the "Find Blog" page. This allows you to connect with "People You Know," but it also provides you with an avenue to further build your community based on specific interests, as you can search for blogs by category. Tumblr has organized potential blogs of interest based on popular categories, such as Beauty, Book Deals, Curators, Fashion, Film, and more.

4. Frequently check the "Activity" button so that you can see what sorts of posts people are liking and reblogging, and if there's an identifiable reason why you are gaining/losing/holding steady with followers. This data can be filtered by date and time.

> **TALES FROM THE TRENCHES**
> **Say "No" to the Hard Sell**
>
> It's worth restating that Tumblr users do not respond well to hard sells on Tumblr. Here's another lesson from the *OJBG* trenches: During the beginning stages of our Tumblr account, we made the mistake of frequently adding captions, such as "Check out OJinBG.com if you are interested in XYZ…" and, consequently, we lost a few followers. Instead of the including URL of the website, instead try linking a relevant word or a phrase to the website. For example, if we were to reblog content related to "women in film," we could write something like "One great thing about our production company is that it is female-driven" and link the words "production company" to our official website. Yet, even things like this should be done sparingly.

Additional Platforms Worthy of Consideration

There are certainly scads of platforms to consider, and new platforms are constantly emerging on the market. Staying relevant hinges upon staying up to date and knowing what your options are. That said, sometimes platforms are overlooked. Here are what I call the "Dark Horses" in the running. They are ones that people sometimes relegate to the margins; however, the benefit to be reaped is immense and can be well worth the effort.

Goodreads

Goodreads is a social networking platform for reading and writing. It allows readers to track everything about books, from compiling reading lists, to rating and reviewing, to interacting with authors. It's also a great platform for authors to connect with readers.

You may not consider yourself an author, but if you do have a script, that means you can publish it! Or perhaps you could adapt it! Or share a free piece of it! And that means there's another platform for you to dabble in. Of course, not every type of content is appropriate for this platform, but if you have a dialogue-heavy script or series, putting it up as a book online may be another way to allow people to discover your content, and it gives your fans another way to experience your show. Remember, you're always trying to give value to your fans. This is just another way for you to do so.

Goodreads was recently acquired by Amazon, so this platform may be subject to changes and to closer ties to its new parent company. Considering Amazon's distribution and retail power, this could be a helping hand to those on Goodreads because it could put your work within a wider distribution network. Selling your script books to fans, having books readily accessible for giveaways, posting a peek or a story-in-progress to your page, or opening up your work for discussion or suggestions — *all of this opens the literary world to you.* as another way to connect and engage with kindred spirits, respected reviewers, future fans, and potential collaborators.

Goodreads is the platform of the quintessential bookworm. It's a robust community of book lovers — these are dedicated readers and lovers of the written word. If you have fans of your show who are also bookworms, then being on Goodreads can be a great overlap. Authors, like yourself, can create special profiles in Goodreads that combine photos, bios, RSS feeds to blogs, upcoming events, videos, reading list, favorite quotes, and more. Goodreads also has an Author widget that you can add to your personal website or blog to show off reviews of your books. Similar to Pinterest, Goodreads establishes who you are by your tastes and preferences. What books have you rated highly? What's on your to-read list? You can make your profile page a dynamic destination for curious users.

Like other social networks, you can have "friends" whose updates you can follow, but you can also have "fans" of you as an author. Thus, within the Goodreads community itself, you can generate a band of followers. Just interacting and building within this community may be sufficient enough. But in case you are an avid reader and writer, with excitement to share about your writing and books — you will want to go the extra mile! Goodreads offers some promotional tools for authors, including advertisements, book giveaways to generate pre-launch buzz, Q&A discussion groups, and forums for groups of readers and writers.

Book giveaways are a great way to get new people interested in your work. The simplicity alone of doing a giveaway makes it worth the few minutes it takes to set up. Goodreads members see the giveaway, but you can easily share it on other social networks, such as Facebook, Twitter, your website, etc. via a simple link or by using a widget. The giveaway gives the option for readers to add it to their Goodreads shelves, thus showcasing your book to all of their friends as well. For those people who enter your giveaway but don't end up being one of the few winners, you can message them with an offer to read the ebook version of your script (if you have one) for free in exchange for a review. Keep in mind, these are voracious readers, many of whom would be happy to read your script for free! And actually having a visual representation of your story and characters in a web series is enticing— people who have invested in your story will want to see it come to life on the small screen of their computer.

For more on self-publishing, see "Self-Publishing" on page 289 ▶

LinkedIn

When using LinkedIn, imagine you are present at a massive networking event. LinkedIn is the largest professional network online, with users ranging from recent college grads to fortune 500 CEOs. Think about the people you want to meet to take your project or company in the right direction. A talented DP? A distributor? A publicist? It's likely that LinkedIn has a systematic way for you to connect with them and to start building a relationship. LinkedIn can be a great tool for increasing your show's and/or production company's visibility. It's extremely useful for researching and networking with potential distributors, for connecting with colleagues within the new media field, and for recruiting staff and crew. According to 2013 data, LinkedIn not only continues to grow — but it continues to do so internationally. With 64% of its users located outside the USA, LinkedIn allows truly global outreach.[8]

8   Alexander, "Social Media Usage Statistics 2013 [Infographic]," AnsonAlex.com, http://ansonalex.com/infographics/social-media-usage-statistics-2013-infographic/

Personal Profile

The first step when joining LinkedIn is to create and fill out your profile. Be descriptive and focus on your strongest assets. Are you an expert in your field; are you advanced in certain skills; or did you work on a really cool project? Emphasize your strong suits, but keep it honest. And make sure you add a profile picture so that people can see they're interacting with a real person and not something simply computer generated. Do keep in mind, though, what makes an excellent Facebook profile picture, may not make a stellar LinkedIn profile make. Think "professional".

A great way to promote your work is to include rich media — such as photos, videos, and web pages — which can be added via uploads or embedded links. These items can be placed within the Summary or Experience sections, and organized within each section by dragging and dropping.

Endorsements and Recommendations

Endorsements and Recommendations allow users to declare public approval or support of each other's work and abilities. You can request that someone give you an endorsement or recommendation (hopefully they'll have something glowing to say about that gig you did together), or someone can choose to do so on their own. Endorsements are used to "thumbs-up" skills and are incredibly easy — just a click of the button — whereas favorable blurbs concerning your qualifications are typically reserved for recommendations. These endorsements and recommendations allow people visiting your profile to see that others vouch for your work, which is especially useful, if someone reputable in your field gives you kudos. LinkedIn allows you to connect to social media sites and to upload your email addresses so that you can link to existing contacts—a great way to get the ball rolling.

Company Pages

If you've started a production company to develop projects, you can create a company page to market your business and to raise awareness of your company brand. These pages allow you to share information about your services to potential clients and to promote job opportunities.

Users can Follow these pages, and your employees can link them to their profiles.

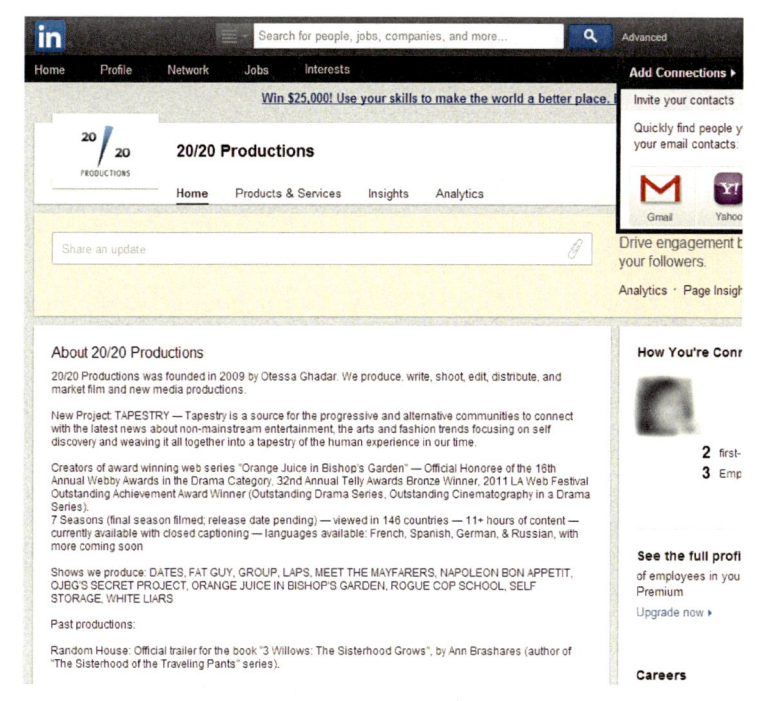

Figure 8.12   Example of LinkedIn company page

Groups

Get involved with Groups. To interact with those you would like to work for, work with, or recruit, hanging out in industry Groups is your best bet. Look for Groups that tackle the subject matter you're interested in and be sure to give fruitful contributions to their discussions, or else you might not be taken seriously.

Search

One of the top uses for LinkedIn is as a search database. With over 238 million members in over 200 countries[9], LinkedIn is one of the best ways to find contact information for individuals and companies around the world. A quick search can get you the coveted email address or phone number of the best in any industry.

9   "About LinkedIn," LinkedIn Corporation, http://press.linkedin.com/about

VIDEO SHARING WEBSITES

When it comes to uploading and sharing your videos, there are many choices. YouTube, Vimeo, and Blip are three of the most popular video sharing websites, and they all offer a myriad of options and features. To help your work reach the widest audience possible, it is wise to have your videos available on all of these major platforms. It's also important to be aware of their inherent differences and modify your strategy accordingly.

There are, however, some universal practices that will best optimize your content on any video sharing website. Listed below are recommendations for your videos, meta-data, thumbnail images, and release strategy that will increase visibility and engagement.

1. *Use more words in the title.* The title should suggest what the video is about. This will make your video better optimized in searches, and less ambiguous to someone seeing the title at a glance. Here's an example using an episode of a web series we'll call *Jane's Journeys*: Episode title "The Jungle" would become "Jane Gets Lost in the Brazilian Jungle"

2. *Episode descriptions should be 3-5 sentences long.* The first sentence should describe what the episode is about. This, again, makes your video more discoverable in searches, and allows for a new viewer of the show to understand the premise of the episode. The rest of the description can be more "quirky". Example: Jane goes into the Brazilian jungle and becomes lost as she searches for secret treasure. Discovering a temple full of hidden traps, will she be able to survive it? And who is following close behind?

3. *Use the description area to include a call to action and links.* Increase traffic to your website, social media profiles, and other videos by including them in the description. Example: See behind the scenes photos on Instagram: http://instagram.com/janesjourneys

4. *More tags.* Start with tags that deal specifically with the episode's description, followed by more general tags. Example: lost in the jungle, brazilian jungle, hidden treasure, secret treasure, treasure

map, booby trap, treasure, jungle, lost, Brazil, Jane's Journeys, web series, web series, new media, funny, adventure, suspense.

5. *Don't include credits.* Most people don't look at the credits and this space can be used to encourage further viewing. Instead, have a "call to action" at the end, such as a clip of a cast member telling the viewer "Subscribe to this channel", "Like this episode" or "Let us know what you think in the comments". On YouTube, you could also use this space to link to other videos on your channel

6. *Use eye-catching thumbnails.* The most engaging thumbnails are close ups on relevant items or people within the episode, with a bright colors, little to no words, and that encapsulate what the episode is about.

7. *Destination programming.* Be consistent with your programming schedule and make it known, so that viewers can be sure of when to expect your next video. Releasing content on a certain day, at a certain time, encourages your audience to develop a habit of coming to your website or channel to see new videos (e.g. Wednesday mornings). Beware—this also means that they could become disgruntled if you don't stick to your schedule or fail to follow through on promises of new content.

YouTube

YouTube is the most famous and widely used video sharing website, and YouTube videos are quickly becoming more watched than TV. Over 4 billion videos are viewed each day, and each month 800 million people visit YouTube from around the world. With videos ranging from cat memes and makeup tutorials, to big-budget serialized shows, the content is vast. But viewers often explore their individual interests and passions. No matter how offbeat or niche your content is, there is potential to build a massive audience and bring in advertisement revenue.

Channel

When it comes to your Channel, the first impression can determine if a viewer ends up spending the rest of the day watching every one of your videos or closing the browser window. Your channel should be eye catching, easy to navigate, and clearly express the premise or mission statement of your content. YouTube allows you to add channel art, a description, links, and customize the way that your videos are organized on the main page. You can even include two "trailers", one for those who are already subscribed to your channel and another for those who are not.

Channel Icon and Channel Art

When customizing your Channel Icon, keep in mind that the image will be the first thing that other users identify with your Channel as they see it around YouTube. The image should standout and also be easy to see even when small in size Example: A close up of a logo, main character or host of your show.

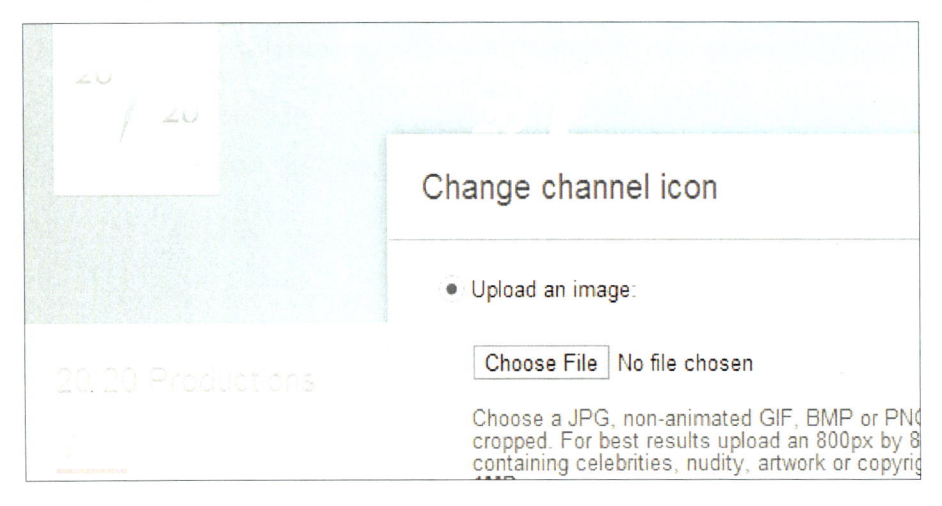

Figure 4.16 YouTube channel icon settings menu

Customize your channel art with your show's logo and theme. The background, colors and font used should follow the style of your show and it's other branding elements. Be sure to follow the specifications for size and placement of graphical items as indicated by YouTube so that your

Channel Art displays correctly on different devices (computer screens of various sizes, tablets, mobile phones, etc.)

Playlists

Organize your content using playlists, which allows someone visiting your channel to easily navigate your videos. For example, a web series could have their episodes added to playlists by season, all of their trailers in one playlist, and bonus videos in another. A makeup tutorial series could have their videos divided by type, such as Celebrity Makeup Looks, Beginner Tutorials, Eyeshadow Tutorials, etc.

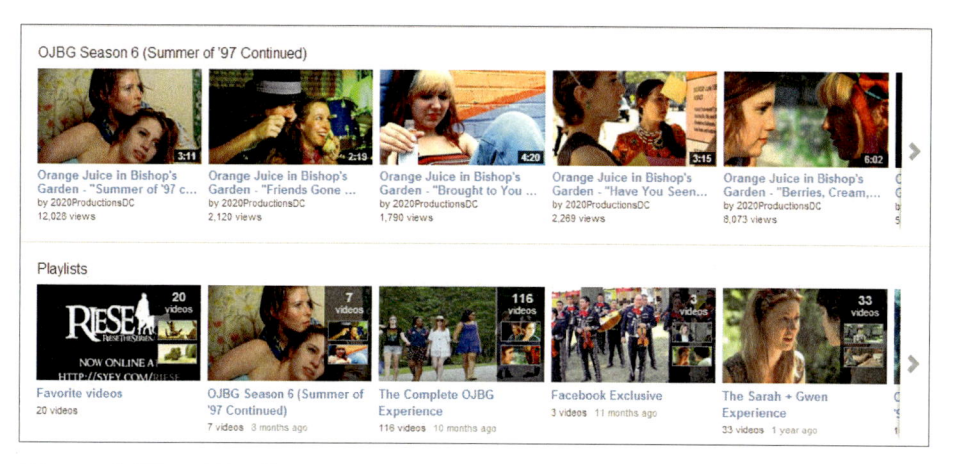

Figure 4.17   Playlists on 20/20 Productions YouTube Channel

Interaction

One of the things that makes YouTube so popular is the social interaction. Users can subscribe to your channel, like your videos, share your videos, leave comments, and send you private messages. Being able to give feedback and get a direct response from the creator of a series on YouTube makes the viewer feel more connected and a part of the action. When receiving comments and messages, reply quickly, be personable, and encourage more interaction. This is a great time to show the wizard behind the curtain, share extra information about the show, and shine the spotlight on subsidiaries like your website, merchandise shop, social networking accounts, other projects, etc.

Another way to engage and drive traffic to your videos is to interact with other YouTubers who make videos that target the same demographic. Leaving friendly comments and giving genuine feedback on another user's video will lead curious clickers to your YouTube channel. Additionally, you should "Like" videos that you enjoy within the same genre or category as your channel. These comments and Likes are displayed in the "All activity" tab of the "My subscriptions" feed of your channel's subscribers, and can help cultivate relationships of mutual "back-scratching" between you and fellow YouTubers (as this will also drive traffic to their videos). Meanwhile, your subscribers will appreciate being tipped off to new channels that they'll potentially find useful or entertaining. If possible, collaborate with other YouTube creators to produce videos that can be cross promoted on both of your channels, so that you can tap into each other's audiences.

Annotations

Annotations are interactive elements that can be added to your video after you upload it. Used in a creative way, they can make your videos stand out and add a new dimension. There are various ways to implement annotations, but the most common uses are call to action links asking the viewers to subscribe to a channel, watch a related video, or watch the next video in a series of video that have been uploaded in separate parts **(Figure 4.8)**.

Annotations can either point to links to another video, playlist, channel, group or search result within YouTube, or an external website that is associated with your YouTube account. You can also create prompts that allow your audience to subscribe to your channel, compose a message, upload a video response, or add their own annotation.

There are some limitations so you shouldn't rely completely on annotations. They won't display on custom YouTube players, or mobile, tablet and TV devices. They also can be turned off by the viewer.

Figure 4.18   Video with a call to action annotation

Captions

Adding captions gives you the opportunity to broaden your audience by reaching the hearing impaired and viewers who speak various languages. YouTube's caption system makes it easy to manually add captions, and even offers automatic captions (available for English, Japanese, Korean, Spanish, German, Italian, French, Portuguese, Russian and Dutch speech) using Google's automatic speech recognition technology (**Figure 4.9**). The results of auto-captioning are not perfect, but can still be helpful if you don't have the time or expertise to add captions yourself.

Take a look at your analytics to determine in which countries you have the highest viewership. Make it a priority to provide captions in the languages of your top countries to bolster viewership even more. Next, focus on common languages like Spanish, Mandarin, Arabic, Russian, or French (or English if that is not the primary language used).

Partner Program

YouTube's Partner Program gives users access to marketing and moneti-

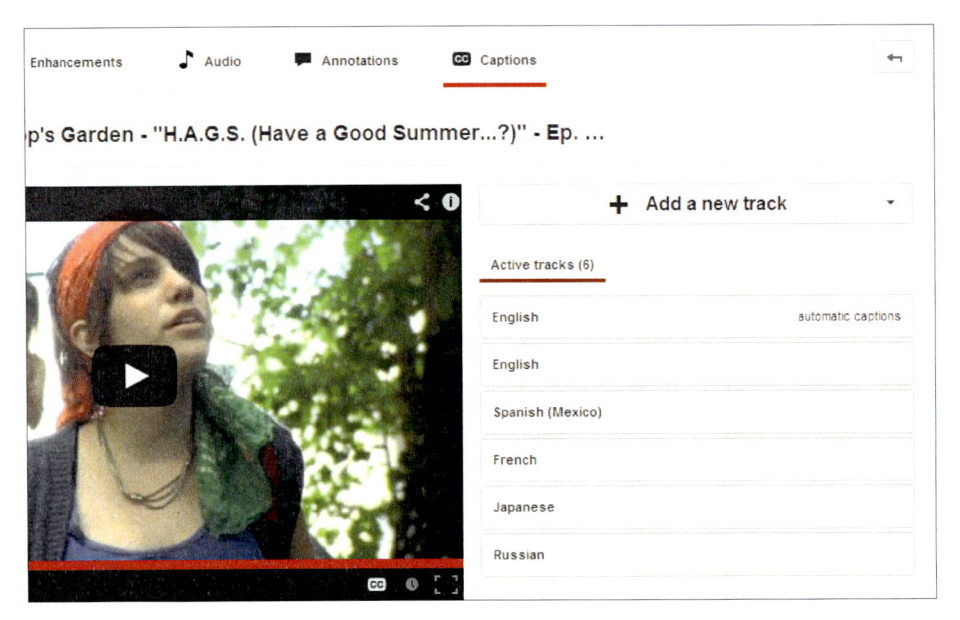

Figure 4.19 Caption settings screen

zation tools that build your audience and allow you to display advertisements on your videos. To become a partner, you must enable monetization on your account and wait to be approved. Once you have at least one video approved for monetization, you're officially a YouTube partner.

To receive payment, you'll have to setup an Google Adsense account and link it to your YouTube. Adsense will allow revenue to be received via checks, Electronic Funds Transfer, Western Union, Quick Cash and Rapida.

Besides monetization, there are other benefits of becoming a Partner. For example, YouTube's Partner Promotion Program (which partner videos in United States, United Kingdom, India, Australia, Germany, Spain, and France are automatically opted-in to) not only features videos throughout the YouTube website, but also across the Internet as a part of the Google Display Network. YouTube offers several programs and resources to help make partners successful and is frequently launching new partner initiatives tailored to the needs of content creators.

Tagging

The tagging system on YouTube is a bit more advance than most video sharing websites. When you begin entering descriptive words or phrases, YouTube will generate keyword suggestions in descending order of relevance and popularity. It is worth using these suggested keywords (if they are indeed reletated to the content's subject matter) to help people discover your work. These tags can also affect the type of advertisements that play alongside your videos.

Common Mistakes

1. *Not posting enough.* If you only have two videos, or upload new content every once in a blue moon, you can't expect viewers to become invested in your show. With short attention spans and lots of options, your audience will look elsewhere for entertainment or information if you aren't keeping them interested.

2. *Videos that are too long.* In some cases, long form videos are necessary or work for the particular subject matter being covered. But, in most cases, those short attention spans kick in and viewers will become bored if your video goes on for ages. Try to be concise and keep the pace moving for non-fiction content, and break your story into shorter parts for fiction series.

3. *Using too many annotations.* Annotations can be a gift or a curse. Speech bubbles and note boxes constantly popping up in a video gets annoying fast, especially if the information isn't especially useful or relevant to the video.

4. *Not being open to constructive criticism.* Viewers of your YouTube channel will have no problem letting you know what they like and don't like. While you should definitely be inspired by your own artistic vision for your channel and/or show, be open to the feedback and suggestions of your audience — especially your regular and loyal viewers. The ultimate goal is to make videos that will entertain/inform your audience, and supportive viewers can help you to develop and improve your content.

5. *Reacting to negative comments or messages.* YouTube is a petri dish for trolls (i.e. people who deliberately post inflammatory, offensive or off-topic comments to upset other users and start arguments). As your channel increases in popularity, you are guaranteed to attract trolls who will attempt to create discord in the comments section of your videos or provoke you by sending rude messages. It is often best to ignore antagonistic comments and even delete them if they are especially distasteful. If you choose to respond, do so in a positive manner, offering a solution or alternative to the commenter's gripe.

Vimeo

Vimeo is often used by creatives in the filmmaking, design, and music worlds, who want a clean and stylish way to showcase their work. There are no ads, and the technology behind Vimeo's video processor and player create a quality unrivaled by other popular sharing websites. It's also preferred by professionals, amateurs, and enthusiasts in these fields, who are looking for useful feedback on their projects. The audience is not as broad as YouTube, but your content will be exposed to people who are interested in quality film and will appreciate it. The Vimeo community is much more supportive and eager to offer constructive feedback.

Albums vs. Channels

Vimeo has multiple ways of categorizing your uploaded videos. While they may seem similar, Albums and Channels have distinct functions that allow them to be used in different ways. Albums are recommended for organizing a collection of videos. They display a group of videos, in any order you prefer, and can be shared with others as a playlist.

Channels, however, are intended to be curated based on a theme. Vimeo users can browse by category and follow channels that they would like to show up in "My Feeds" on the homage. This allows for your entire series to be easily discovered by your target audience. Channels are also useful for showcasing multiple series on the same account.

Groups

Groups are like forums for videos of a particular subject or theme. Like Channels, they can be browsed by category and followed. In addition to creating you own groups, you can add uploaded video to groups created by others, thus sharing to users who are following.

Password Protection & Video Downloading

A useful and sometimes forgotten feature on Vimeo is the ability to password protect a video. This could be used for a myriad of reasons, including sharing rough versions of your work to collaborators without worrying that it will get into the wrong hands. Vimeo also allows for video files to be downloaded in various formats (including the original, high resolution version), which is something that you don't see on major video sharing sites.

Common Mistakes

Not taking advantage of Groups as a way to share your work. Groups are probably the most socially active spaces on Vimeo, so you would be remiss to ignore them or to underestimate their importance. Be sure to create Groups, add your videos to Group created by others, and go onto these Groups to participate in the conversation.

Expecting tons of feedback and social interaction. If you're looking for tons of feedback and sharing of your videos, don't hold your breath. On Vimeo, your audience will be much more targeted than, say, YouTube, so you won't have as much wide-open visibility. Up side: fewer trolls.

Not upgrading your account. For basic users, Vimeo puts restrictions on the size, frequency, and number of uploads; customization; and the ability to add Groups, Channels, and Albums. If you plan to use Vimeo as a distribution platform, it may be worthwhile or even necessary to upgrade to a Plus or Pro account.

Being too passive in social interaction. Although Vimeo pales in comparison to YouTube when it comes to social interaction, it's still important to engage others and to try to build relationships. Vimeo is a great place to connect with other creatives who share your interests. Leave comments, engage in Group discussions, and show support. You may learn some new techniques or build relationships with people who you could work with in the future.

Blip

Blip is a video sharing website that caters specifically to web series and fosters growth therein. There is a screening process, which requires you to submit your show information, proposed release schedule, marketing plan, and video. Not all applications are approved, but getting picked can unleash a bevy of web series specific tools and one of the best ad revenue rates among similar sites. Unfortunately, Blip is not among the top visited video sites on the web[56], but it tries to make up for it by distributing shows to various platforms, including Roku and iTunes. You can even have your Blip videos automatically transferred to YouTube. However, like Vimeo, there are limitations on the amount of uploads, if you choose not to upgrade your account.

Other Video Sharing Sites

Break: This is a platform more for short, funny one-offs. It might be a good fit for your content if you have a concept for a series, which you are just starting or have not completed. Break makes a strong platform for testing those waters. Or maybe you just want to share your one-offs all in a row — Break also makes a good home for these types of endeavors.

DailyMotion: There all kinds of video content on this platform. It's a European-based company, and you can get medium level exposure. Many views from this platform are through mobile-viewing. You just want to make sure having content on this platform isn't cannibalising your other

---

5   "Top 15 Most Popular Video Websites | September 2013," eBizMBA Inc. , http://www.ebizmba.com/articles/video-websites, Accessed: September 2013
6   Blip TV Network, Quantcast Corporation, https://www.quantcast.com/blip.tv, Accessed: September 2013

views. You want to syndicate your show on DailyMotion, but you probably don't want to make it a top priority, as there are no real revenue based opportunities on this platform.

Funny or Die: This platform actually does have a web series section to upload to. However, you will be competing with celebrity content and not solely fellow independent artists. It seems more difficult to break out on this platform. But if you want to be associated with celebrities, it may be a beneficial place to be.

Just the Story: Just the Story is an ad-free subscription based service. For a few dollars a month, viewers have complete access to content. The monthly-subscription fee means viewers will want and need a reason to subscribe. Just the Story works well for those who already have an established fan base or a modicum of fame.

Justin TV: Justin TV is a life-casting mega-hub. Justin TV began in 2007 as a California based start-up. Justin TV can be said to have had two reincarnations. The first is as the beginning of a type of broadcasting called 'life casting,' which is similar to the basis of modern reality television. Justin Kan, the original creator and namesake, wore a camera every day, broadcasting his daily activities and making the average American life something to be viewed from a public perspective. This generated so much press that it led to the second generation of Justin TV.

Justin "2.0" consists of thousands of channels of multiple people 'life casting' or putting whatever else they deem view-worthy on the site. You may have heard about the 2008 incident of an 18-year-old named Abraham Briggs who overdosed live on Justin TV, before the horrified eyes of the many watchers who were currently tuned-in. Though the segment was quickly taken down, and explicit content can only be viewed by those 18 or older, this incident called into question the appropriateness of having public spaces invade that of the private sector. Because of this, if you are considering putting your videos on Justin TV, be warned. It is a free broadcasting service that reaches many people, but it has a turbulent history and reputation. Just food for thought, when you are considering your image in terms of distribution.

Koldcast: Unlike many of the others sites listed, Koldcast is a curated video platform. Content must go through an application process, and there is no guarantee you will be accepted. The nice thing about a curated experience is that it is self-selective. People go to Koldcast to watch Internet programming and web series specifically. This means shows are less likely to be lost or buried. With Koldcast, you can gather tremendously high view counts. Yet, unfortunately, you won't know who's watching or where they come from. The analytics and tracking program on the back-end of its site is somewhat useful, but extremely basic. Its best asset is that Koldcast does do some social media and blogging, via its "Fourth Wall" platform, which directs high volume traffic to your work *when it happens*. Additionally, Koldcast does offer some third party platform opportunities, but that list can change without much notice. Koldcast is a great place to reach additional viewers, but it probably works best when bundled together with other options and platforms, as part of a larger strategy.

Vuier: This is a relatively newer option that allows you to choose your own distribution strategy. With Vuier, you pick a price to sell your content (either per video or by season), and then Vuier takes a standardized cut of the profit. This is neat because you can offer the pay-per-view episodes exclusively or as an additional option available to fans. You set your own price. You get almost all of the return. It's not just about sharing ad revenue per thousand views.

Tales from the Trenches
How to Deal with Troublemakers

Unfortunately, people aren't always polite or even civil in the virtual Internet arena, especially when they're not inhibited by fears of face-to-face communication. With *Orange Juice in Bishop's Garden*, I received complaints from a myriad of people for a variety of reasons, not all of which were justified. There was distress or even unprovoked virtual lunges that the next season was taking too long being released. Sometimes viewers were incensed about how a character was behaving-he or she "couldn't have done that "to a friend or enemy. Sometimes people breathed fire about a season costing money...or because a season was in the vault and they would have to purchase it to view it, never mind that 80% (or more) of the content was free. Sometimes viewers had selective memory about old plot points and they didn't understand why A and B led to C...this could make them feel cheated or betrayed, as though the story-telling was arbitrary or poorly planned. And sometimes people will just hate your work and by extension you.

Remember that there will always be haters no matter what you do or how you do it. The good news about (most of) this is that it means you have a *loyal following*, people who are *excited* about future installments and just can't wait to find out what happens next. A sign of good work is that your viewers feel personally involved with your characters and story- but that doesn't mean you should feel abused by those you are providing content for. How do you respond to the wrath of frustrated and impatient fans?

In general, it helps to keep in mind these three rules, when responding to not-so-pleasant posts:

1. Kill them with kindness

2. Place the agency on them

3. Never say no (but don't say yes) aka the yes, but...

So, for example, I'd often respond with something along the lines of: "Thanks so much for your comment! I love hearing from my loyal viewers out there. We're fast at work on the next season, but in the meantime, check out *OJBG*'s newly-released books, which feature the entire scripts of each season."

Sometimes people make mistakes or are confused about details. And sometimes people can lash out about money. Expect to get some unpleasant notes about how something costs crazy amounts of money to download or to order, etc. — even when this may not be the case. A few times, people would complain about processing fees that were wildly expensive, so I would respond with: "Woah, that *would* be crazy if it cost $8.99 to download that episode! But, if you check again, I think you'll see we don't charge that much :)." If it just so happens that you do charge a reasonable amount and people are complaining, kindly remind them that you need some source of resources in order to produce the art/work/web series/what-have-you you release free each week, and to provide them with that next season/installment/what-have-you they are so keen on. Also, if you offer a giveaway — as I tried to do with *OJBG* — you can point them in that direction. You don't have to give them the episode for free. You don't need to grant every wish and demand. But, you can offer them an alternate. Re-direct them to something you are already doing, which they might not know about, which is free or exclusive, and which they just might enjoy. This is an example of "never say no (but don't say yes". I call it the "yes, but..."

Finally, if you really want to turn away complainers, sweetly ask them to upload their thoughts via video, and then you'll happily respond via another video. Even better would be a venue like an on-air Google Hangout — which brings you face to face with another across the dissociative web. Looking people in the eye is important, and you may find that you both have greater sympathy and mutual-appreciation that initially suspected. You can even offer to promote the conversation by social media, to give them a larger platform from which to speak. When you put the agency on them and have them try to create their own video, they'll quickly realize making videos is not an easy task — and then, perhaps they'll have a little bit more respect for you the next time they feel it takes a little too long for new episodes to be released.

Sample Post:

ONLINE COMMENTER: Everything should be free — how dare you charge!

ME: Thank you so much for sharing your thoughts with me — and thank you for caring about my work. Yes, I so wish I could provide everything I make for free to those who love it. But unfortunately :(then I would not be able to create the show or make you more episodes. BUT, I am giving away — completely for free! — this song/scriptbook/poster this month, and I hope you enjoy it :) Also, if ever you would like to share your thoughts again — please know that I always appreciate and encourage people to send video responses. I make sure to respond in kind :)

Chapter Nine
ANALYTICS

If social media is like your agent and marketing team, analytics is your business development team, providing you the insights into how to make your online presence reach its full potential. Analytics will help you to determine if efforts to solidify your brand are truly successful. After investing so much time developing a website, executing a social media strategy, and deciding on a release schedule for your content, you don't want to just "throw darts" blindfolded. But how do you tell if they're working? You need to know what people care about, who is watching, who is visiting your pages, and who is leaving… enter analytics programs. These programs will aid you in learning your audience's habits and in building your strategy around them.

Analytics essentially compile people's digital footprints. Each analytics source bleeds information that can be useful in gaining insight on viewer awareness of your brand and response to your content online. Analytical information is so valuable that one social network, Facebook, already has two data centers in the U.S. the size of 11 football fields, and it is currently building another one in Sweden, simply to collect and process the data.[1]

The best analytics will put statistical data into context. They will identify patterns and trends, helping you make smarter decisions. Some of your conclusions will be reached through estimation and guesses, but they will be informed by real data that is constantly being updated. Analytics can help you capture data to understand attitudes, opinions, and trends, and allow you to manage your online reputation and impact. They also allow you to predict and to improve upon how people interact with your

---

1   Bradbury, Series: On social media marketing: Effective social media analytics, Guardian News and Media Limited, http://www.guardian.co.uk/technology/2013/jun/10/effective-social-media-analytics

content. You can create customized campaigns and promotions, and track how well they do. You can also identify the primary influencers within specific social network channels and get connected through them.

TIPS TO KEEP IN MIND WHILE LOOKING AT ANALYTICS

Make Projections: Based on the data you receive, make educated guesses and judgment calls. Keep an eye out for trends and pitfalls. Constantly learn from your mistakes and successes to adjust your strategy.

Investigate Why: The numbers you receive from analytics reporting are great, but it would be doubly useful if you could help point out why the numbers are where they are. Is it the time of year? week? day? Is there a holiday or major current event happening? Did somebody post a link on his or her site? Anything you think can explain why you're seeing what you are would be very helpful in guiding your social media outreach.

Compare Yourself: Study how your niche-neighbors and competitors use the digital landscape and its social media platforms. Look at what days and times they are active and how they interact. How many views do they have on Youtube, for example? How many posts do they have per day on various platforms? What voice do they use for in response to comments from fans and how fast do they respond? Where have they been mentioned or done interviews? Much can be inferred from this use — train yourself to intuit what this means for your analytics. Learn to track the trends of others, even without the benefit of inside-information.

Analytics may seem very technical and difficult to understand, but with a little patience and curiosity, anyone can use them. The following section will walk you through an analytics report and show you how to be efficient and strategic.

GOOGLE ANALYTICS

Google Analytics is probably the most important analytics tool available.

It's robust; it's easy to install, and it's free. Google Analytics tells you who came to your site, how they arrived, and what they did while they visited. You can use it to track a website, social networking sites, and even apps. It also can be used to measure revenue for advertisements placed on a website.

If your objective is to promote new content, advertise an event, or cross populate traffic from various social media accounts, data collected by Google Analytics will quantify your success. You can even create customized reports to manage specific goals and track your progress.

Understanding the Basics

Definitions:

Visits

"Visits" tell you how many people click on the site as a whole. This is useful so that you don't have to rely on guesswork regarding whether your outreach strategy is effective. Note that, if someone comes back to the site, his or her visit will be counted again.

Unique Visitors

"Unique visitors" are the number of distinct individuals who have ever been to the site. This number refers to the *person* and is not affected by the number of times said person visits over time. This number helps to determine whether your presence in the internet world is growing.

Pageviews

"Pageviews" reveal the number of pages visited *in total*. Multiple or repeated visits to the same page by the same user are also counted.

Pages/Visit

"Pages/Visit" tells you the number of pages the average person views while he or she is on the site. This information reveals how engaged people are when they are viewing the site. The more pages users visit, the more likely they are paying attention to what they're seeing.

Avg. Time on Site

"Avg. Time on Site" is similar to "Pages/Visit" in that it, too, reveals whether people are paying attention to your website. When people spend a lot of time on the website, it means that they are finding things on the website worth staying for.

Bounce Rate

The "Bounce Rate" tells you the number of people who visit the site and then immediately leave. The "Bounce Rate" is opposite of "Avg. Time on Site" because it reveals if people are not finding things on your site worth staying for.

New Visits

"New Visits" is the number of times a new visitor views the site. If there are more "New Visits" than "New Visitors," it means that the new visitors are returning to the site.

Interpretation:

The way you study and use your web analytics will depend on the goals set for your sites and data your sites acquire. However, a basic starting point for all users can be found in the Overview statistics, which can provide insight on your site's overall performance.

The following section will use the OJinBG.Com website as a guide. The Google Analytics reports referenced do not mark any major events in the performance of the site, but that does not mean that the data is useless. Analysis of the reports show examples of "learning from your mistakes" and did affect later decisions on how content was released and promoted.

In the month of February 2012, Google Analytics stats reveal there were a total of 2,414 Visits to the OJinBG.com website. These are visits to the OJinBG.com site and they do not include any of our other various platforms and thus should not be studied "in a bubble." Third party knowledge of your home page and web site may not always be easy to build, which is all the more reason to track it. You want to make sure people are aware of your brand or content in a specific and personalized way — and are not only viewing from a larger source or framework (like YouTube or Facebook). Always compare, contrast, and add these home page metrics to a study of your video platform viewership, social media stats, and any ancillary sites or content you may have.

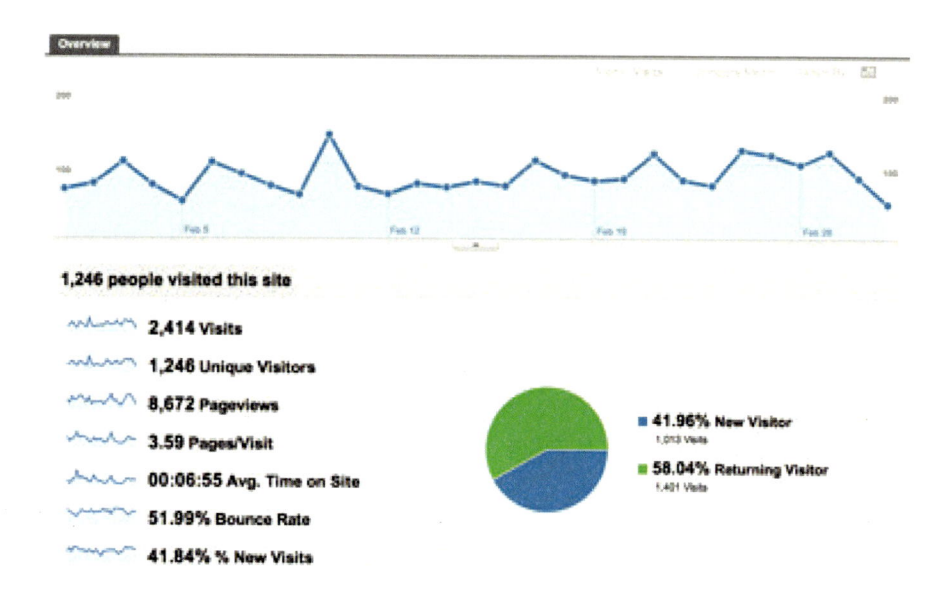

Figure 9.1   February 2012 Google Analytics Overview for http://orangejuiceinbishopsgarden.com

Of those visits, 41.96% were "New Visitors" while 58.04% were "Returning Visitors." Based on this data, a general conclusion can be made: Knowledge of the OJinBG.com website is still spreading to new people, while managing to retain a core audience. Ultimately the best ratio of New-to-Returning vistitors will depend on the site you have and the type of content you are sharing. For a serialized digital program, like *OJBG*, it is especially important to retain continued and sustained interest — a.k.a. returning visitors. New visitors are always great, but you want to make sure you keep your visitors, too, especially with serialized and buildable content.

When looking at your analytics, do you find that your returning viewership is too low? Make certain that it is clear how fans can stay connected. Consider the placement of your subscription buttons and social media widgets; also make sure that your release strategy or content schedule is clear to even the most cursory glance. On the flip side, would you like to improve your "new viewership"? Re-visit your outreach and promotional strategy — you may find that it needs shaking up. Also, consider including some collaborative efforts, ancillary (but related) links, guest content, or third party elements.

Figure 9.2 January 2012 Google Analytics Overview for http://orangejuiceinbishopsgarden.com

In comparison to January 2012, our "Visits" in February slightly declined. However, the "Bounce Rate" decreased and the "Avg. Time on Site" increased, meaning retention on the site is increasing — an important discovery. Further in the report, we will delve more deeply into the strategic analysis of "Bounce Rate," but do keep in mind that you want this rate to be as low as possible because it means people are not simply navigating away and "X'ing out" the site.

This part of the analytics report tells you what pages people are viewing when they visit your site. This information is valuable because it tells you what visitors are specifically interested in. The top five most visited pages this month were Home, Watch, Episode 5.5, Episode 5.4, and lastly About the Characters.

The top five most uniquely viewed pages were: Home, Watch, Episode

5.5, Episode 5.4, and Episode 5.6. This is interesting to note and relatively positive as it means that unique views are not microcosmic — in fact we are seeing that the repeat views and page view counts reflect the same information and interests.

	Page	Pageviews	% Pageviews
1.	/	2,851	30.35%
2.	/watch/	796	8.47%
3.	/5-5-signed-sealed-delivered/	280	2.98%
4.	/5-3-secrets-lies/	225	2.40%
5.	/category/characters/	214	2.28%
6.	/5-4-what-the-cards-hold/	205	2.18%
7.	/5-6-trial-expired/	184	1.96%
8.	/5-1-summer-of-97/	168	1.79%
9.	/1-1-orange-crush/	166	1.77%
10.	/5-2-the-audition/	129	1.37%

Figure 9.3 February 2012 Google Analytics pages viewed http://orangejuiceinbishopsgarden.com

Looking further into the analytics report for February 2012 reveals that the most "Visits" for a single day occurred on Friday the 10th, which is the day Episode 5.5 "Signed, Sealed, & Delivered" of *Orange Juice in Bishop's Garden* premiered. With new episodes being released every Friday, this begs the questions: why was this Friday the most successful of the month and why was Episode 5.5 the most successful episode of the month? Did a new marketing strategy for the video prove successful? Did a random event of relation to our content spark an unforeseeable pique in interest? Or, perhaps, the storyline in this episode became viral within a particular demographic of viewers and was heavily shared by this group.

Keep in mind that merely looking at the analytics is not enough. An outsider might not draw the same conclusions because he or she doesn't know the backstory or day-to-day operations of your business. To gain insight on the question of *why*, consider your insider knowledge and compare it with Google Analytics' more advanced analytical information, such as traffic sources, keywords, and demographics.

Delving even more deeply into Episode 5.5: the episode was what we internally called a "New Kids" episode, as it revolved primarily around the new, younger characters in the story world. Previously, according to YouTube comments, social media intereaction, and raw video view numbers, the "New Kids" episodes had always under-performed and suffered from a real "backlash" from fans. So, are we seeing a reversal or a "coming around" to these characters and storylines — or is it something else?

Here we have an example of our "insider information" actually creating more of a mystery, rather than less. A strong next step is to study the traffic sources and audience metrics. What were the referrals and demographics for the home sites overall, as well as Episdoe 5.5 specifically?

Traffic Sources and Audience

2,601 people visited this site

- **42.87%** Search Traffic
  1,115 Visits
- **35.22%** Referral Traffic
  916 Visits
- **21.80%** Direct Traffic
  567 Visits
- **0.12%** Campaigns
  3 Visits

Figure 9.4   Example of Google Analytics traffic sources statistics

Definitions:

Direct Traffic

"Direct Traffic" refers to the amount of traffic you receive from people simply typing in your website address.

Referral Traffic

"Referral Traffic" reveals how many visits are from referrals from other platforms. This number reveals how people are finding out about your website if they do not find it through a search engine or through coming to the site directly.

Search Traffic

"Search Traffic" tells you the number of people who are viewing your site through search engines. If the majority of people are viewing your site through search engines, it means they were either searching for keywords that happen to be related to your website without your particular business in mind, or they learned of your business somewhere else and then looked through a search engine.

	Keyword	Visits	% Visits
1.	orange juice in bishop's garden	466	41.79%
2.	(not provided)	128	11.48%
3.	orange juice bishops garden	72	6.46%
4.	orange juice in bishops garden	63	5.65%
5.	ojbg	42	3.77%
6.	orangejuiceinbishopsgarden.com	16	1.43%
7.	orange juice and bishop garden	14	1.26%
8.	orange juice in bishop garden	14	1.26%
9.	ojinbg.com	12	1.08%
10.	cherry girl orange juice in bishop's garden	11	0.99%

Figure 9.5   Example of Google Analytics key words statistics

Google Analytics also lists the keywords that lead people to your site when doing a search. It is important that your website includes relative keywords so that search engines suggest your site to those seeking the type of content you provide. Track that people are using your selected keywords; also be open to using new keywords based on positive results from search terms you had not previously considered. If you're not satisfied with the traffic acquired from searches, a change to the text and meta data on your site could be a solution. (See Web Design Chapter for more information on using keywords to increase Search Engine Optimization)

Demographics

"Demographics" give you a breakdown of visitors by language, country, and city.

Technology & Mobile

"Technology" lists specific site usage stats by web browser, operating system, and internet service provider. This could be useful when optimizing your content and sites for use on these platforms. "Mobile" will allow you to see what type of devices are being used to browse your site — e.g. desktop, mobile, or tablet — and even what model the devices are.

Campaigns

The number of visitors you receive from "Campaigns" tells you how many people are viewing your site as a result of online advertising campaigns. It can be a paid campaign through something like Adsense or it can be an unpaid campaign through your blog. This tells you whether your online campaign is effective.

	Country/Territory	Visits	Pages/Visit	Avg. Time on Site	% New Visits	Bounce Rate
1.	United States	1,618	3.26	00:05:56	39.00%	58.03%
2.	France	313	5.42	00:11:39	47.60%	37.06%
3.	Canada	115	3.62	00:06:59	28.70%	53.04%
4.	Australia	100	3.30	00:05:13	17.00%	25.00%
5.	United Kingdom	82	2.80	00:04:42	46.34%	51.22%
6.	Spain	70	3.17	00:08:49	48.57%	47.14%
7.	Germany	32	3.44	00:06:32	53.12%	40.62%
8.	Romania	26	3.62	00:08:04	11.54%	57.69%
9.	Brazil	24	2.04	00:02:02	87.50%	50.00%
10.	Italy	17	2.29	00:04:25	76.47%	35.29%

Figure 9.6   Example of Google Analytics breakdown of visits by country

Interpretation

In February, there were many different traffic sources.

OJBG's top five referral sources were: Google searches, direct traffic, Facebook.com, Bing searches, and Univers-l.com (a site that features our French translated lesbian story line in its online directory).

The big point of interest and surprise is that Univers-L.com (a French lesbian media site) continues to be such a high source of referrals because February's new episodes had not even been translated into French yet! The lesson here is clear: keep up the relationship with France! It is a healthy one of mutual support. Foster its growth and hurry up with more subtitles!

Next, it is always recommended to look at what new or curious traffic is specific to the month. There was additional visitor direction from La Teta Extranjera, Lez Media, Fashion Grunge, Shewired, and Sidereel. The visitors from these sites also spent *significant* amounts of time on the website — a rough average of 20 minutes for all of the above. People from these sources actually spent about three or more times the amount of time on the site than that of the average site visitor, or of visitors coming from say Google or Facebook.

The point of interest here? We are continuing to really resonate with our niche and core audiences. The Sarah and Gwen lesbian storyline continues to draw real attention via LGBT sites (Univers-l, La Teta Extranjera, Lez Media, and Shewired). The 90s grunge fashion element continues to hit the mark with fashion blogs, a la Fashion Grunge. These viewers are visiting the site, watching perhaps more than one episode and delving into additional content.

Now, about Sidereel, this viewership is actually tied to pirate viewership. No one from this end at *OJBG* had posted any content to Sidereel. When we visited Sidereel to scope out the situation, it became clear that some episodes had been illegally ripped and posted to external sites (for which we got no analytics, no advertising revenue, and no credit). However, a few other episodes had been added that did refer to OJinBG.com. The lesson here? Take control of the pirate-plundering. It is great that people are craving content. So, reign in that desire. What we ended up doing was posting all our episode links on Sidereel.com so that viewership was directed to the home page — and not to an outside site with illegally ripped videos of poor quality.

Also, during the same month, the percentage of our international audience moderately increased. The top viewing countries remained relatively the same compared to other months in recent history.

In particular, France continues to be the top performing international country, despite the fact that the most recently released episodes have not yet been translated in French. However, there were prior seasons available in French, and we had a pre-existing relationship with France, so the fact that there were no known additional efforts on our part would instead suggest there is a slow-but-steady "snowball" effect. If we study up further, there might actually be some traffic coming from alternate/additional Spanish and Italian bloggers. AND, those additional new Euro bloggers can be potential new contacts with whom we can connect and thank, whether by commenting on blog posts, tweeting, et cetera. Always strive to connect personally in these instances — it turns one-time visitors into fans and blog posts into actual IRL relationships.

Checking the top pageviews per international (non-English-speaking) countries, we see that the most viewed episodes this month are all over the place. Viewers are delving into old content that has been translated and also into new content, which has not been translated yet.

Lesson learned? Keep translating. Offer even more languages. Make it a major initiative.

All of these insights led us to undertake a massive translation effort over time, thereby encouraging international viewership and making the show even more inclusive.

Also, the international viewership is high, which we eventually determined was sticking out as a noticeable trend because we were failing to optimize our domestic viewership. We eventually determined (over the course of many months) that domestic viewership was better on Wednesdays — and was not good on Fridays, nor around the holidays, especially not the winter holidays. We determined this by tracking our social media plus cross-platform analytics; we then decided to "try and test" releasing video content on another day and then did a "compare and contrast" of the numbers.

So, what does all this mean for Episode 5.5? "Signed, Sealed, & Delivered" has no obvious demographic significance to LGBT media. Could the traffic to Episode 5.5 be related to another site? In point of fact the answer is not really. Traffic to Episode 5.5 is coming predominately from direct visits, Google searches, and Facebook referrals, a.k.a. the usual suspects. Country viewership to 5.5 is also from the usual suspects. However, if we break down the 5.5 page viewership domestically, by city, we see a blip. Philadelphia is performing much higher than we are used to seeing. Interesting corollary: the episode's lead actress had recently started her first year of drama school in Philadelphia. We could be seeing a focus of interest from an entire university population.

This still doesn't completely solve the mystery of 5.5, but that is okay. Sometimes you'll have anomalies that may never be solved or that will be revealed at a later date. In particular, relative to the plight of the "New Kids" episodes, it will continue to be important to track performance and see if audiences are starting to come around. In the meantime, you can also search your ancillary metrics (like YouTube, Facebook, et cetera) to gather more insight.

YOUTUBE

YouTube allows you to really see behind the scenes with detail and transparency. You have access to a strong (but basic) overview — but it is just a jumping off point. From there you can dig into the nitty gritty to gather a rather advanced view of your metrics.

Per your YouTube analytics, you will want to compare and contrast them to your other cross-platform metrics. This is somewhat like comparing apples to oranges. However, you can still glean some important information. In particular something that is good to look for is consistency and, alternately, any blips or mysteries. If your basic numbers, stats, breakdowns, et cetera look similar from your home page to YouTube to Vimeo — then you can safely assume you have a strong baseline from which to view. Now, if you do have any blips or divergences, these can be incredibly informative sources. You want to get to the bottom of these to the best of your ability. Often these supposed "blips" are actually indicators of bellwether activity, trends, successes, failures, or areas deserving focus.

In addition to doing your cross-platform analyses, you should definitely focus on doing month-to-month and year-to-year analyses of the same platform. With YouTube analytics, much like Google analytics, you can specifically determine the time range you wish to study.

In this case, we will take a look at the YouTube stats for February and March of 2012. We will compare them to each other and then consider them also in relation to the Google Analytics we just consumed so thoroughly.

YouTube's overview tells you your performance (full episode views) over that time. It also lists your "engagement," broken down by the number of likes, dislikes, comments, shares, favorites added, and the subscriber net change over your selected time range.

YouTube viewership continues to surpass the OJinBG.com web page. It's not really a shocker considering YouTube is the top destination for online videos. However, you still want to make sure that when people view you on YouTube, they are aware of and can access your other sites. This is a good way to make sure they are fully aware of your larger brand's entity.

Performance

VIEWS
30,639 ▲

Performance

VIEWS
42,324 ▲

Figure 9.7   Total views in February (left) vs total in March (right)

For *OJBG*, YouTube viewership really jumps from February to March. Remember when we were saying the holidays and winter were not optimal posting times? Here is a prime example: we see that trend affecting views as we transition into spring. It's a trend we continued to see across platforms and across months and years. It took us awhile to "wise up," but we eventually "got the picture." As a general rule, viewership will warm up with our seasons.

You can also view your "Top 10 Videos." This list arrangement not only tells you which were most viewed, but it also tells you what the "Subscriber Net Change" was per each episode. The subscriber net change tracks how many subscribers were gained and lost, while a viewer was watching that particular video.

In the current YouTube analytics system, "Subscribers Net Change" is now just called "Subscribers." Also, the "Subscribers" info is no longer included in the "Top 10 Videos" list on the Overview page; instead, "Estimated Minutes Watched" is listed in its place. "Estimated Minutes Watched" is something relatively new that they weren't yet tracking in March 2012. "Estimated Minutes Watched" tracks how long your average viewer stuck with the video viewing experience. This is certainly a good factoid to have at your fingertips. And as to the "Subscribers" — fret not. You can still access that information; it has simply moved to a different area of the YouTube report and can be found on a separate Subscribers page.

The Overview is great, but really, you will need to examine more critically, so as to gain a firm grasp of trends. Think of your analytics as a living microcosmic entity. You need to perform a biopsy to know what exists within and under the surface. More detailed information can be found in further reports under three categories: Views, Engagement, and Earnings.

Next up analyze who is viewing. What's the gender and age breakdown? Does it look like what you would anticipate or what you have come to expect? Is it more or less consistent over time and across platforms? Are there any surprises?

In our instance, we have continued to see a relatively steady gender breakdown. We have also continued to see some interesting numbers on age. Specifically viewers have consistently been high in the 45-54 age demographic. Now, we have already discussed how there are vagaries to how metrics are compiled, and sometimes the numbers are not as representative as you would hope or expect. (e.g. sometimes with metrics programs, especially advertising based ones, age may be inferred and not determined. Similarly, sometimes the age listed is that of the account holder and not the user). That said, we have continued to see a real interest in the older age group across time and platforms (in addition to the younger demographics). One can take this to mean that we are successfully enticing and drawing the "nostalgia audience," a la the Wonder Years, and we are simultaneously drawing the interest of the current young adult audience. As this was the primary target of the work, all seems to be going to plan.

As for viewing countries, the YouTube countries are relatively on par with the information coming from Google vis-a-vis the home page web site.

What are some of the stand outs or anomalies? Saudi Arabia in particular. Also, Turkey.

> ### Random Blips and Unsolved Mysteries
>
> Mobile viewing in Saudi Arabia was particularly high this month. While sometimes you just can't "get to the bottom" of these trends, you can instead use them as a springboard for positive thought. Since interest in Saudi Arabia is high, perhaps reaching out to Saudi Arabian blogs about syndication would be a good bet. Also, it is worth mentioning that this trend may have been buried in the analytics were it not for the fact that our domestic viewership was somewhat lackluster at this time. While we eventually determined that Fridays were not a good release day for new content, if it were not for trying out Fridays, we might have lost out on the fact that our content fared so well in Saudi Arabia.

Additionally, we posited (although cannot officially prove) that we garner a lot of views and interest from countries that censor LGBT content and/or marginalize "non-traditional" stories. Note to self: continue to advocate for human rights, get more political, seek out translations specific to countries that censor.

How are people watching? From February to March this changes rather drastically. What is an even spread of playback locations in February becomes extremely weighted by March. By March, close to half (42%) of views are from the native YouTube page, 28% are from embedded players, 26% from mobile, and 4% from the YouTube channel page.

Why the big change? How come there is such a sudden increase in the proportion of YouTube views? Does this mean that more random traffic is stumbling our way? It seems so. Okay, so what does that mean? Because the "YouTube suggested video" viewership was also significantly up come March, there could be a correlation. Perhaps the tag choices on our newer videos have been an improvement, meaning that our views are showing up as more correctly targeted suggestions to viewers.

VIMEO

Vimeo's metrics are pretty basic. (Lucky you). Vimeo arranges your data into an overview listing your plays (a.k.a. full video views), loads (how many times a video was accessed, but not watched in its entirety), likes, and comments.

Figure 9.8   Section of Vimeo "Advanced Stats" page

Again, all of this information can be broken down by date range. Comparing month-to-month and year-to-year is both possible and useful.

When studying your analytics over time, keep an eye out for days of high performance and high engagement. Was there a special initiative on those days? What have you been doing, or not doing, that has been transferring into success, or lack of success?

Vimeo also allows you to see which countries are viewing. Are those countries changing over time? Are they similar to the countries of viewership on other platforms and sites? If not, what are the anomalies and what can you infer or determine from these?

On Vimeo, we are seeing that China, Russia, Malaysia, India, and Brazil are performing higher here on the country list than they were on either the home page or YouTube. Since YouTube and our OJinBG.com page allows for easy embedding of subtitling and closed captions, it does make sense certain countries would flock more to the sites that cater to them.

Vimeo doesn't allow for the super-simple subtitling option, so we may be seeing country viewership that reflects that. And again, the prevalence of viewership in countries that censor or marginalize LGBT or "non-traditional" stories continues to be noteworthy and worthy of our sustained support and outreach.

As a penultimate note, take a peek at the most viewed episodes. Which ones are the most played, the most loaded, liked, commented, and embedded? Was a particular episode high on the loads, but not so high on the full plays? Was there an issue with the file size or compression — or perhaps was it just a turn off to your audience? Ideally you want the loads and plays to reflect each other.

Lastly, another useful option is being able to see on what external sites your videos have been embedded and how many loads and plays they received on those domains. This allows you to track embeds — perhaps there were embedded videos of which you were not even aware. In this case, you have a new fan source to which it would behoove you to reach out, thank, and further foster. Or you may want to measure the performance of videos that you have embedded on your own website, especially as compared to video's played directly from Vimeo. Are embedded videos performing better than direct plays from Vimeo? And, which sites are most inclined to embed. All of this can tell you more about your niche interest groups and audiences.

BLIP

Blip offers a simple Statistics panel within its Dashboard that has a strong focus on revenue. The Summary screen provides an at-a-glance view of total Revenue, Views, Monetizable Views, In-Player views, and Monetizable RPM.

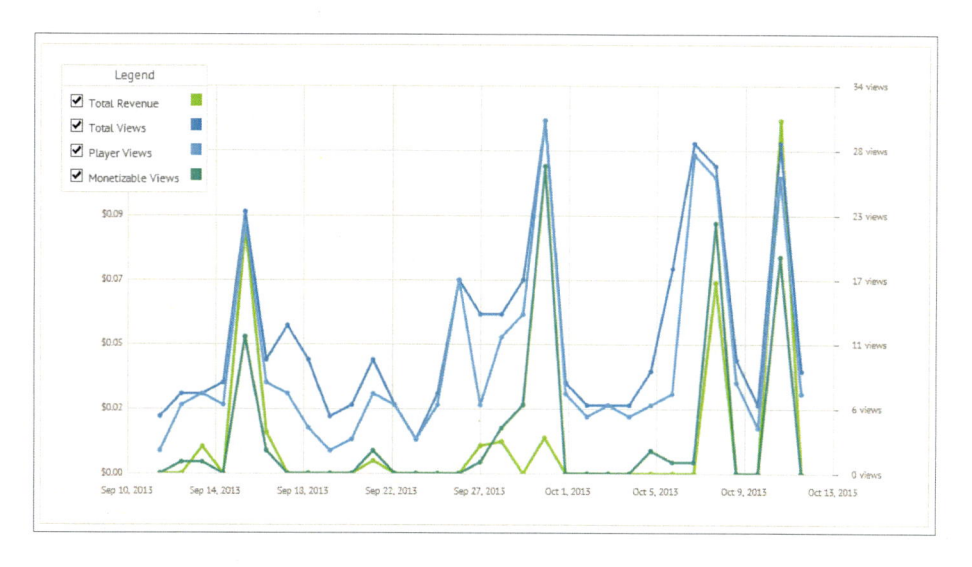

Figure 9.9 Section of Blip "Views and Revenue" page

The Views and Revenue page takes things a step further, breaking down the stats totaled on the Summary page by date and episode. Traffic Sources allows you to track views by "Synsicator," which includes Blip, its third-party distributors, and any external embeds. You can also track from where views are being referred, like Blip's Apple iOS app or a search engine like Bing.

Analytics in the Engagement report are bare bones. An ambiguous graph compares the rate of Percentage View to Percentage of People.

An important note: Blip does not allow you to access data more than one year old, so be sure to save any information that might prove useful to you in future analysis. You can download some of the Views and Revenue data as CSV files.

FACEBOOK

The best way to encourage your fans to engage with your content and to share it on Facebook with their friends is to find out what the fans you want to reach care about. Facebook's "Insights" give you the metrics you need to do just that. While website statistics generally focus on the number of visitors and how long they spend on your site, Facebook's data revolves around who your visitors are in terms of age, gender, and country of residence, and how they engage with your posts.

How

On your main Facebook insights dashboard, you'll see the total number of likes (and whether this is increasing or decreasing), the number of friends of fans available (the potential number of people you can reach), how many people are actively talking about your page, as well as your total weekly reach.

The overall reach on Facebook refers to the number of unique visitors who have seen any content associated with your Page within the given timeframe (this includes ads and sponsored stories that point to your Page) (**Figure 10.10**).

The "Talking About This" data refers to the number of unique people who have created a story about your page during the given timeframe (**Figure 10.11**). A story is created when someone likes your Page; posts to your Page Wall; likes, comments on, or shares one of your Page posts; answers a question you posted; responds to your event; mentions your Page; tags your Page in a photo; checks in at your location; or recommends your location.

Your dashboard will also show your latest posts and their corresponding

Overview

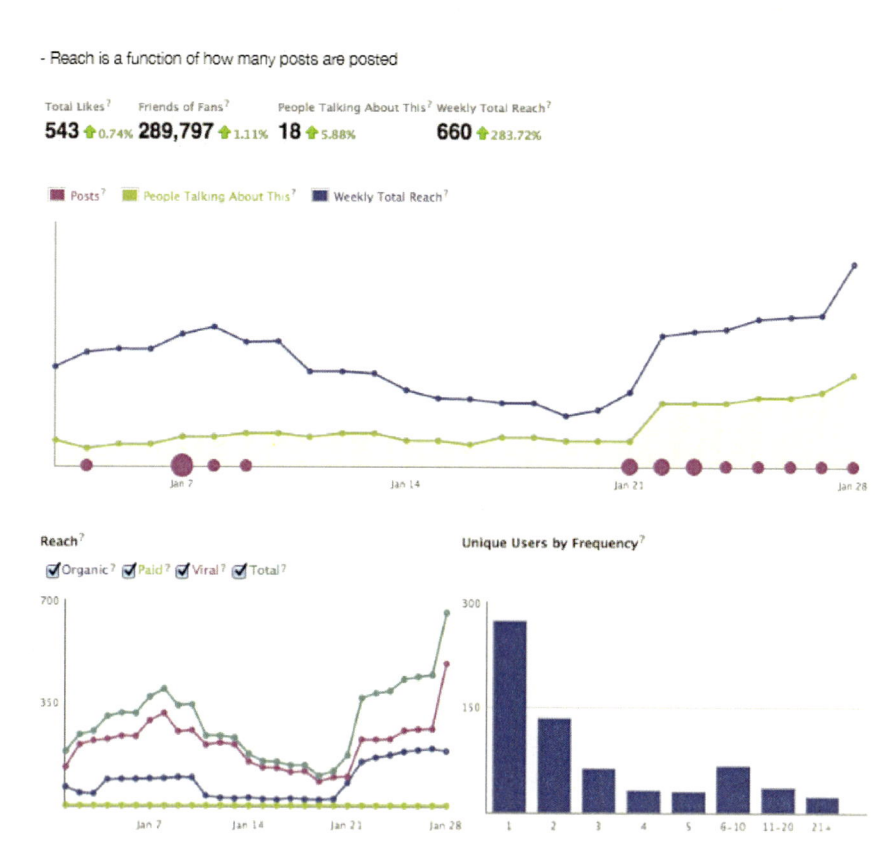

- Reach is a function of how many posts are posted

Total Likes Friends of Fans People Talking About This Weekly Total Reach
543 ↑0.74% **289,797** ↑1.11% **18** ↑5.88% **660** ↑283.72%

Figure 9.10 Example of Facebook Overview

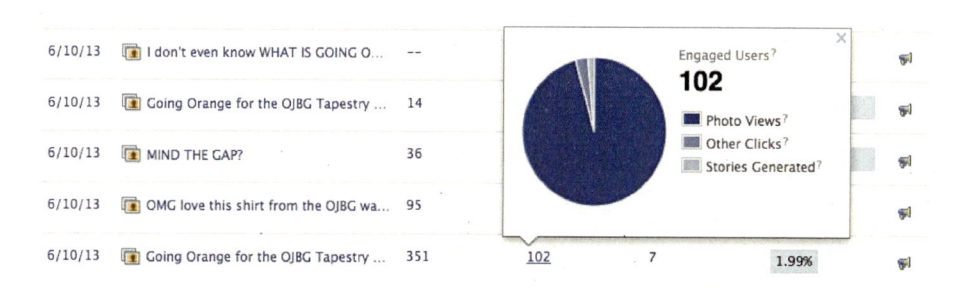

Figure 9.11 Example of Facebook "Talking About This" and "Engaged Users" data

virality. This is especially useful if you would like to see which posts were the most successful. You can sort posts by all post types, photos, links, questions, etc. Instead of sifting through all the posts, you can simply sort by types in order to find the success of a specific, singular post. You'll be able to see the date the post was made, the title of the post, its reach, how many users engaged with that particular post, how many spread the word about it, as well as its virality in a percentage form.

Engaged users are unique people who have clicked on any one of your posts (**Figure 10.11**). You can click on the number of engaged users to see more details, such as the stories generated, whether there were links clicked, photo viewed, etc.

Virality is the percentage of people who have created a story from your Page post out of the total number of unique people who have seen it.

If you click "Likes," you'll be able to see the demographics, as well as the locations of your fans.

You'll also be able to see their age groups. In this case, the *Orange Juice in Bishop's Garden* fan page has a much larger female fan base than a male fan base. Most users are also located in the United States, France, and United Kingdom, and hence posts can be customized accordingly.

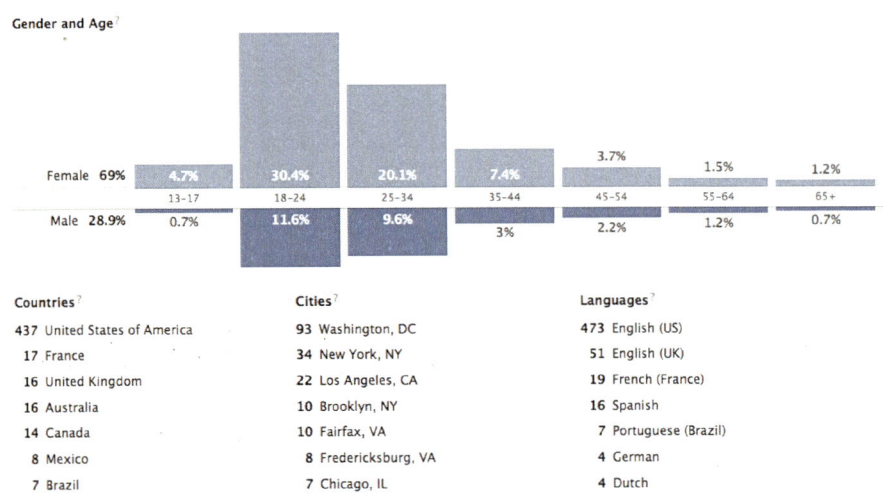

Gender and Age

	13-17	18-24	25-34	35-44	45-54	55-64	65+
Female 69%	4.7%	30.4%	20.1%	7.4%	3.7%	1.5%	1.2%
Male 28.9%	0.7%	11.6%	9.6%	3%	2.2%	1.2%	0.7%

Countries	Cities	Languages
437 United States of America	93 Washington, DC	473 English (US)
17 France	34 New York, NY	51 English (UK)
16 United Kingdom	22 Los Angeles, CA	19 French (France)
16 Australia	10 Brooklyn, NY	16 Spanish
14 Canada	10 Fairfax, VA	7 Portuguese (Brazil)
8 Mexico	8 Fredericksburg, VA	4 German
7 Brazil	7 Chicago, IL	4 Dutch

Figure 9.12   Example of Facebook Demographics stats

The geographical location of your fans will be useful in scheduling posts due to differing time zones. Also, if you choose to target your posts, you can do so based on age and gender, if you have something that may be of interest to a particular segment of your fanbase (or will be a disturbance to others).

> **WOULD YOU LIKE TO KNOW MORE?**
>
> According to an article posted by AllFacebook, April 2013, the determining factors for how Facebook dictates what is considered "top" updates on news feed is by an algorithm called EdgeRank.[1] As described, Edgerank uses four pieces of information to circulate FB news. The first two can be divided by individual participation and the last two as communal participation.
>
> 1. The relationship and communication level you have with another(s) FB user. Whether that be through liking, commenting, sharing, tagging, writing on walls, invitations to events as well as personal contact through FB-chat and messages.
>
> 2. The various types of posts that you respond to positively will increase your visibility to that type of post, e.g. photos, status, video, etc.
>
> 3. If a large number of people responded positively to a post, you are more likely to see it.
>
> 4. If a large number of people responded negatively to a post, you are less likely to see it.
>
> ---
>
> 1   Lafferty, "INFOGRAPHIC: Understanding Facebook's Post-Sorting Algorithm ," Mediabistro Inc., http://allfacebook.com/infographic-understanding-facebook-algorithm_b115269

You can also search by new likes and by unlikes. For example, on the above graph, you can see that our fan page had some unlikes. No matter what you do, there will always be some people who unlike your page. It would be useful to go back to your page to see what posts you wrote on those days and to find out if there was something posted that provoked those unlikes. Your previous posts may be able to give you an indication as to what went wrong. Maybe you weren't entertaining enough or were posting too frequently, or posted too many links and not enough images. If you don't investigate the cause, these analytics just become useless data.

The pattern of highs and lows with Facebook data depends on the content you're posting. What is causing a surge or a drop in interest and interaction with your page? The important thing to learn from Facebook data is to understand how your content trends over time. You may find that it takes some time for your content to reach many people. This can be helpful when planning promotions and other time initiatives.

Facebook also provides you with the option to download your insights as an excel sheet with the Export Data button. Once you've downloaded them, they will become rows of data and various data sheets containing information such as key metrics, daily like sources, daily viral reach, etc. Sometimes looking at the tabulated data can give you more insights than graphs can to find out more about your fans and social media impact.

(Just a note, Facebook only provides insights for Pages with at least 30 likes. Also, keep in mind that Facebook's insights show analytics for Page posts from the past 28 days. For data about older posts, you can download it using the Export Data button).

What

Using Facebook analytics, we discovered that *Orange Juice in Bishop's Garden* ideal new episode release day is Wednesdays, but the time at which we post it varies by month, season, etc. This means when we release new episodes, we can maximize the number of people who come across it by posting on the day our fans are most active online. We were also able to see that many of our fans were returning to our page, sometimes up to 21+ times! Therefore, we know that what we're doing is working because fans specifically come to our page to find something interesting.

Other things to consider and look for:

Timing:

- What day of the week do you have the most engagement/reach?
- What time of the day do you have the most engagement/reach?
- How does the peak time for weekend and weekday posting compare?

Your most popular posts:

- When were they posted (day of the week, time of day)?
- Do they use any tags?
- What was the language used? Did it pose a question?
- What was the topic?

Users:

- Who are your most engaged users on Facebook?
- When are most Facebook users online?

Apps:

- Which apps on your Facebook page are people visiting? (Such as Pinterest, Etsy, Youtube, Etc.)?

TWITTER

For such a large platform, Twitter doesn't collect analytics internally (except if you pay to have a promoted post or ad), but instead allows third parties to do so. The ubiquity of Twitter and ease with which developers can sync with the platform has resulted in a plethora of analytics programs for Twitter users that can give you information on anything from who's not following you that you're following, to what your most influential hashtag is, to how to get connected with other influential tweeters in your extended Twitter network. However, take heed that these applications come and go as fast as Twitter updates! Each application has its own particular use, but there's no telling how long it will last! Also, newer, better Twitter applications that perhaps even integrate more than one specialty feature will continue to be released. For example, Hootsuite consolidates all of your social media platforms into one web application where you can post to Twitter, Facebook, LinkedIn, and other platforms. It also provides you with analytics reports based on how many clicks you get, etc.

The analytics reports for Twitter will most likely differ from those you receive from Facebook or Tumblr. Each platform has its optimal time to post and different types of content will be successful. Because Twitter is more conversation/dialogue based, interaction with others will most likely be a larger factor in your Twittersphere influence than it would be on Facebook.

Specific questions that can be answered through one of the various Twitter applications include:

- What day of the week do you see the most interactivity? What time of day?

- Do trending hashtags make a difference? Are they worthwhile to use?

- Are there any particular hashtags or terms within the larger web series/film/documentary and other communities that you should be using?

- Who are influential Twitter users in your sphere that you should interact with?

- What day of the week is best to gain new followers? Hold a giveaway? Release new content?

- What is the growth rate of your follower base?

For your reference, here are some platforms that @OJBishopsGardens has used in the past with success:

Tweet Archivist (http://www.tweetarchivist.com/): No longer free, Tweet Archivist allows users to select three things for it to 'archive' or track — such as a hashtag, user, or term — for $14.99 a month. The site will then analyze the results of the archive, allowing users to identify top influencers, images associated with terms, language breakdowns, and more. With a subscription, you are also able to export Tweet Archivist's findings for future use.

mentionmapp (http://mentionmapp.com/): The site provides a map of people a user has mentioned and who has mentioned that user. With this map, you can also view what users identified on the map are talking about.

Twitonomy (http://www.twitonomy.com/): Essentially the goldmind of Twitter analytics, Twitonomy will compile basically everything related to Twitter, from tracking clicks on your links to easily identifying who the users are that you're following who aren't following you back.

TwitSprout (https://twitsprout.com): Compatible with both Facebook and Twitter, TwitSprout tracks activity for both social media platforms and allows you to see how you measure up to your competitors. It also has the ability to handle multiple accounts and offers you the opportunity to then group those accounts and cross-compare. The data can then all be exported. But, depending on what you want TwitSprout to do, its services might not be free. If you're only interested in three Twitter accounts, then you're fine — but, if you would like to see more accounts or Facebook results, then prices start at $10 a month.

LINK SHORTENERS AND TRACKERS

In the age of short form content for entertainment, news, etc., everything is becoming abbreviated — even links! And if you want to stay in the game, you need to know where your traffic is coming from and what links are generating the most popularity.

A quick way to shorten links and to keep track of how many people are clicking your links, where they're coming from, and from what type of device can all be learned from bit.ly or similar link shorteners like goo.gl, Ow.ly, and Su.pr.

Aside from eliminating the visually unappealing look of a long link, using a URL shortener offers the benefits of providing data useful to managing a website or to trying to keep track of social media marketing. Shorteners also make links manageable and allow you to monitor and analyze their performance. You can be assured that the statistics are updated in real time and reflect accurate clicks that measure your performance.

Figure 9.13   Example of Bit.ly stats

It's especially interesting to see from which countries people are clicking your links. You'll have a visual representation of where your fans are located, and thus, be able to give them special recognition or readjust your promotional strategy and further increase your influence in those areas.

A benefit of using a link shortener is that all of your links are accessible wherever you are. When you save a link with a bit.ly account, you can find it in your bitmark list. View your shortened links at any time when logged into your account.

One potential drawback of shortened URLs is that they disguise the original links and make it somewhat difficult for others to determine if the link will redirect you to a good or parasitic site. With websites having longer and longer URLs, a shortener can be a handy thing to have.

- What are our most clicked links?

- What platforms are people clicking from? (FB, Twitter, etc.)

- What are the top countries where clicks are coming from?

PINTEREST

While few developers have worked on creating metrics for this platform, Pinterest has created its own. Unfortunately, the functionality is somewhat meager and is still being fleshed out. However, you should still consult any metrics available because something is obviously better than nothing. With Pinterest's innate metrics, you can graphically see pins, pinners, repins, repinners, impressions, reach, clicks, and visitors.

If you wish to delve even deeper, these are some excellent, outside platforms you can look at:

http://www.repinly.com/

http://www.reachli.com/landing

http://www.curalate.com/

But, even better, Pinterest recently gained the capability of allowing Google Analytics to be installed to users' platforms. [2]

---

2   De Vivo, "Pinterest Analytics: The Ultimate Guide to Tracking Your Site's Performance on Pinterest ," Search Engine Watch, Incisive Interactive Marketing LLC. , http://searchenginewatch.com/article/2273658/Pinterest-Analytics-The-Ultimate-Guide-to-Tracking-Your-Sites-Performance-on-Pinterest

INSTAGRAM

Because there is no HTML available on Instagram, the analytics provided for it are barebones, in comparison to the analytics available for other social media platforms. There are a couple of sites, however, worth looking at for somewhat comprehensive results.

Statigram (http://www.Statigr.am) is an excellent choice if you are looking for Instagram analytics. Statigram is a website to which you allow access to your account, and as a result of this access, it provides statistics and information regarding the number of total likes, comments, and followers you've received. The website also gives you information regarding new followers, lost followers, and follower growth. It doesn't end there either; Statigram breaks down your feed according to most popular post, most engaging filters and tags. It even suggests the best days and times for posting, based on your post history. In addition, the website provides information about your "scores," in comparison to other Instagram users.

Another worthy site to dive into is Webstagram (http://www.Web.stagram.com). One of the elements that makes Webstagram so compelling and relevant is that it constantly keeps tabs on which topics or tags are trending or popular and which filters are most used. The top tags, as of September 2013, are: #love (265,437,824 photos), #instagood (141,467,744 photos), and #me (122,777,402 photos). Surprisingly, using no filter at all is the choice for 40% of photos posted on Instagram, while Earlybird, X-Pro II, and Valencia are next in line. Webstagram also provides an as-it-happens run down of popular photos and feeds, which can be an eye-opening pedagogical (or procrastination) tool for users.

Nonetheless, make careful use of what statistics and analytics you collect — if you do this, plus focus on uploading photos with proper captions that will interest your intended audience, then you should find it easy to reach a wide audience.

TUMBLR

Through Tumblr's dashboard, you can access a skeletal analytics system by clicking on the "Activity" button on the right-hand side of your screen. There, you can view your traffic for up to a month-long period. You can also see how many followers and likes you've earned, who your biggest fans are, and what your top posts are. A running stream of all the latest notes is also compiled. But, as stated, this is all pretty basic. So, if you want to obtain a clearer picture of your Tumblr analytics, install Google Analytics to your account.

Chapter Ten
SELF-DISTRIBUTION AND FESTIVALS

SELF-DISTRIBUTION

Wohoo! You've finally actualized your artistic vision, and so now you're done, right? Well, not quite. Guess what, you haven't even begun to fully realize it yet. You might think you're done, but what on earth are you planning to do with your project? You've created this thing and now you need to let the world know. You need to distribute it.

But before you go about distributing it, make sure to consider what the ultimate goal for your creative vision is — why did you make it in the first place? Once you know this, then you can begin to decide how to distribute your content. Your goal could be exposure, networking, fame, money. Whatever it is, the distribution plan you use should help you achieve it and should reach your target audience. It's not just uploading; the upload isn't even half the battle. You don't want any random pair of eyeballs watching your content; you want to reach people for whom it was made — that's the true value in what you're creating. You create value around your show by reaching your target audience and by building a community of engaged fans around your show.

Also, keep in mind that growth happens organically, so it's not all going to happen immediately. But there are some things you can do (and should avoid doing) to help pilot this growth.

Helpful Tips to Avoid Common Mistakes

Let's go over some common mistakes and misconceptions about self-distribution:

1. Don't try to make your web series like a TV show. The TV and the web are two fundamentally different mediums. First, there are different audiences watching them. Second, the web is an inherently interactive medium, where you should interact and engage with your audience throughout your whole process. On the other hand, TV is broadcast *at* an audience. It's inherently *not* interactive; even if you can call in and vote for your favorite singer on *American Idol*, it's mostly a passive experience. Audiences can't just message a creator and voice their opinion about an episode ending and have some kind of creative input like they can with a web series. Your web series could potentially land you an opportunity on TV. But, even then, there's a reason why web series remain on the web and don't easily make the transition to broadcast. They're different mediums, and their structure, audience, and distribution differ accordingly.

    Also, consider that people crave quality content all the time, so "deadzones" for TV may well make for your digital bread-and-butter. In particular, consider that the digital medium means you can access your fans at times and in places that are completely off-limits to forms like traditional TV and movies. For example, many people have long commutes or passing times between classes — these times are standardized, frequently boring, and just aching to be filled. You can make your online content the go-to destination for just such occasions.

    Additionally, web content is not (yet) policed by the same ratings and content boards to which TV and movies are subjected. And especially in countries that control or censor content, the web is frequently an uninscribed place, which has greater freedom of content. In China in particular, commuters turn to web series and micro-movies to watch un-censored programming. And they tune in in droves.

2. Distribute your web series on multiple platforms, not just one. There are so many places to distribute, each with different audiences in different places. YouTube, for one, is huge. But there's a much different community on Vimeo and Blip, which both have more creators as users and more original content. Putting your web series on different platforms will allow you to reach new audiences. Especially in the

beginning, when you are carving out your niche, diversify your platforms. Diversify, diversify, diversify!

Every web series has a different distribution plan that is specific to the kind of show and audience that watches it. This can be according to genre or determined by if it's a daily or monthly show. The plan can depend on factors like your bandwith, what you have time for, and what your audience is used to. For example, Fridays may be good for some people but not for you, so don't decide to release your show then.

Yet, no matter what you choose to do, do not release all of your episodes at the same time! This will spell a certain death for your web series. Timing is important! You want to have a specific distribution schedule with specific days and times for each different platforms. Each episode helps you build audience, which takes time. Build a consistent release schedule and consistently message to your fans about release dates with links.

3. Do not assume that if you shoot a pilot episode, somebody else will give you money to make the rest of your series.

Pilots are great; they show an audience what kind of show you're going for, and you can build your fundraising efforts around it. But, honestly, you're better off doing as much as you can with the resources you have than praying for some big shot to fund you. Using all your resources together at once and shooting as many episodes as you can is your best bet. In the end, you just need to get your work out there. Otherwise, you're limiting your potential by waiting around instead of producing and being creative with what you have. You'll be surprised at how much you can do with so little!

4. Massive production value means a massive reception. This is just not true. Viewer engagement and audience reception make for a multi-faceted beast of an issue.

Consumers everywhere are fickle, but especially on the web. Web audiences are pretty savvy, and they're always poised to click away at any time something isn't interesting or entertaining — no matter how good the video quality. This is an instance where substance is style. While a good looking web series can make people say "wow," what's going to keep them watching is if the content is not just beautiful but also captivating. The work must be worth watching.

Not every element of your project needs to be glossy, polished, expensive, or gorgeous. Your style may be haphazard but charming. The most winning elements should be your story and how you share it. This means that if all you had was an iPhone to shoot with — or if you lack deep pockets for prints and advertising — don't fret! Refrain from stressing overmuch about video quality — and besides, the iPhone shoots HD. If you have a story worth telling, it will resonate with audiences regardless of your video resolution. So go ahead and tell it! If you're obsessing over video quality and the depth of your pockets, you may be misplacing your energy. Alternatively, high video quality and big bucks are not something you can rest on. You have to make sure your content is interesting; you have to share content and engage with your audiences. Remember, you are your own agent. You alway have to be active in promoting yourself as a creator. The web is saturated with other high quality video content; you are the factor that will make yours stand out.

5. The most important thing is to get as many people as possible to watch your web series. Then, you can make money from your views

    Low views don't necessarily mean your show is a failure. Views are not what creates the ultimate value for you as a creator. For different web series, there's a range of views in which shows are considered successful because they've reached their _target_ audience. The true value in views is about reaching your target audience, creating a community of fans around your show, and making sure your audience is engaged (e.g. they watch past 30 seconds of your video or past the first episode in your series).

    Along with this is the assumption that if you get a lot of people to watch your content, you will make a lot of money off of views. This may be true, but it really depends on how many views you get. Most web series don't get millions of views, but even if you did, it really doesn't amount to as much ad revenue as you probably think. If you do the math, a typical first web series that has a run of 100,000 views across all episodes is worth between $200-$700, if it's getting a decent ad rate. This amount is probably what you would spend on production, so in the end, you may just barely break even. So, if your ultimate goal is to make money off your web series, you're going to have to find other ways not solely associated with your views to make money. Most likely, if you're going viral on YouTube, any significant money you make will probably come from the exposure and the offshoot opportunities that manifest, and not the actual views themselves. Monetizing digital content isn't easy. It takes planning, commitment, knowledge, and a lot of organization about the scope of options to reach and build your audiences across the variety of places where they can discover your show.

Designing Your Distribution Plan

How do you design your distribution schedule? Believe it or not, your production schedule largely determines your distribution schedule.

Before you even launch your series, you must think about your distribution. Your basic distribution production equation will be how many episodes you need to have before you launch. This number will dictate how much time you have to produce all of them. If you're shooting 10 episodes at a time and releasing once a week, then you'll have about three months' worth of content. This means you would need to shoot once every three months. The formula is pretty straight forward.

Deciding on a distribution schedule depends on a few factors. How many episodes are you planning to make? Is it 10, 20? How often do you want to distribute an episode each week? Once a week, once a month? Additionally, there are two kinds of programs. The first is a seasonal or serialized show: it has a beginning, a middle, and an end. It has a first and a last episode within a collection of pieces that constitute a season. And each season should also function similarly within the larger organic whole. The second type of program is that which has no definitive or set ending — it is an ongoing show.

Is your work seasonal? If it is, you would benefit from stacking up your work according to season. Or is your program on-going? Then, it makes sense to shoot/edit/distribute as you go. You just need to pick and lock down a schedule.

> ### A Note on Release Schedules
>
> How you decide to release your show, whether once a week, bi weekly, or monthly, depends on both the type of show you have and also on how much work actually goes into creating the final product. For example, *Web Series Watch* by Cindy Jenkins and Patty Robinson is a web series that releases video weekly. Their show reviews and recommends other web series programs. It only features them and has simplified locations, occasionally making use of green-screen. The setup is simple, the needs are not exorbitant, and the content is cute but informational. For them it is possible to crank out successful episodes at this energetic rate. For a massively labor-intensive show, this would be neither advisable or possible.
>
> As an ongoing show, Cindy and Patty's *Web Series Watch* releases episodes one after another with no clear end in sight. Episodes do not hinge on each other and work well as stand-alones, so grouping episodes by season is unnecessary. Instead, due to the constantly evolving nature of the web and the informational nature of the content, the show needs to stay current with constant, timely updates. Akin to a TV Guide, *Web Series Watch* provides these updates weekly.
>
> This is the best distribution schedule that worked for this show in particular. You'll want to base your schedule off of your specific needs and abilities.

If you haven't shot all your episodes and are creating an ongoing series, you still need to make a release schedule. Doing so will make you hold yourself accountable and ensure that you produce and edit consistently for you and your audience. Get your audience accustomed to your times and don't switch the schedule on them, as doing so will only annoy them. Your audience will care about these things. People who follow you and are looking for regular releases from you will care. And these are precisely the people you want to cater to. Consistency is important. Maintain an episode archive on your site. A successful web series builds itself on a community of fans, and this is one step toward establishing one.

If your episodes are already shot and in that proverbial can, you'll still have to figure out a release schedule that works with what you already have. Pick a day of the week and a specific time to release your main episodes, and maybe the same or different day and time for exclusive content. And when you're making your announcements to your audience on social media, mark on your calendar and follow through! Give people a heads up before you release your content, tell them the day of, and then give them a reminder to watch after it's been up for a few days.

Task: Choose a web series with a similar audience and model out its distribution plan. When does it release? At what times? Find a few web series you love and study what worked for them. Look at their different channels and see how they describe their content's release on social media. Then think about what you want to do with your show and create a calendar with your distribution and production schedule.

Programming

Once you have all your footage and are ready to distribute, an important question to consider is: how to package what you have? How many episodes do you need before you launch? How long should each episode be? And why is bonus content important? You should certainly have considered these questions in pre-production, but now is a time to re-visit your strategic conclusions.

A good aim is to try to have at least 10 episodes at a bare minimum — whether per season, for a serialized show, or for an on-going show.

Having a minimum of 10 episodes will help you grow your audience as you go through the distribution process. Also, keep in mind, if you are actively seeking third party distribution, distribution companies are much more interested in work that has been fleshed out and sustained. A brilliant idea with only one piece of content or only one episode in the can is too great a risk for them. However, a project that already has a season or series of episodes under its belt is something an audience can sink its teeth into, which means that a distributor can, too. It is shocking how many projects fizzle out after a few episodes or don't make it to a second season. (It's so endemic to the industry that I've coined it the "Second Season Curse"). Just think, why should a third party spend time, money, and other resources on a small and unfinished body of work? Wouldn't the safer bet be to throw in with a known quantity or with at least a body of work that is hefty and completed? More content means better return on an investment for the distributor. It's just the bottom line.

As for the format of content and episode length, for the most part, this is flexible according to your genre and to other factors and conventions that dictate the optimum format for your show. There is no hard and set rule for how long your episodes should be. It really depends on the kind of show you want to make. However, do consider that to diversify your viewing, it pays to be mobile-friendly. Most smartphones can't handle the influx of too much content — so keeping an episode around the six to seven minute mark will encourage that mobile viewing.

See **"Script and Story" on page 15, "Ready, Set, Go" on page 117, and "Web Site Basics and Web Design" on page 241 for greater elucidation of this principle ▶**

That said, sometimes you can even go shorter… micro-short even. Sketch comedies, for instance, could be as brief as the two to five minute range. Just think about how long you can sustain the laughs and compare that to how much character and narrative building you actually have. In a sketch comedy, the over-arching narrative may be simple or almost non-existent, and the characters may be studies, not people your audience needs to fully know; this means you can get in and out more quickly. As for news or review shows, keep them two to four minutes tops. News viewers want in and out; they are there for the information, so no fluff.

Drama, sci-fi, fantasy, and horror episodes, however, may be a bit longer. You want your viewers to be more invested in your world and characters, and sometimes it takes an audience a little longer to get to know them. These generally should still stay under the 10 minute mark. Action, similar to comedy, appeals to short attention spans. The audience wants to watch something fast, something gripping. For this genre, in particular, longer episodes can also mean significantly higher costs, so shorter is better. If your series is subject specific, like a cooking show or make-up tutorials, you have more of a range, but within five to 10 minutes is still a good target range. Talk shows can, as a general rule, get away with being longer, up to 30 minutes, because people who tune in are there to listen to you talk.

Bonus Content

In addition to your normal episodes, you'll want to distribute and share bonus content for people to watch in between the releases of your main attraction. Bonus content helps you build your fan base so that they're always engaging with your creative content — even when you don't have that main attraction ready for sharing. In the vast, swirling, enormity of the web, carving out a niche is hard. And even if you do that, being remembered and being memorable is harder still. More content means less chance of losing people's attention. It means more days and times of meeting the expectation of that programming schedule. You want to become destination viewing for people. Every Wednesday at 9am EST, say, you need to be there and active and artistic, to burn an incendiary mark in people's memories. And then you need to gently maintain that over the rest of the week. Moreover, giving people something extra is not just another way to engage them; it turns viewers into fans. The additional content means you are going the extra mile for them and consider your viewers special. When these in turn fans begin actively telling others about your show, they create a perpetual motion machine. In such cases, extra content will be extra valuable to share.

Bonus content can constitute any type of content. It could be wallpaper, a theme song, a bonus video, or a copy of the shooting script. It can be a creator's vlog with you talking about what it was like creating your work. Was it difficult? Was there enough money? Did your main actress fly to Paris and never come back? Another option is character vlogs where characters in your story talk to the camera in character. Other content includes bloopers, deleted scenes, and behind-the-scenes footage. All

Tales from the Trenches
Crossing Platforms

OJBG had a plethora of additional content (bonus videos, cast interviews, wallpaper images, songs, deleted scenes, behind-the-scenes, sneak peeks, memes, and more). And that is all great. But it also helps to think outside of the box in terms of **packaging** your work.

OJBG was packaged seven ways to Sunday. Viewers could access individual episodes. Or viewers could have series of episode comprising full-seasons of content. Plus, the seasons were put together as feature-length films. There were free viewing options, plus rental and purchase options. But it didn't end there, *OJBG* was also packaged in book form, as scriptbooks for each season and as a *Director's Notebook*. Character "diaries" were also available on the blog, as a way to peer deeper into certain issues and plot points.

Cross-platform meant we could reach more members of our audience. *OJBG* passed in front of more interested eyeballs. And when it did, it could be used/shared/watched with ease, in many different ways, suited to many different habits and tastes.

It all comes down to making your content as easy to use, as easy to access, and as readily available as possible — and in making it so to the greatest section of your audience possible.

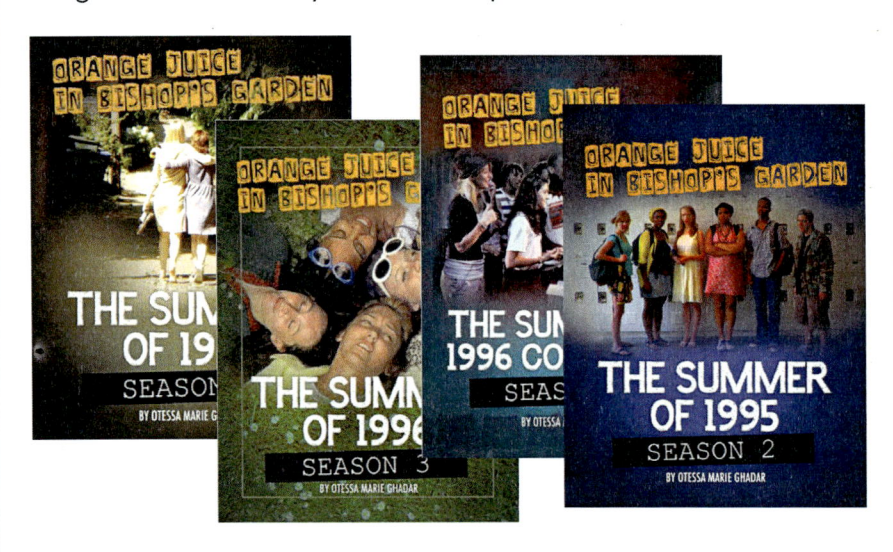

of this adds extra value and makes your work more immersive. Again, this doesn't have to be complicated or super sophisticated. This could just mean someone filmed onset with his or her phone and you turn it into a bonus video. Another easy way to create bonus content is to create extended episodes or "bonus versions." Consider adding another ending to an episode, and then you get twice the bang for your buck because you get to distribute it a second time as something totally new. Alternatively, you can have bonus content that is totally extra, like a field trip or anything related to your theme. Bonus content will give your audience something to watch, and then it will want to stay invested in your show.

Even better, try always having some bonus content available for free to download. It need not be something large, but giving back to those who give to you is priceless.

Task: Pick a known-commodity digital program. What type of story or work is it? Using the genre or type of story as a guide, choose your target number of episodes; determine the ideal length for each episode or content piece.

Building Your Audience Before Launching your Series

Now that you have your content, it's time to make sure you have all the details worked out to prepare you for a successful launch. You already have a title for your work, now secure your domains. This means on a website and on Facebook, Twitter, Instagram, Pinterest, Tumblr, et cetera. These are streams around which you'll want to be part of to build communities. It sounds like a lot — and it is! — but each audience is different. What you're going to say to the audiences in those places will differ. You'll want to design your distribution campaign around things that make sense for your show as well as for the channels you're using.

See "Social Media" on page 149 for more on using various social media platforms, as well as how to utilize video sharing sites and channels ▶

See "Web Site Basics and Web Design" on page 249 section for explanations on registering website domains and setting up your website ▶

First, decide how many episodes you want completed before you actually launch. Then, if you don't already have trailers or teasers, you should make those. Those are tweetable, shareable, easily digestible bits you can throw out to entice people and to start building your audience.

With your newfound social media empire, consider holding contests to build hype and awareness for your launch. Post pictures on Instagram, ask fans to link to or like it. What social media will be doing for you at this point, when you don't have any episodes out, is providing your audience with an engagement opportunity. Engage people with questions. Think about what might be relevant to their lives and also connected to your show, while still being specific to each social media channel. But, most importantly, secure some kind of website domain for your content. This is deeply important; it helps you build your brand — not just as a show, but also as a creator.

Task: Complete your social media and website land grab. Figure out what domain names you want linked with your title. Connect with your target mentors/creators, who are already out there, and see how they can be helpful to you, and you to them.

> Before you begin distributing your own series, try making a list of your favorite web series creators or YouTubers. Email them and tell them you enjoy their show, and ask if they'd be interested in being involved in your show. Offer them something you can do for them — tweeting, blogging, helping out at an event, etc. Ask them later on to tweet about your show, and they probably will. This is the general atmosphere of web series creators: they want to collaborate and help each other. And this is how many web series often succeed: through collaborative relationships with people who already have a following. Consider cross promotional deals to do with them, reciprocal shout outs. But, please, give people a specific thing you want them to do and give them something specific back, whether a tweet about a launch date or a like on Facebook.

Pre-Building Audience by Crowdfunding

What does pre-building your audience mean? This may be a foreign concept to those who don't have their work completed already or to those who are not ready to launch. All pre-building means is getting people ready, telling people about your show and that it's "coming soon." So, how do you create this pre-existing audience? How do you make people want to watch it and feel like they are in some way affected, before it even comes out?

Crowdfunding is a great way to do this. Crowdfunding for your launch might not be a bad idea. Even crowdfunding for finishing funds can be turned into a distribution strategy. Don't forget that any crowdfunding efforts are simultaneously great places to build advance buzz, both through pre-production and also through the disbursement of perks. Holding a campaign can make people invested in your work. Your ultimate goal with a crowdfunding campaign is not necessarily to get a high dollar amount, but a high *level of investment* — backers who believe in YOU.

Crowdfunding allows you to reach people who aren't just in your immediate social network; you can go beyond that.

See "Rounding Up Your Resources" on page 51 for an expanded view ▶

> The Bridegroom is a great example of building an audience outside your immediate sphere. It's a feature film and not a web series about a gay couple who is unable to get married because of family differences. There's a built-in fanbase for this film among the gay community who would find this kind of story really interesting. By doing a crowdfunding campaign, they could tap into that crowd, that audience, and present their film as a story they want to tell. People who identify with that story will want it to be told. Crowdfunding will be an effective way to get people invested in hearing your story, or at least in learning more about your subject. It will also allow you to hit your niche audience.

Even if you've raised all the money you need for your digital production, you can crowdfund for something else, like a launch party. Hold an event for your artistic endeavor; you can raise money for distribution and marketing plans, while simultaneously hosting a marketable event. Your team has much to celebrate, so bring them, their networks, and your fans together. An event is something nearly everyone can find value in. After the event, you will have news to share and new contacts with whom to network. Your event could even spark an ongoing and defining event for your show or artistic community.

TALES FROM THE TRENCHES

Before releasing the seventh and final season of *Orange Juice in Bishop's Garden*, 20/20 Productions held a web series festival to honor and spotlight the industry contributions of the Mid-Atlantic region. At the event, web series creators across the region were honored, and their showreels and trailers were screened. It was also a chance to screen a sneak peek showreel and recap of some of 20/20's recently commended work and newest projects.

It was a screening turned network-builder and major industry event, with the likes of *The Washington Post* covering the goings-on. It later led to additional screenings at the larger International Washington D.C. Film Festival (Filmfest DC). The web series festival is now planned to be an annual event.

Task: Create a crowdfunding campaign purpose. What would it accomplish? Think outside the box. How to make your campaign stand out? Keep it simple; set up a campaign; shoot a teaser; get it done.

Pre-building an Audience Without Crowdfunding

We know some of you are averse to asking for money and want to avoid holding a crowdfunding campaign if you can help it. That's fine; there are alternative non-monetary ways to pre-build your audience. In this case, your best bet will be through grassroots buzz building. This can be done through old school email gathering, and there are a few ways of doing this, some more guerilla than others. If you're outgoing, social, and like being around people, or you know people who are like that, think about some places your audience is going to be. If you're doing a food show, maybe they're at a grocery store or a kitchen shop. Do they like action movies? Will they go to the movie theaters to watch the newest Batman flick... and what about a comic book store? Go to those places. Talk to those people. Tell them what you're doing and ask them if they'd like to know more about it later. If they say yes, sign them up on your email list. This is a somewhat guerilla tactic, but building your early watchers — the people who will help you build your show later on — is crucial to your success. Until you have those first people watching, it's harder to get your content off the ground. Once you build a base following, then you can really grow.

With your list of emails, make a campaign. Make newsletters that are entertaining, not annoying. Let them know what your distributions options are, when you're planning to launch, etc. Give your audience members an early exclusive access to stuff related to your show before anyone else. Perhaps schedule a sneak-screening for them. Or include some beautiful still images and photographs in your newsletter. Always think of ways to give back to your audience.

Now, if you prefer not to go places and instead want to utilize your computer, that's also a good thing! Web series and digital art are online and on mobile devices after all! If you can find where other people are watching shows like yours, that will be a gold mine. And remember to have fun with this process! Don't think about it like you're spamming people or stealing another's audience. You're doing everyone a favor by giving early access to your show, getting their feedback, adding to the wonderful wealth of content online. A lot of those communities are hungry for new content, new shows, new ideas that are interesting. A way you can also drive engagement is to do a little testing pre-launch. Ask the public for tips and ideas, and if you implement any of them, tweet them thanks or give them a shoutout on Facebook!

Task: Pick five to 10 people to reach out to, with the goal being to build them into your base audience. Use this as the springboard, or first degree of separation, to build on and out from. Seek out physical places, online communities, and places where kindred spirits and similar works connect. Come up with a list of 200-400 emails. This is the core group you will target and engage with for your initial launch.

Releasing Content to Create Fans

Timing is important for your episode releases and for building your audience. By offering your fans a first "exclusive look," you're giving them something special. You can then later put the content in other places, at other times. But putting it exclusively on your site first is the best way to get people acclimated to visiting your site in the first place.

TIP, TRICKS, TOOLS: Remember that you can craft your distribution release schedule around this principle. You can make your content exclusively available on your own site, or another preferred site, before it is available on others. This can be an excellent way to direct an audience to the site of your preference and to build an audience base for your own website.

Rule #1. Figure out where to release when. The first place you put your web series is where you want your fans to see it. Fans are people that follow you; they're looking forward to seeing your show. Somebody who stumbles upon your show once or randomly isn't a fan; he or she is only someone who subscribes.

Rule #2. Wait a day or some specific and consistent amount of time before you release the same episode in another place. For example, if you release content on your website on Tuesday, release it onto YouTube on Wednesday or Thursday. The window of time before the first and second release is called an exclusive window release pattern.

Rule #3. When you put your content up on secondary platforms, make sure you tell people about your early release and show them where to access it. If people don't know that you're giving it to them early, why would they go to your site? You've got to communicate the message to people and guide them with links.

Review "Video Sharing Websites" on page 214 for a more in-depth view of video platforms and how to use them ▶

Picking Your Distribution Platforms

Where to put your show — this is what you've been waiting to know! But, before talking about where you should put your show, it's necessary to discuss *who* your audience is and what that means for you. Different distribution platforms sometimes have different audiences, and sometimes they have similar crossover audiences. For example, similar audiences watch both YouTube and Blip, but not everyone watching on YouTube is also watching on Blip.

So, who is your audience? Think broadly about whom your audience might be so that you can reach everyone possible. Also think specifically about whom your niche audience is. Is it solely knitting moms, guys who like to woodwork, or simply people who like funny stunts? Try to identify what they like.

Task: Write down target audience(s), who make sense for you and your work. Follow them and encourage them to follow you back. Think outside the box for your audience and even consider peripheral audiences. Ask around to see who else may find your show interesting.

Now that you're ready, which distribution platform do you use? Here's an overview of a few with their advantages and disadvantages listed:

Review "Video Sharing Websites" on page 214 for a more in-depth view of video platforms and how to use them ▶

High Traffic

YouTube: All kinds of digital content and web series exist on YouTube. It offers the biggest exposure and is definitely a top tier distribution platform. You can't ignore YouTube; you have to use it. There really is no way around this platform, unless you don't want people to know about what you're doing, or if you're specifically trying to isolate your content from Youtube for some reason. YouTube is a great marketing engine with great analytics to back it up. It is easy to share, like, and comment across platforms. Videos can be embedded, and the player can be customized on your site. Videos are even natively playable when they are linked within a Gmail message.

You can now also become a partner and earn ad revenue if you choose, but this means there will be ads on your video content. YouTube also has a ton of other great features — one being that it has the biggest video community online. It's also quite collaborative, which is something you should be looking for as a pioneer of new media. The downside is that YouTube's "Help Center" is anemic at best. At the same time, YouTube itself is massive, so you're competing with vast swaths of content, which is barely categorized and difficult to wade through. Also, there's no web series brand on YouTube yet, so finding your niche market can be trickier. That said, YouTube is the original standard. It is the first and the last, but maybe not your everything.

Vimeo: The wonderful aspect of Vimeo is that it offers audiences an ad free experience as an embedded player on your own website or as a channel on Vimeo. The Vimeo player is clean and visually-appealing, and the playback is notable for being high-quality and retaining the look and color of the original material. Vimeo can work well for views, but, again, there is no real section or brand for web series or other forms of digital art. It has a reputation of being filmmaker-friendly and is largely composed of a community of the like.

Boutique Traffic

Vimeo: Vimeo is placed in both "High Traffic" and "Boutique" categories, as it is an excellent, filmmaker-centric community, while also serving up a high volume of views.

Blip: A solid, commendable platform for original web series, Blip is a platform that specifically cultivates the web series form. Surprisingly, original content is often hard to find on the web. While YouTube is cluttered with repeats, revamps, and cats with cheeseburgers (and maybe there's nothing wrong with that!), creatively original content with a story or concept is more likely to live on Blip. This platform provides good ad revenue return — probably one of the highest out there, which is a reason a lot of creators like it! There are ads, though, so keep that in mind. Blip is a great place to build your own audience. There's also a big community of web series creators, so it's great for networking. On the back end, Blip offers quality analytics, so you can track how you're doing, how many views you're at, and from where and on what devices. Blip also has a deal with Yahoo! and AOL, so it can pipe some of its shows to these larger platforms, but these are probably going to be used for bigger shows only. That said, it does offer third party opportunities for "the rest of us," namely Roku and iTunes podcasts. Lastly, the Blip player embeds on websites and is customizable, so you can really brand your content.

Koldcast: Unlike many of the others sites listed, Koldcast is a curated video platform. Content must go through an application process, and there is no guarantee you will be accepted. The nice thing about a curated experience is that it is self-selective. People go to Koldcast to watch internet programming and web series specifically. This means shows are less likely to be lost or buried. With Koldcast, you can gather tremendously high view counts. Yet, unfortunately, you won't know who's watching or where they come from. The analytics and tracking program on the back-end of its site is somewhat useful, but extremely basic. Its best asset is that Koldcast does do some social media and blogging, via its "Fourth Wall" platform, which directs high volume traffic to your work *when it happens*. Additionally, Koldcast does offer some third party platform opportunities, but that list can change without much notice. Koldcast is a great place to reach additional viewers, but it probably works best when bundled together with other options and platforms, as part of a larger strategy.

Intermediate Traffic

DailyMotion: There all kinds of video content on this platform. It's a European-based company, and you can get medium level exposure. Many views from this platform are through mobile-viewing. You just want to make sure having content on this platform isn't cannibalising your other views. You want to syndicate your show on DailyMotion, but you probably don't want to make it a top priority, as there are no real revenue based opportunities on this platform.

Break: This is a platform more for short, funny one-offs. It might be a good fit for your content if you have a concept for a series, which you are just starting or have not completed. Break makes a strong platform for testing those waters. Or maybe you just want to share your one-offs all in a row — Break also makes a good home for these types of endeavors.

Funny or Die: This platform actually does have a web series section to upload to. However, you will be competing with celebrity content and not solely fellow independent artists. It seems more difficult to break out on this platform. But if you want to be associated with celebrities, it may be a beneficial place to be.

Low Traffic

Just the Story: Just the Story is an ad-free subscription based service. For a few dollars a month, viewers have complete access to content. The monthly-subscription fee means viewers will want and need a reason to subscribe. Just the Story works well for those who already have an established fan base or a modicum of fame.

Justin TV: Justin TV began in 2007 as a California based start-up. Justin TV can be said to have had two reincarnations. The first is as the beginning of a type of broadcasting called 'life casting,' which is similar to the basis of modern reality television. Justin Kan, the original creator and namesake, wore a camera every day, broadcasting his daily activities and making the average American life something to be viewed from a public perspective. This generated so much press that it led to the second generation of Justin TV.

Justin "2.0" consists of thousands of channels of multiple people "life casting" or putting whatever else they deem view-worthy on the site. You may have heard about the 2008 incident of an 18-year-old named Abraham Briggs who overdosed live on Justin TV, before the horrified eyes of the many watchers who were currently tuned-in. Though the segment was quickly taken down, and explicit content can only be viewed by those 18 or older, this incident called into question the appropriateness of having public spaces invade that of the private sector. Because of this, if you are considering putting your videos on Justin TV, be warned. It is a free broadcasting service that reaches many people, but it has a turbulent history and reputation. Just food for thought, when you are considering your image in terms of distribution.

Vuier: This is a relatively newer option that allows you to choose your own distribution strategy. With Vuier, you pick a price to sell your content (either per video or by season), and then Vuier takes a standardized cut of the profit. This is neat because you can offer the pay-per-view episodes exclusively or as an additional option available to fans. You set your own price. You get almost all of the return. It's not just about sharing ad revenue per thousand views.

Task: Pick the distribution platforms that you're going to use as they relate to your goals. Remember why you wanted to create this work in the first place and who it was supposed to be for! Factor all that information in to find the platform(s) you're going to use.

Considering Bigger Brands and Third Party Deals

My Long Distance Relationship is a popular web series on Hulu. This begs the question: should you make something for self-distribution or get some bigger company to fund it and distribute for you? You can try to do either option, but be aware that you could be limiting your options if you go after a bigger company as opposed to self-distributing.

Here's the reality. Unless you have a pre-established digital audience, it's going to be a tough sell for bigger companies to consider distributing or even funding your show. It's even more difficult if you don't have a celebrity in your show or a big-wig somehow associated or affiliated. Many "big-name" companies (hello, Hulu) do not even accept unsolicited materials, and if your rolodex or address book is underwhelming, you may feel powerless. It's getting cluttered in the web series world, and it is no longer just the realm of the independent artists. Bigger names are barging in, and sometimes it can feel like the little guys will be squeezed out if they're not vigilant.

> *Battlestar Galactica: Blood & Chrome* is a ten episode science fiction web series, which functions as a prequel to the re-imagined and much-beloved *Battlestar Galactica TV* series. Created by sci-fi heavyweights Michael Taylor and David Eick, it was distributed through Machinima.com and then later by SyFy as a TV movie. With beaucoup pre-existing production money, it's almost no surprise that the series did so well. If you don't have a big name or major franchise readily available, don't bank on getting a big name company to take notice of you. That doesn't mean you shouldn't try! It just means that it shouldn't be your only strategy.

That said, even if you can do it, make sure that you want to first. With the rise of box digitals — sites like Hulu, AOL, Yahoo! — and more host web series online, the chance of getting in the door is even slimmer. So, perhaps making it a Season 2 goal, after you have an established audience, is a bit more realistic.

The advantage, of course, of being distributed through a bigger company or of securing a major third party deal is the marketing and exposure you will get out of it. You do gain some stability. But you also give some things up, including perhaps the DIY appeal, your connection to your fans, your creative control, even your ownership. Once your content is on the larger distributor's site, it's out of your control — many sites will not even allow you to have your work up independently on your own website. This takes a bite out of the personal and DIY nature of the art. Having full creative control, plus a direct and meaningful connection with your fans, is so much of what makes this art form special, radical, powerful even. This heady mix is also frequently what attracts artists to the medium. Take away the alchemy of these elements and you may yourself be left with something that no longer captivates the mind. If you do go the big business route, try to maintain a strong and personable social media presence. This can mitigate any audience dissociation with your show.

Maybe you do want to at least try to make it with a bigger brand. Maybe you have a buddy who knows another buddy at a big company who can try to buy and distribute your show. If you have connections, by all means use them! If that doesn't pan out, look into contests. Contests can bring attention and recognition to you and your work. Occasionally contests come in the form of "one off" videos rather than as a series, but do your research and give it a try.

What about web series studios? Companies like Machinima, Vuguru, Endemol, Digital Broadcasting group, and MyDamnChannel have makers' studios that help people make shows like yours. Whether they decide to help your show comes down to where you are in your web series career. Have you already made a few shows; do they have a big following? If you haven't and are still working on your first series, you'll most likely have to do your first series on your own, which is perfectly fine and doable! These places usually have difficult selection processes. At times, it doesn't even come down to your content. Sometimes they prefer to work with people they've already targeted or worked with in the past.

You may think you'll have near complete freedom with these makers' studios, but you're probably going to have to give up some level of ownership and revenue stream. If you independently keep control of your intellectual property and distribution rights, everything that goes into the brand you're creating and working on is all yours. This isn't the case with larger brand names. So rather than working with a huge brand, collaborating with smaller companies could be a good distribution option.

Working with small companies is a bonus because they're more accessible; you can approach them more directly. If you cater to the same audience, you can easily propose making something together that they fund and that you can work on creating. You can reach out to these companies via email to gauge their interest. This is sort of like "cold emailing" and a bit guerilla, but it is effective! Send them a link to a short film or a teaser where they can check out your content, and then gauge their interest. If they bite, set up a call and pitch your show. And if a deal doesn't' happen, let them know you're still doing it, and maybe they'll get involved later down the road.

Still searching? Consider consulting a list of distributors and companies that attend major film and new media markets, and send queries and EPK's to companies that look like a good fit.

See the **"Best Practices for Your EPK and The Literary Pitch" on page 297** for more information on how to create an EPK for the distribution hunt ▶

For example, MIPCOM, an annual TV and entertainment market held in Cannes, releases a list of participating and exhibiting companies after each event. This would be an ideal starting place to identify companies in various countries. Information and offers they send to you the first time will most likely be more one-sided in their favor. It's OK to negotiate to get what works best for you and your fans, but you should also know when to stop. What are your deal breakers? What performance guarantees do you require? A 50/50 net split, while one of the most standard you'll find, is just one type of deal. Something else might suit your needs better. Do some digging and determine what is best for you and your work.

Task: Pick a local brand or smaller brand that you'd like to try to get to underwrite your show and reach out to it. Use traditional outreach methods in addition to social media.

> A great example of starting small and independent before going big is The Guild. The show premiered on YouTube in 2007. Then its later seasons two through five were distributed by Microsoft's Xbox Live Marketplace, Zune Marketplace, and MSN Video. It's now one of the most well known web series.

Social Media as Distribution

We already went over social media in great detail in the previous chapter, so there is no need to beat a dead horse. [insert link to chapter].

Instead, in this section, you should think of social media AS a form of distribution. Social media is a part of your life now; there's no avoiding it in business, filming, and distribution. If there are people in these places on social media, it means it's a place where you can distribute. Think of Facebook and Twitter as individual distribution platforms you need to consider and schedule in addition to Blip, YouTube, etc.

Why? Because it's not just your personal network of friends on social media. If you're creating a page for people to like you as a creator or a page just for your content, then you have a possible community. Social media sites provide a neutral, controlled ground for fans to interact with you besides your website. And the great part of most of these platforms is that people don't need to leave the site to interact with you or to see an update or an event. It's a place where you can put teasers, funny jokes, ask questions, contests, etc., all while promoting your product.

And remember, grasshopper, Twitter, in particular, is great for teasers, trailers, and little clips, and, most importantly, extends beyond your immediate social network because your tweets are accessible to the entire Twittersphere.

Task: Create a "Like My Page" campaign for Facebook and try to get your likes up to 100. Also, create a Twitter hashtag for your show. Start interacting with people on Twitter and get your followers up to 100. It's amazing how well people respond to challenges, such as if my post gets 100 likes, I'll do this crazy thing. Maybe set up your page with a description that if you get so many likes, your audience will get a sneak peak.

FESTIVALS

Film Festivals for Web and New Media

Hallelujah! You've successfully distributed your web series or at least have a plan fully thought out, and so you're finally done, right? Well, technically, you could be — but it'd be nice to get a little recognition (aside from your slew of loyal fans, of course), for all your hard work! Enter in, the festival. AKA another wonderful chance to get the word out there about your fantastic new show. But, beware, it's not as simple as just submitting to any old festival. Namely, be wary of the "Old Fart" Festivals — they will require national or worldwide premieres — this means your work cannot be ONLINE. How does this help you? It doesn't. Be careful to strategize your festival plan around web-friendly festivals!

HollyWeb Festival
Early - July - $50/60 (Short/Long Form)
Regular - November - $60/70
Late - January - $70/80

Holly Shorts
Early - February - $40
Regular - April - $50
Late - May - $60

New Media Festival
Early - September - $65/60 (Regular/Student)
Regular - November - $75/70
Late - February - $85/80
Extended - May - $90/85

LA Web Series Festival
Regular - October - $50
Extended - December - $75
Late - February - $90

The Webby Awards
Early - October - $275/150 (Commercial/Personal)
Regular - December - $295/150
Extended - January - $295/150

The Streamys Festival
Official Entries - November - First Category $125, Each Additional $50, 7+ Categories $400
Audience Submissions - November

Tellys Festival
Regular - March - $80/165
Extended - May - $95/180 (Single/Campaign Entry)

Marseilles Web Fest
Regular - April - Free

ATL Webfest
Regular - September - $50
Late - October - $75

Raindance Web Fest
Deadline - July - £20

Disposable Film Festival
Deadline - October - $5

Melbourne WebFest
Early - April - $40
Late - June - $70

LA Web Fest
Regular - October - $50
Extended - December - $75
Late - February - $90

Vancouver Web Fest
Early - October - $50/60 (Short/

Long Form)
Regular - January - $60/70
Late - March - $70/80

FirstGlance Film Festival (Web Series Pilots category)
Earlybird - September - $30
Regular - October - $40
Late - November - $50

New Media Film Festival
Early Bird - September - $65/60 (Regular/Student)
Regular - November - $75/70
Late - February - $85/80
Extended - April - $90/85

SharpCuts Indie Film Festival
(Web Series Category)
Earlybird - May - $15
Regular - September - $20

DC Web Fest
Deadline - February?
(Nothing Really Announced)

The Future of Viewing
Where Have We Been? Where Are We Going?

The herd mentality versus lone wolves:

In the digital age, it's hard to say what the end product of viewing films at festivals will be, especially with the emergence of festivals exclusively for web series. Nonetheless, it is interesting to note the evolution of the traditional film festival. Screenings for film festivals used to be watched by a committee, in one place, in one time. They, the committee members, watched together as a *group*, most likely on a large screen. Nowadays, committees make festival selections separately. Members watch submissions via personal computer (which is not the way the film was originally intended to be viewed), and reports are sent in individually and electronically. Even the final committee discussion, in which votes are discussed and reviewed, may be orchestrated over Skype or Google Hangout.

Similar to these festivals, many web festivals have both a selection committee and an audience choice category, which is determined by, say, view count, likes, and interactions made from their festival page. These web festivals generally use screening methods that make sense for the format, in that viewers watch on separate, personal devices. However even these new festivals (weirdly) end the same way that a traditional film festival does — with a screening on a large screen that belies the original form and intention of the work.

Because of this, there may be a change in the future. What exhibition or festival strategy would better suit the "small screen" and its inter-connected web? As the adage goes, only time will tell.

Task: What would solve this dilemma? What festival format would more accurately reflect the new media experience? What do you think the future will bring?

Chapter Eleven
SELF-PUBLISHING

Within the past few years, the self-publishing industry has been completely transformed by new media. Technology has made it so distribution costs are going down, while quality design and marketing platforms are cheaper and more readily accessible. Most self-publishing services today are designed for a large number of clients, who have relatively small budgets (that means you!). Small self-publishing companies offer legitimate alternatives to the mega-publishers, thanks to the power of the Internet. Undiscovered writers of all kinds can get their book designed, edited, published, distributed, and marketed in a matter of weeks for a fraction of what it cost 10 - 20 years ago. Just to get a few hundred copies of a book published required thousands of dollars in upfront printing costs! With publishing in demand, this entry obstacle has been essentially removed. And, occasionally, a self-published author ends up with a huge hit, like J.K. Rowling and her *Harry Potter* series. While she's the exception rather than the rule, the point is that self-publishing makes such success stories *possible*.

Publishing? Books? Harry Potter? You may be wondering what any of this has to do with you as filmmaker/web series creator. As an independent artist in new media, you'll often find yourself reincarnated in many forms and being active on many different platforms; self-publishing can be one of them.

Do you want to build a following and interest in an idea you have — but aren't ready to shoot yet? What about drawing additional attention to work you have already created? You already have a script and it can be so much more than just a pre-production tool — so much more than just a means to an end. Your story is a secret source of power.

After your web series has been filmed, and while it's being distributed, think about publishing your script books as a way to further promote your show. This gives fans another way to experience a show they enjoy and a chance to support you by purchasing your book. Book giveaways as part of promotional contests are also a useful tool. If you're feeling especially ambitious and want to offer something more than just a script book, consider creating a director's notebook for your series. This can include the scripts for your series, but it also can include behind-the-scenes images, character descriptions (maybe the same as on your EPK), personal notes and thoughts, letters from the cast and crew, etc. In one sense, it's making the most out of stuff you already have: the script, pre-existing photos, and stills from your series.

And remember, people do judge a book by its cover! You're a film creator—you should have a plethora of stills or images to choose from that represent your content! You want your book to be equally as visually compelling as and representative of your show.

> A special "making of" book was made based on the 2009 movie adaptation of the classic children's book *Where The Wild Things Are*. *Heads On and We Shoot: The Making of Where the Wild Things Are* features interviews with the director, animators, key crew, as well as cast members and lots of behind-the-scenes images.
>
> *Orange Juice in Bishop's Garden* was made both into script books for its respective seasons and a final "director's notebook" for its final three seasons. All the books were self published and offered in paperback or as digital ebooks. They were used promotionally as giveaways and were also sold online.

PLATFORMS

If self-publishing is so easy, how do you do it? There are a number of great platforms for self-publishing and, like all new media platforms, each has its own advantages and disadvantages.

Amazon

Amazon is both a great print and ebook self-publishing platform. Not to mention, it has a wide and well-developed online retail space for you to directly sell and distribute your finished product.

Amazon's Kindle Direct Publishing (KDP) offers ebook-only publishing. It's very user-friendly, and Amazon provides an easy formatting guide for authors to follow before publishing to the program. This service allows authors to bypass traditional publishers and deal directly with Amazon, which can publish books digitally within hours. Kindle Direct Publishing doesn't offer editorial services, but it does provide a booklet of detailed technical specifications for publishing your ebook successfully on its platform. There are no upfront charges to self-publish on KDP. You can choose your own list price and are offered two royalty options. Authors can receive 35% royalties or 70% author royalties, each with its own set of parameters and benefits.

Importantly, the Kindle Store provides KDP authors with a distribution channel. Kindle owners can purchase KDP content on the Kindle Store, and readers who don't own an e-reader can also read on their PCs or Macs by using Kindle software, or on their mobile phones with the Kindle app. Amazon online merchandising also includes cross-promotion in areas as "More Items to Consider," "Customers with Similar Searches Purchased," and "Customers Who Bought This Item Also Bought."

Another advantage of KDP is that authors and publishers can enroll books in the KDP Select Program, which offers unique ways of reaching more readers and making more money. Enrolling your book in KDP Select you will make it exclusive to Kindle for a 90-day enrollment period; and it also becomes eligible to be included in the Kindle Owners' Lending Library. Books borrowed from the Kindle Owners' Lending Library earn a share of a global fund established for KDP Select users. Additionally, users have access to a new set of promotional tools that allows authors and publishers to offer enrolled books for free to readers for up to five days every 90 days. These free giveaways are promoted by Amazon and are a great ways to get extra eyes on your work. When you choose KDP Select for a book, you're agreeing to make the digital format of that book available exclusively through the Kindle Store. You cannot distribute your book anywhere else, unless it is in physical format, or in any format other than digital.

Amazon's CreateSpace allows authors to publish paperbacks of their books. And for basic books, there is no set-up fee. You can either pay someone to do the formatting for you (and that will save you a lot of hair-pulling) or do it yourself, in which case InDesign will be helpful in this endeavor. The free set-up option includes an "Interior Reviewer," which flags common manuscript issues, and a Cover Creator tool that enables authors to create a basic, custom book cover design. For additional fees, you can get an array of different book development and editorial services. Like KDP, the author sets the price of the book. The author retains the rights to his or her book, and CreateSpace awards 60% royalties to the author, minus production cost. CreateSpace also offers seamless access to Amazon's book distribution channel, as well as an easy ebook conversion through KDP. In addition, books may be sold directly through a personal and customizable CreateSpace eStore. For an extra free, CreateSpace also makes books available for Expanded Distribution through bookstores and online retailers, and to other distributors, libraries, and academic institutions.

An added bonus of using CreateSpace to publish books is that it provides you with a free ISBN or International Standard Book Number. This number is used by book stores, book retailers, and libraries to identify books, and it is required by most publishers. Your CreateSpace printed book will also include an ISBN barcode. A CreateSpace-assigned ISBN can be used on Amazon as well as on a wide selection of book stores, online retailers, libraries, and academic institutions. However, a Custom Universal ISBN must be purchased from Amazon or a third-party seller to ensure your ISBN is useable with any publisher.

NOOK Press

The book retail chain Barnes & Noble is still standing, and it's most likely the Nook that's kept it alive, while its competitors have crumbled under the weight of technology and change. B&N now has its digital-only self-publishing platform called NOOK Press (formerly called Pubit).

There are no delivery fees or production costs; it's free to use from start to finish. NOOK press offers collaboration, content creation, and publishing tools. An interesting feature it provides, too, is the ability to upload a manuscript once and to continue to edit or make changes directly within the NOOK system, no re-uploading necessary. There's a two or three day turnaround for its services. The NOOK Press publisher/authors can price their titles between $0.99 and $199.99 and can receive a royalty based on the given price. And, like Amazon, you have access to distribution power of its powerful online bookselling force. Downside? It rejects information like advertisements (even if they are ads for the book or author), calls to action (ex: "Please review this book."), hyperlinks, and publisher/author contact information.

Smashwords

Smashwords is an indie publishing site. For authors looking to publish on other ebook retail sites, such as Apple, Sony, Kobo, and others, Smashwords is the platform to use. You can upload your ebook to Smashwords using its formatting guidelines, and Smashwords will distribute your ebook to the different retailers.

Smashwords offers authors a lot of control over pricing and access to their work. As a service, it requires the author take a measure of responsibility over the quality of the work that is uploaded to the service, as well as other aspects of the process. It doesn't offer editorial services for the book's content or design guidance for the creation of the work, but it does provide extensive instructions for document formatting to ensure successful ebook downloading. What is especially great about Smashwords is that it takes an uploaded Word document and creates files that are compatible with a variety of e-reader formats and other readable formats, such as EPUB, LRF, .PDB, HTML, .Mobi, etc. There are no upfront charges; books are paid for by the reader when the ebook is downloaded. The author chooses the price for his or her own book, and Smashwords earns revenue by taking a 15% commission on all net sales.

Smashwords is another platform that offers free ISBNs, but your book must first be accepted into the Smashwords' Premium Catalog to be eligible. Note that when obtaining an ISBN, Smashwords will be registered as your book's publisher, but you retain all the rights to your book.

Other Platforms

Lulu.com and Blurb.com are two of the more respected elders in the world of self-publishing. A few other sites include: Lightning Source, Xlibris, iUniverse, and Book Country, among others.

HOW TO PREPARE YOUR BOOK FILES

eBooks are available in a variety of formats, and which ones you should create depend largely on what platforms you expect to make them available for. The good news is, generally, each format starts as a .doc file, and that file can then be converted into multiple formats.

Each major e-reading platform (Kindle, Nook, Smashwords, etc) provides recommend specifications for submitted files, which can be found on their websites. But some rules generally apply across the board:

1. Don't use headers, footers, or page numbers. Ereaders display books with flowing text, meaning that the text automatically adjusts to the shape and size of the device being used. The text is continuous, it does not just exist on certain pages. This gives the reader better control of the visual experience, allowing charge over font size, line spacing, and paragraph alignment. Headers, footers, and page numbers will not work in this format.

2. Limit the use of other formatting. Because the text is at the mercy of the device and the device's user, keeping the text as simple as possible will insure the best reading experience. Avoid indentations, tables, drastic differences in font size, or font colors other than black. Hard returns don't display well either, so use page breaks instead, at the end of chapters.

3. Insert images instead of copying and pasting them. This will ensure they are embedded into the file and don't get left behind when exporting.

4. Don't embed your cover art into the .doc. This image will be uploaded separately on most sites.

Once you're settled on your ebook's layout, some services, like Kindle, will allow you to upload your finished .doc and will complete the conversion process for you. Others will require you to upload an ePUB or MOBI version. To do so, you must first save your .doc as a Web Page, Filtered (*HTM & *HTML) (for PC) or Web Page (.htm) (for Mac) format. To check for formatting issues, open the Web Page file in a web browser. The browser will render the file in a similar way an ereader will render the ebook file. Note: Kindle offers an online previewer during its upload process and has a downloadable Kindle Previewer program available on Windows and Mac which allows you to see how your ebook will look in its various devices.

Calibre, a free program for Windows and Mac, can then be used to convert the Web Page file to various ebook formats. This program also allows you to edit metadata, such as the title, description, and keywords, which will be embedded into the file. **Calibre** - http://calibre-ebook.com/

PDF's

Some ebook platforms allow or even prefer PDF versions. There are no hard-and-fast rules for formatting these files because the text is not continuous like in other formats. With PDFs, headers, footers, page numbers, and creative colors are fair game. You have creative freedom, but it's also important to make PDF versions easy to navigate and pleasing to the eye. It is suggested that you follow the basic format of the typical book. Look at other books in the same genre for examples.

Printed Books (for CreateSpace)

CreateSpace has very strict guidelines for it's interior and cover files. The CreateSpace websites offers templates, which make the creative process easier. Download a template for your desired book dimensions and number of pages, and use this template as the outline of your book layout. You can be creative, but you must remain careful of layout mistakes that can prevent your file from being approved, such as the size of your margins or using images that are not of a high enough resolution for printing purposes.

MARKETING YOUR BOOK(S)

Then the really hard work begins: Getting people to buy what you've written! But, by now, you should be prepared with an arsenal of social media tools and tips to keep you afloat. Plus, there are a bevy of websites, plus Goodreads, Twitter, and Facebook accounts dedicated solely to the promotion of indie publishing, for free or very low cost. Though talked about briefly in the social media chapter, it's worth noting again that Goodreads, in particular, is an invaluable resource for marketing your book(s). A social media platform devoted exclusively to everything related to books, Goodreads is an excellent way to entice all those book lovers out there, who literally devour words. Not only can you get in touch with potential audience members through joining in various groups' conversations and through friend requesting, but, as a Goodreads author, you can also host giveaways. These are a great way to get the word out about your new book(s), and you only have to give away a few copies of the actual book, so the cost is minimal. Just remember to actually send the book out to your lovely winners, along with a thank you note. Another good practice, if possible, is to offer the "losers" free ebook copies in exchange for a review on your book's profile. This helps to increase traction on your profile, hopefully bringing in more readers.

See "Goodreads" in "Social Media" on page 149 ▶

When it comes to all platforms, market your books as a bonus or extra feature of your larger body of work. Remember, the point here is not to become a best selling author—you're a new media artist, after all! You want to offer your fans another extension of your content, an exclusive inside look into its making. And on the plus side, it's another way for fans to socially, emotionally, and financially support you and your passion.

Learn how to market your book via "Social Media" on page 149 ▶

Chapter Twelve
BEST PRACTICES FOR YOUR EPK AND THE LITERARY PITCH

THE EPK (AKA ELECTRONIC PRESS KIT)

We have spoken at great length about how in the new, indie, and digital world, you will have to wear many hats. And here again is no exception.

Since you will have to act as a representative not just of yourself but also of your work, it is important to have all the weapons in your arsenal ready. The EPK, or electronic press kit, is one such tool.

The EPK is a representation of all the key, salient points about you and your work or project — presented in an accessible, visually-appealing layout. It should be brief enough that no one should grow bored half way through. Even if someone merely flips through, he or she should be able to glean the heart and soul of your work — at a glance. And, the press kit is electronic, so it can be emailed/shared/printed with the greatest modern ease.

Now, let's break it down more specifically...

Best Practices for Your EPK

It is advisable to create both a SHORT version and a LONG version of your EPK. The short version is what you will woo people with, and if your intended express interest, then you can whip out your longer version. But let's face it, many people, particularly industry big-shots, will be put-off by a 10 page document. They receive oodles of mail, oodles of pitches, oodles of EPKs and they value their time. So, save the lengthy version for once their interest is piqued.

In addition to having a short and long version, you should tailor each EPK to the specific people or entities to whom you are pitching. Do your homework: know them well. Why are these people better than all the others for your work? What projects are they currently distributing or backing? What are their areas of expertise, their genres, their scope, their geographic reach, their niche? What makes them such a good fit? And, if they are not a strong fit, should you be bothering?

Just as one should always tailor a resume and cover letter so that it is relevant to each and every job… the exact same principle applies here.

Key points to pay attention to:

1. Put Logline and key quotes from top sources and awards on page 1

2. Give more detailed information aka a brief description on page 2.

3. Include a link to a REEL showreel or preferred video

4. Give information about yourself, aka the filmmaker

5. Full list of awards, honors, etc. on later page

6. Include key bullet points that are impressive

7. What's your mission statement? — include that!

8. Contact Information

9. Extended version can include longer descriptions and even CHARACTER bios!

10. Try to make the look match the look of your work or show. (e.g. the cool crumpled paper, the super saturated images, the font choices, and canted mage placements in **Figures 12.1 - 12.4**)

Best Practices for Your EPK and The Literary Pitch 299

ORANGE JUICE IN BISHOP'S GARDEN

20/20 PRODUCTIONS

Awards:
- Webby Awards Honoree
- Webby Award Honoree
- The 32nd Annual Telly Awards Bronze Winner
- Official Selection Hollyweb Festival 2013
- Indie Fest Nominee
- LA Web Series Festival 2011 Award Winner — Outstanding Drama Series
- LA Web Series Festival 2011 Award Winner — Outstanding Cinematography in a Drama Series
- LA Web Series Festival 2012 Award Winner — Best Supporting Actress, Donnis Collins
- LA Web Series Festival 2013 Award-Winner — Outstanding Lead Actress, Ellen Winter

"Do you remember what it was like to be a teenager? When high school was your world filled with first crushes, parties without parents and nostalgic music that brings you right back to that first kiss? Budding filmmaker Otessa Ghadar does, and her fond memories [...] have made way to the screen of your computer."
— **NBC WASHINGTON**

"There aren't many non-reality web series that manage to be creatively, critically and commercially successful, but the teen drama Orange Juice in Bishop's Garden definitely achieves the trifecta"
— **TV WEEK**

Named by the **ADVOCATE** as a reason to have pride in 2012

Recognized by the **HRC** for making a positive contribution to the LGBTQ community

"captures the experience of a generation"
— **DIGITAL CHICK TV**

"[Orange Juice in Bishop's Garden] follows those totally crucial and always entertaining drama-fueled teen years and oh! The costuming! The music! The awkward sexual awakenings! [...] It's My So Called Life meets Skins"
— **BRIGHTEST YOUNG THINGS**

Otessa Ghadar
reply@twentytwentyproductions.com
(202) 588-5891

7 SEASONS · VIEWED IN 146 COUNTRIES
FINAL SEASON FILMED (RELEASE DATE PENDING)
11+ HOURS OF CONTENT · CURRENTLY AVAILABLE WITH CLOSED CAPTIONING
French, Spanish, Japanese, German, & Russian Subtitles available, with more coming soon

Figure 12.1 Example of page 1 of press kit, from *Orange Juice in Bishop's garden* EPK

What is OJBG?

You know that summer, right... the summer where EVERYTHING changed? "Orange Juice in Bishop's Garden" (OJBG) is that summer and Bishop's Garden is where it all happens. An unexpected romance between two young girls, Sarah and Gwen, begins to blossom and their epic first love will redefine and lie at the heart of their teenage experience.

What is OJBG about?

OJBG is a genuine story of young adult experience without the filter and glamorization often found in the mainstream media and Hollywood production companies. The series gives a voice to young adults through its frank and unfiltered portrayal of teen life and issues. OJBG continues to resonate with viewers in countries where discussions of such topics (such as LGBT relationships and identity issues) are not publicly acceptable and are often censored. Hitting home across multiple demographics -- OJBG really resonates with current YA audiences, as well as those Gen X and Yers who lived their teen years in the grunge era.

In this emotionally charged young adult drama series, nothing is taboo, nothing too personal, and nothing too intimate to share. Freely available online, OJBG utilizes the unique web series medium to fill a void for youth audiences all over the world. With viewership in over 146 countries, the series has gained a devoted global following.

Have a Taste of OJBG... watch here:

www.OJinBG.com/webby

The Creator

Globally viral, much-beloved, and highly-lauded show "Orange Juice in Bishop's Garden" is created by award-winning independent film maker, Otessa Ghadar. She is also Founder and President of new media production company, 20/20 Productions.

Otessa created OJBG in 2007 when the idea of internet television was still in its infancy. As one of the medium's earliest adopters, she is a true forerunner and pioneer of the wild west of film. OJBG is now one of the oldest and longest running web series and continues to release new content. Otessa was recently named as Filmmaker of the Month by the DC Office of Motion Picture and Television Development and has been awarded as an "ITV Innovator."

In April 2013, she organized the first Web Series Festival in Washington, DC and the first web series screening at the 27th Annual Washington, DC International Film Festival. With viewership in over 146 countries, Otessa provides closed captions for her series and is actively adding subtitles in French, Spanish, Japanese, German, and Russian, with more languages on the way.

Through fiction and film, Otessa and her show seek to empower and connect young adults around the world and advocate for tolerance and freedom within media. Much like Otessa, OJBG is thought-provoking and sincere; it embodies the rebelliousness of the '90s grunge era while tackling social issues that surround youth, such as sexuality, bullying, peer pressure, and intolerance. OJBG has been recognized by the Human Rights Campaign for making a positive contribution to the LGBTQ community. The online accessibility of OJBG fills a void in entertainment for those whose stories are under represented and under-served. Presenting an honest and diverse portrayal of teen life, Otessa aims to give voice to the non-Hollywood young adults of the real world.

Figure 12.2 Example of show reel link, show and filmmaker information from *Orange Juice in Bishop's garden* EPK

Press

Apr 29, 2013	*The Georgetown Dish*	– Interview with "acclaimed pioneer of the web series format", Otessa Ghadar
Apr 6, 2013	*Washington Post*	– D.C. Web Series Festival (featuring Orange Juice in Bishop's Garden) listed in Going Out Guide's Events Calendar
Apr 6, 2013	*Washington Examiner*	– "This weekend's best bets for fun...DC Web Series Festival", interview with Otessa Ghadar
Feb 17, 2013	*Broads*	– "Proudly holding it down for DC, Orange Juice in Bishops Garden is like Skins meets The Perks of Being a Wallflower while totally giving off the home-field advantage vibe to all local residents... what's not to love?"
Dec 5, 2012	*The Eagle*	– "Welcome to the grungy 1990s, where angsty D.C. teens face the hardships of growing up, as they mature from adolescents into young adults."
Nov 10, 2012	*AllVoices*	– Featured article, "Ghadar casts actual teenagers from her Washington DC area as characters in the show, letting the teens tap into their real life emotions for the roles."
Jul 06, 2012	*PandaHead*	– OJBG Short "Bottle Pop" premiering at End of Summer Bummer during The Fridge's Fresh Produce Festival
May 18, 2012	*Advocate.com*	– Featured as one of 181 "Reasons to Have Pride in 2012"
Mar 17, 2012	*BC Living*	– Featured article, "This award-winning web series pushes the envelope of edgy teen drama"
Jan 10, 2012	*ScoutMob*	– "Otessa Ghadar Reveals the Secret Cinematic Spots in DC"
Jan 10, 2012	*The Pink Line Project*	– "DC-based teen web drama Orange Juice in Bishop's Garden preserves an analog past in the digital present"
Jan 9, 2012	*TBD*	– "Orange Juice in Bishop's Garden new season debuts Friday with even more '90s-era clothing"
Dec 7, 2011	*memburn*	– Featured as one of "9 web series worth watching"
Nov 10, 2011	*TBD*	– "The French can't get enough of this D.C.-based Web series"
Nov 1, 2011	*WashingtonPost.com*	– Mentioned in article as "another popular D.C. Web Drama"
Aug 2, 2011	*The Watch List*	– "Midnight, Hunter's Moon, Pt. 1" A Webseries Review
Jul 11, 2011	*The DC Ladies*	– "The Juice is Definitely Worth the Squeeze"
July 2011	*DC Office of Motion Picture and Television Development*	– "July Filmmaker of the Month - Otessa Ghadar"
Jun 26, 2011	*Digital Chick TV*	– Featured series in playlist for 2011 Pride Web Series Marathon
May 2011	*Cherry Grrl TV*	– Featured series, with weekly recap of new episodes
Apr 30, 2011	*One More Lesbian*	– Episode 4.1 is the featured video on the homepage

Figure 12.3 Example of press page from *Orange Juice in Bishop's garden* EPK

Characters

SARAH

The Bishop's Garden group is my family; a clique that, for the majority, has known each other since middle school. At times, I get caught up in the moment, and in that one instant when I'm not being cautious or over-analytical, I make a mistake. People have expectations for me: I need to be smart, I need to be chill, I need to be the perfect friend. But all of the different images that others think I'm supposed to uphold only make me think harder and deeper about myself: someone who, at age 19, I'm still getting to know. When I met Gwen, an older girl from school, I unexpectedly found myself being exposed to a new way of seeing things, and myself. I'm beginning to explore new possibilities and create my own image of who I want to be-- a totally badass and fearless girl.

GWEN

I'm the confident, outgoing girl of the group. I always know who I am. Once Sarah and I OFFICIALLY began dating, everything felt spectacular. But when Sarah makes plans to go off to college and I realize that I'll be the loser still stuck at home, serving coffee to yuppies in the coffee shop, I freak out. NOT the future I imagined. And even though I love Sarah, I up and leave for New York to make a name for myself. Long distance relationships can work, right? I keep telling Sarah they can... because I want to be strong for her -- not that she needs it, but I like to be strong -- but honestly I'm not sure.

ALEX

I'm the sweet girl with an edge. I know how to party and get down with the best of the OJBG gang. I knew grunge was dead long ago. Raves, ska-- that's where it's at. Although, a rough encounter with a creepy dude at a club has kind of rattled me and now I'm feeling vulnerable. To top that off, my boyfriends have not always been the most upstanding guys, I'm fighting with my BFF, Tamsin, and then I finally FINALLY find a nice boy, someone I can watch Star Trek re-runs with...and it turns out he's gay. I don't even know who I am anymore. And I don't know who I want to be. Is the person I was just some projection that made things easier for everyone? I'm just robo-tripping solo like a loser and it's almost like I do it because I'm hoping someone will call me out -- because at least it means I exist. And...now I'm having weird sexy dreams about Sarah... Underneath my layers of flannel and hard-edge demeanor, I'm really just a lovesick puppy---but I'm kinda feeling like I'm getting kicked more than pet lately. Being a person is hard!

Figure 12.4 Example of characters page from *Orange Juice in Bishop's garden* EPK

THE LITERARY PITCH

So you have an amazing book/graphic novel/SF epic/short story collection/film script that you are turning into a novel/emotobook/the list goes on? But… you don't have an agent. And so… you don't have an publisher. Or, even if you do have some form of representation, perhaps you're unhappy with it and would like to expand your horizons.

It used to be that you had to create a ferocious manuscript and then you could write a slamming query letter. And if, and only if, you had an agent would you have a chance at publishing success.

You can still go that route. And here you will find some tips, tricks, and overviews for doing so.

But please remember, don't limit yourself. You are not beholden to this old school method. There are many other routes leading to literary success.

The internet has provided more than just a collection of cats who "can haz cheeseburgers". The interwebs are a font of information for writers. You can research your craft, enroll in e-classes, and even study successful pitch letters. The web created a forum for reaching out, tweeting to, and following the blogs of more serious, top-level agents, authors, and reviewers.

You can build a frenzied following without an agent and without even publishing in the traditional "paper" sense. You can put your work up on sites like Smashwords and Goodreads and interact with like-minded, kindred spirits. You can give and garner reviews and feedback. You can place your ebook in the Amazon marketplace and set up a Kindle Direct Publishing giveaway, which will generate a great deal of traffic toward your work.

And, if you crave something more tangible that you can hold in the palm of your hand, with the wild advances in self-publishing you *can* print and publish your own work… it can exist and you can hold it. And you don't even have to do bulk orders. Through a site like Amazon Create Space, you can print, buy, and order as few as one.

And to build a buzzing hive around that honey, you can create a giveaway on Goodreads, which is a sure-fire way to focus the eyes and ears of a literary community on your work. You will be amazed at how many people will enter.

Simply put, it's all about building a name and a network for yourself. You want to build a cult of personality around you and your work. Whether the agents take note, or whether they pass, you can and should still do as much as possible to build a name and fan base. Who knows, it may just make you more interesting, more google-able, and more savvy for when it comes time for "Query Writing: Round Two".

But, if you insist, here is a "Baby Steps" guide to the traditional query letter process. Definitely ameliorate it by brushing up on

See **"Social Media" on page 149** and **"Self-Publishing" on page 289 for tricks and tools** ▶

Query Letter: Baby Steps

- Much like the EPK, a query letter should be short. One page. No longer. This is important. Anything longer will only serve as a turn-off to the important person whose time you are imposing upon.

- Next, the query letter should represent and introduce you and your story. It is not a friend request. It's not a dissertation. It's not a loosely woven tale of your personal trials and tribulations. It is a professional outreach tool not meant for overly emotional or tangential jargon. Don't be a buffoon. Keep it concise and professional — keep it on point and on task.

- Kind of akin to those annoying keyhole essays you had to write in secondary school, the query letter has a set number of parts. Although, in this case, the magic number is three and not five. The three components are: the bumper-sticker, the blurb-y expansion, and the bio. THE BUMPER-STICKER: Sum up your story in a one sentence logline. This should be pithy, precise, and alluring to the reader. You need to hook them to reel them in. Turning a fully-actualized, long-form work into a sentence is an abominable task. But you must do it. Think to yourself: what is the "bumper-sticker version" of your work. If you were to cut in front of someone and speed away and all they saw was a cloud of dust and a one line bumper-sticker… what would this be for your work? What words would leave a lasting impression? If you are still at a loss, try to think of your work in terms of the setting, character, and scenario. These may give you a jumping off point. Take inspiration from the thesis of a paper. You have one sentence to sum up everything to your reader: go!

- THE BLURB-Y EXPANSION: Thought the bumper-sticker was hard? Well, relax because now you get to expound on it. You have a whole paragraph to synopsize your work. It's difficult but doable.

- THE BIO: Who are you, as a writer? Keep the bio focused on your writing and your life only as it relates to your story. Don't provide tangential information. The only non-writing information you want to provide is information that directly informs your work and makes you an insider or expert. And, if you have any relevant awards, commendations, degrees, blogs with epic site traffic, etc., mention them here. It can be difficult to toot your own horn; however, if you do not, no one else will. So try to put your best foot forward, without being pompous. Now, flip the focus. Talk about the agent. Specifically, why is this agent better than other agents for you and for your work. Do your homework and make sure you are familiarized with this person's taste and catalogue of other represented works. And last but not least…

- SAY GOODBYE: Briefly thank your reader for his or her kind consideration. Having sufficiently researched your agent(s), you should be familiar with each one's submission process. Some will accept sample chapters. Some will not. Be sure to offer sample chapters and/or the whole manuscript accordingly. And make sure that you actually have the whole enchilada finished and ready for consumption. Do not offer what you do not have. When snail-mailing your query, make certain to enclose a self-addressed, stamped envelope for their reply. Now, get out there and good luck!

Chapter Thirteen
WEB SITE BASICS AND WEB DESIGN

You need a website. Even if web design is completely beyond you, there is no excuse for not having one. Before your work is ready to face the world, you should be building an online platform where current fans, potential fans, and possible funders and distributors can find in-depth information about your work. It's important to create a website that clearly illustrates a mission statement—what is the premise of your work and who has created it? Your website should embody the theme of your program and should serve as a one stop shop for all things related to your show: you, cast, crew, news, updates, where you are in the production process, merchandise, ways to contribute, ways to connect via social media, and, of course, your videos.

Unfortunately, creating a website can be expensive, so it helps if you can do as much as possible on your own. If you do hire a web designer, understanding the basics of web development will help you to play an active role in both the creative and technical decisions in its development, and will help you be better equipped to self-maintain your site once it's been launched.

BASIC STRUCTURE OF WEB PAGE

A web page consists of many elements and programming languages, which translate into what we ultimately see when visiting a website. HyperText Markup Language, or HTML, is the main markup language for creating web pages and other structured content that can be displayed in a web browser. A basic webpage consists of various HTML elements and attributes, and you don't even need to be connected to the Internet to view them. HTML files can be viewed in web browsers such as Chrome,

Firefox, Safari, or Internet Explorer, and can be edited in a simple text editor (of course, more advanced web development applications, like Adobe Dreamweaver, have a ton of additional tools and options for editing these kinds of files).

Here is what a very simple web page would look like if you opened the HTML file:

```
<!DOCTYPE html>
<html>
  <head>
    <title>My First Web Page</title>
  </head>
  <body>
    This is my first web page
  </body>
</html>
```

An HTML document includes tags. Tags mark the beginning and end of an element. In the above example, "<title>" and "</title>" are tags, "<title>My First Web Page<title>" is a title element. Note: Some tags close themselves and do not have a closing tag.

doctype: Each HTML document needs a Document Type Definition (DTD) declared at the beginning. There isn't just one type of HTML, and some tools that process HTML need to know what type of document is being used.

html: The html opening tag is the root element of the entire document. Everything between that and the closing tag (</html>) is an HTML document. The document is then divided into two main sections: the head and the body.

head: The head section contains the document title and other meta data, and links to related documents that load along with the HTML document.

body: Everything you see on a web page is contained inside this element. This can include headings, paragraphs, tables, lists, images, videos, and much, much more.

Here's a more complex example of an HTML document.

```html
<!doctype html>
<head>
  <meta charset="utf-8">
  <meta name="viewport" content="width=device-width">
  <meta name="description" content="Here we would put an accurate description of this website.">
  <title>My Very Awesome Website</title>
</head>
<body>
  <h1>My First Heading</h1>
  <p>My website has some <em>really</em> awesome content.</p>
</body>
</html>
```

Note the followings tags included in the <head> section. These optional elements don't actually appear on the web page, but can affect how the elements within the body are rendered.

meta: Meta data describes the document with information, such as the title, key words, and character encoding. Often, the title is used to define the heading that appears in the browser's title bar or when the web page is added as a favorite in a web browser. Meta is also important in providing indexing, categorical, and ranking information to search engines.

link: Links refer to resources, such as style sheets and scripts.

object: This defines an embedded media object, like audio or video.

script: Used to embed a script, such as a JavaScript, or to point to an external script.

style: Style elements define style information and are used for embedded CSS styles. CSS files provide instructions about how to style the various elements on the web page. In fact, the main CSS file is called the "style sheet". When using pre-made templates to build your website, the style sheet can be edited to customize the colors, font, background, etc. So, CSS is particularly useful to familiarize yourself with.

Other terms to know:

attribute: Attributes, the opening tag, provide additional information about an HTML element. Example: <p attribute="value"> This is my first web page </p>.

script: Scripts provide rich functionality that cannot be achieved with HTML alone, making them more interactive and dynamic. For example, a script could be used to create a fade effect when hovering over images; conversely, a script is also used for some non-aesthetic functions, such as tracking visitors to a website.

WEBSITE LAYOUT

When designing your website or selecting a premade template, keep in mind that your website should be easy to understand and should shine a spotlight on the most important information. An overly cluttered or difficult to navigate layout can turn people off, confuse them, or keep them from seeing the main attraction.

Basic Principles

1. Your layout should be easy to understand (**Figures 13.1 and 13.2**).

2. Your landing page should clearly link to all the salient features of your work that you want to share with the interwebs. At a glance, people immediately should be able to tell what your work is and how they can access it. In the case of a video or series, they need to know how to watch! In the case of a written work, make the writing easy to access. Photo-based? Galleries should be eye-catching with clear navigation. These are just a few examples, but the key point is shared across a myriad of expressions.

Figure 13.1 Example of website layout with options that are easy to navigate and clearly display the most important content

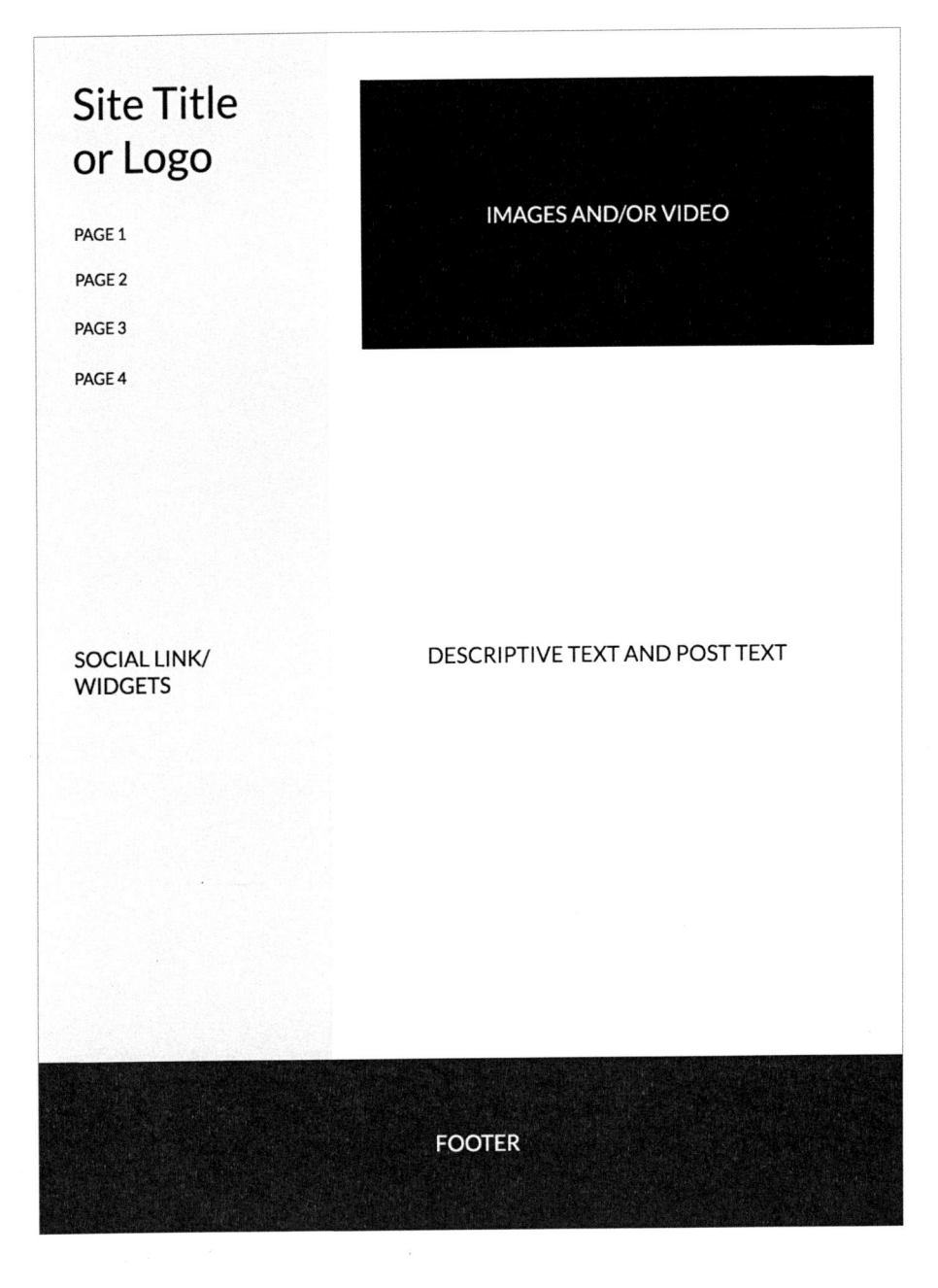

Figure 13.2   Example of website layout with options that are easy to navigate and clearly display the most important content

3. Your branding and theme should be unique and also tell people what your show is about. This can be achieved with fonts, color schemes, and images that match the style of your series.

4. Include Social Media links and have them readily available... remember "sharing is caring," and you want to make it easy for your visitors to do so.

5. Maintain a blog to give updates on your work and to show some of your personality. In addition to writing about your own content, write posts on pop culture, news, fashion, etc. that is topically related to the premise or theme of your work.

6. Include a BLOG ROLL — A blogroll is a list of links to blogs that the blogger likes — or some interaction with other sites with which you can exchange traffic. This means new viewers and visitors for both parties.

7. Photo galleries are important. Everyone enjoys seeing a beautiful photo or funny, behind the scenes moment. Use imagery to catch people's eye and to give them something to share with others.

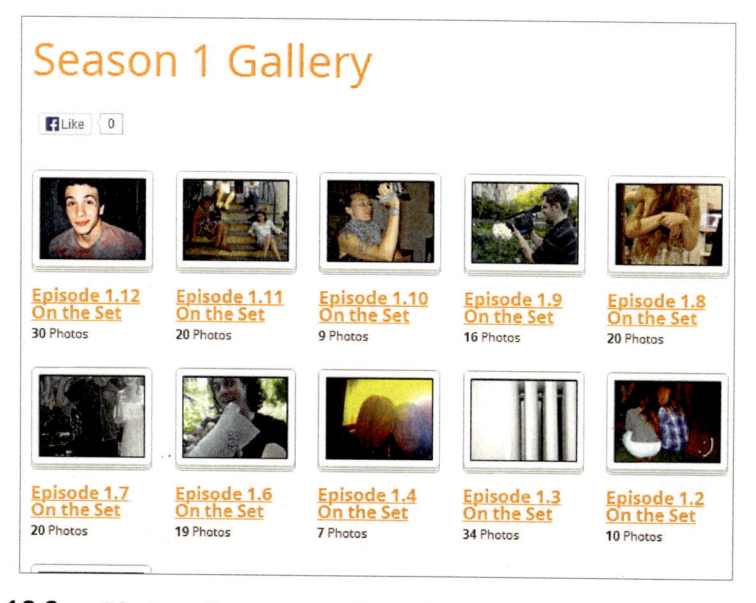

Figure 13.3   Photo gallery page on http://orangejuiceinbishopsgarden.com

8. People also love to know as much as possible about the origin of their favorite projects and the people involved in creating them. Share information about the cast, the crew, and how your project came to be.

9. PRESS — you definitely need to include THIS. Good press gives legitimacy to your work. It gives potential viewers and financial partners an extra push to check out your content.

10. Merchandise. In the Wild West of Film, monetization is still yet to be mastered, so it's wise to bring in revenue from as many streams as possible. Merchandise can be an easy way to bring in extra bacon, and it doesn't have to be a complicated process. Many existing online shops (Zazzle, CafePress) allow you to upload images and attach them to t-shirts, posters, mugs, etc.—only taking a small percentage in exchange. You can also sell stuff—on, say, Etsy—that you already have: wardrobe, props, signed scripts from the cast.

SEARCH ENGINE OPTIMIZATION

Search Engine Optimization (SEO) is key to making sure that your website is easily discovered when searched for on Google, Yahoo, Bing, and other search engines. In order to get a high ranking when the title of your show or key words related to your show are searched, there are steps you can take to improve the visibility of your website and to receive more visitors from search engines. When optimizing a website, it's important to consider your web pages' content and the way you code the HTML because both can affect your website's relevance in searches. This can be a complicated task, but there are some easy ways to quickly increase optimization.

1. As mentioned earlier in the chapter, meta data, included in the <head> section, plays a role in how your site is indexed by search engines. The head section should include key words related to the type of content on your website. For example, the falafel website in our previous example may have the following key words: falafel, food, recipes, DIY, do-it-yourself, chef, cooking, lunch, dinner, Arab food, fried food

2. Include keywords in the title tags, as well. The title should describe what the overall site is about in addition to the current page.

   Example: <title> Contact Us – Falafel World: A website devoted to falafel recipes</title>

3. Include keywords in your urls.

   Example: http://falafelworld.com/recipes/traditional-chickpea-falafel as opposed to http://falafelworld.com/p=?uyyub6rnhuj

4. Use social sharing buttons.

5. Remove duplicated content on your website. The same text should not appear multiple times on your web pages.

6. Search engines want to provide users with the most useful and relevant information, so consistently adding new content that is relevant to the topic of your website will help move it to the top (or keep it at the top) of the rankings.

WEBSITE HOSTING

The files that make up a website are similar to the files and folders on your computer. They're stored on a server, which is a system of software and computer hardware that provides storage and can be accessed over a network, such as the Internet. Because maintaining such a server is not a simple or easy task, web hosting companies provide hosting services to allow people and organizations to make their website accessible on the web.

Web hosting companies usually offer a variety of packages and pricing options. The more complex your site will be, the more comprehension a package it will require. If you're working with a web designer, this is something very important to discuss before purchasing a hosting account. You must ensure that the features included in your package are sufficient for the functionality you expect to have on your website. If you're building your own website and are unsure, talk to a representative from the web host.

Recommend Web Hosting Companies
Some popular and reliable hosting providers:

HostGator - http://www.hostgator.com/
DreamHost - http://www.dreamhost.com/
GoDaddy - http://www.godaddy.com/

Content Management Systems

A web content management system (CMS) is a bundled or stand-alone application to create, manage, organize, and deploy content on web pages.

> **WOULD YOU LIKE TO KNOW MORE?**
> **IP Address vs. Domain Name vs. URL**
>
> An IP address, or "Internet protocol address", is a unique identifying number given to any machine connected to the Internet. They consist of segments of numbers and/or letters, separated by dots or colons.
>
> e.g. 123.0.0.1
> e.g. 31CA:D3:0:5R7B:2AA:FF:FI28:3C4G
>
> The Domain Name System, or DNS, is the most recognized system for assigning addresses to web servers. This system helps to give web servers an easy-to-spell address, and keeps the complicated IP address invisible for most viewers. While the IP address remains the true identifier of a web server, the domain name is a memorable redirector to help people find it.
>
> e.g. 123.0.0.1 = falafelworld.com
>
> A domain name is commonly part of a larger web address called a "URL". A URL goes into much more detail than the domain name, providing more specific information, like the protocol language or a specific page. In the following URL, the domain name is in all caps:
> http://www.**FALAFELWORLD.COM**/about/f-a-q.html

Web content includes text and embedded graphics, photos, video, audio, and code that displays content or interacts with the user.[1] In most cases, your CMS of choice will be installed on your web hosting server and used online. To streamline the installation process, many web hosts provide one-click installation of popular CMSs, such as WordPress, Joomla, and Drupal.

WordPress

WordPress is an open source, user friendly, and industry standard software to create and manage websites. You can easily install a one of the thousands of free and premium website templates available for WordPress on the web, or create your own custom layout. You don't need to be a web savvy genius to make this work (although it can be just as powerful as other, more complicated CMSs).

Joomla & Drupal

Joomla and Drupal, along with WordPress, are in the top three of most used CMSs on the web.[2] These are more complex content management systems that are popular among experience web designers and developers. They're both open source and great choices if you know, or want to learn, what it takes to bring the best out of them.

Free Web Hosting Service Providers

Free website publishing services usually come with an easy to use, built in CMS, and a reasonable amount of allocated hosting space for your web content. Registered users can create a free url, which is perfect if you're just starting out and don't have $10 to slap down for a custom domain name, but it will include that company's branding (Example: yourwebseriesname.tumblr.com as opposed to youwebseriesname.com). A downside to using free web hosts is that there will be limitations, e.g. the layout of your website may not be completely customizable, or you may find that

1	"Content management system ," Wikipedia, http://en.wikipedia.org/wiki/Content_management_system#cite_note-5
2	CMS Usage Statistics , BuiltWith , http://trends.builtwith.com/cms

the restrictions on the amount of data that can be used for your website is not enough. These sites often require paid upgrades to unlock more advanced features. Also, having your website hosted by a third party means that it stores and has control over your files.

WordPress (Website)

WordPress.com is a free web hosting service provider from the creators of the WordPress CMS software. Hosted websites use the same CMS technology as the open-source system, but you must sign up for an account and are subject to certain conditions. Some features (including customization of available themes, removals of ads, video uploads, and storage upgrades) are available only as paid options.

Tumblr

If you don't want to figure out the inner workings of a Wordpress site, you can alternatively use Tumblr. It's easy to embed videos and other media, which, in the beginning, may be all you need. Many people are using Tumblr as a free option for their website because of the wide variety of templates available and its inherent sharing capabilities. This is a great choice if you plan to keep things simple and don't want a bunch of frills.

Blogger

Blogger is another popular, free hosting service. It's primary focus is blogging, so the ability to make customizations are more limited than other options. The main draw to Blogger is its existing blogging community. If your blog is the main attraction on your website, this could be the optimal choice.

CHOOSING AND REGISTERING A DOMAIN NAME

Many web hosts also provide registration of custom domain names, but it is wise to register your domain name with a separate company. That way, if you ever have issues with your web host, you don't have to worry about it locking down on your domain name, thus preventing you transferring that domain to a different hosting company.

When deciding on a domain name, sometimes it's as simple as using the name of your show. But what if the title is long, unavailable, or you promote multiple projects on the same website. In this case, the solution would be to come up with a name that is easy to remember and accurately describes what the site is about. falafelworld.com tells us that the website will most likely be all about... falafels!

It's also recommended to use the .com extension, as opposed to other options like .tv, .biz, .me. Sometimes using one of these extensions is necessary, but, because .com is so common, using something different could be confusing and could cause you to lose traffic.

Recommend Registrars
Some tried and true domain name registrars:

Namecheap - http://www.namecheap.com/
1&1 - http://www.1and1.com/
GoDaddy - http://www.godaddy.com/

HOW TO INSTALL GOOGLE ANALYTICS

As explained in the "Social Media" chapter, Google Analytics is a very powerful tool used to track the traffic of your website. Google Analytics is installed by inserting a script in the <head> of your HTML document. Accessing this file varies by CMS; you can contact your hosting provider or web designer if you're unsure.

To find the script that must be inserted:

1. First log into Google Analytics.

2. Next, navigate to the account for your website.

3. At the top right, click Admin and then select Tracking Info.

Here you'll find a textbox with the script. It will look something like this:

```
<script type="text/javascript">

 var _gaq = _gaq || [];
 _gaq.push(['_setAccount', 'UA-XXXXXXXX-X']);
 _gaq.push(['_trackPageview']);

 (function() {
   var ga = document.createElement('script'); ga.type = 'text/javascript'; ga.async = true;
   ga.src = ('https:' == document.location.protocol ? 'https://ssl' : 'http://www') + '.google-analytics.com/ga.js';
   var s = document.getElementsByTagName('script')[0]; s.parentNode.insertBefore(ga, s);
 })();

</script>
```

4. Copy this script and paste it just before </head>, the closing of the head tag. Navigate back to Google Analytics to make sure that the tracking code is transmitting data.

Now that you've choosen a domain name, web host, and CMS; designed your website; and installed Google Analytics; it's time to attract some attention.

See **"Social Media" on page 149 for some tips** ▶

Refresh on how to use Google Analytics to track your site in "Analytics" on page 175 ▶

Chapter Fourteen

FORMS, PAPERWORK, AND IMPORTANT DOCUMENTS

This chapter includes example and sample forms, agreements, documents, paperwork, exercises, and planning materials that can be used or referenced during various stages of the production process.

ACTING EXERCISES

Acting exercises are a vital part of ensuring that your cast becomes the characters you're aiming for them to be. We can all agree that the goal is for the actors is to "become" the people that the script lays out for them, but there is disagreement in the acting community on how to get there. Some schools of acting focus on complete emotional embodiment, while others on the objectivity of the characters. But it isn't necessary to subscribe to one singular school. Your actors can fulfill their roles by combining several different games and using a variety of techniques.

Time/Space Travel

A lot of the time, actors become overly comfortable in the spaces in which they practice. They get used to the blackbox theatre, the couches they sit on, and the props they use. But the mark of a good actor is when their character can be anyplace, anytime. You want your characters to be able to move beyond the screen- you want them to stay with their audience, and the way to do that is to ensure that they can put themselves in any environment and still stay in character. Versatility is key- it shows dedication and commitment to character. Take scenes from your script and change the setting- if the scene is in a bedroom, change it to be in a park or restaurant. You want actors to be comfortable in character wherever they may be- especially in intimate moments. Make sure they use different props and utilize space. When they come back to the bedroom, it will surprise you how much more the actors feel like they have to work with.

The Question Game

Sometimes it's difficult for actors to "out with it"- or, in simpler terms, they choke. Not being able to get the words out is very common with younger actors because most haven't completely found their voice yet. Your job is to help them find it- and in time for your series to begin shooting. Young actors need to be comfortable enough with themselves before they recite anyone else's lines. The question game is pretty basic. You ask two or three actors to get on stage, and recite questions to each other. No periods or fragmentations allowed. The questions must make sense in the context of a conversation, and whoever stalls first loses. Ever see the musical Damn Yankees? There is the famous "Who's On First?" dialogue that uses this technique, the only difference there is that questions are mistaken for statements by the actors in character. It's a grown-up version of the Question Game.

A sample game: (choose any location, but make it one that you can utilize later when you're shooting)

Actor 1: Ever been to our shop before?
Actor 2: Can you believe how hard it is for me to choose?
Actor 1: Did you say you were looking for boots or heels?
Actor 2: Do those wedges make your feet hurt?
Actor 1: Perhaps try our sister shop?

Make sure there are the correct emotions there- the shopkeeper above should look like he/she is visibly tiring of the possible shoe buyer. This is a traditional improve technique and it really makes sure actors are thinking on the feet. Plus, the added bonus is competition. At any age, people love to win. This game encourages listening- to succeed, you must rely in the other person in the dialogue.

AGREEMENTS

LOCATION AGREEMENT

The following will serve to confirm the agreement between ("Company") and you as follows:

1. You hereby grant to Company, its producers, artists, employees and directors the privilege to enter and use the premises known as _____, and located at _____, ("Premises") for the purpose of producing a videotape or film ("Shooting") on the following dates:_____.

2. Company shall maintain in full force and effect, at its own expense, during the period of this agreement, a comprehensive policy of liability insurance. Said policy shall insure and protect Company and you against any and all claims, liability or litigation arising out of or directly connected with the Shooting on the Premises. Company shall have in effect coverage for Company employees against workers compensation claims, as required by law, in the statutory amount.

3. This agreement is subject to immediate termination by you or Company in the event of riots, strikes, acts of God, or any other legitimate conditions outside your or Company's control rendering use of the Premises dangerous or impossible. If possible, should the above termination be required, the production of the Shooting may be rescheduled under the same terms and conditions as stated herein. In no event shall (a) you be liable for any damages to Company for such cancellation; or (b) Company be liable for any damages to you for such cancellation. Company and its licensees shall have the perpetual right to use all footage of the Premises for any purpose and in any media.

The undersigned represent and warrant that they have full authority to execute this agreement.

AGREED TO AND ACCEPTED:

_____   _____

(Print)   (Print)

_____   _____

Title: Title:

SYNCHRONIZATION AND ARTIST/MASTER USE LICENSE

Licensor grants to ___Otessa Ghadar, 20/20 Productions___ ("Producer") the non-exclusive and irrevocable privilege, right, license, and authority to record, edit, dub, perform, and otherwise reproduce the Composition and the Recorded Performance listed below in synchronization or timed relation with the Production and the soundtrack thereof and for promotion thereof. Licensor will receive credit in the project's credit section, along with a copy of the final project. Producer will promote Licensor through social media efforts and video footage. This license agreement shall become binding on the parties hereto upon the signatures of both parties.

Production: "_____Orange Juice in Bishop's Garden_____"

Compositions/Recordings: _____

Composer(s): _____

Publisher(s) (if any): _____

Artist: _____

Record Label (if any): _____

Use and Timing: ___Full songs (or less)___

Media: All media now known or hereafter devised

Commencing: Upon being signed by both parties.

ADDITIONAL TERMS AND CONDITIONS:
REPRESENTATIONS AND WARRANTIES: Licensor represents and warrants that it has the full right, power and authority to enter into and fully perform this agreement and to grant all of the rights granted herein and that the consent of no other person or entity is required to grant such rights; and that use of the recording will not infringe the rights of any person, firm, corporation, artist, union or guild.

ASSIGNABILITY: This license shall run to Producer, its successors and assigns, provided that Producer remain liable for the performance of all the terms and conditions of this license on its part to be performed and provided further, that any disposition of the Production shall be subject to all the terms herein.

AGREED AND ACCEPTED:
PRODUCER: DATE:

LICENSOR: DATE:

If Licensor is under 18 years of age, please have Parent or Guardian sign as well.
PARENT/GUARDIAN: DATE:

ORANGE JUICE IN BISHOP'S GARDEN

TALENT / MODEL RELEASE

Authorization to Reproduce Physical Likeness

For good and valuable consideration, the receipt of which from <u>20/20 Productions</u> (producer) is acknowledged, I hereby expressly grant to said production company and to its employees, agents, and assigns, the right to photograph me and use my picture, silhouette, biography and other facsimiles of my physical likeness (as they may appear in any still camera photograph and/or motion picture film or videotape), in and in connection with the exhibition, theatrically, on television or otherwise, of any motion pictures or videotape in which the same may be used or incorporated, and also in the advertising, exploiting and/or publicizing of any such motion picture or videotape, in perpetuity, throughout the world, but not limited to television or theatrical motion pictures and may be released in any other future media.

I further give the said company the right to reproduce in any manner whatsoever any recordation made by said company of my voice and all instrumental, musical, or other sound effects produced by me.

I hereby waive any claim for further compensation in connection therewith except as described in this document. Further, I waive any right to inspect the finished work or approve the use to which it may be applied.

I hereby certify and represent that I have read the foregoing and fully understand the meaning and effect thereof and, intending to be legally bound, I have set my hand this Day of _____, 20___.

    PRINT NAME: _____
    SIGN NAME: _____
    ADDRESS: _____
    TELEPHONE: _____

TO BE COMPLETED IF PARTICIPANT IS UNDER 18 YEARS OF AGE:

Parent/Guardian   Signature: _____

Dated:_____ , 20__   Print Name: _____

CREW DEAL MEMO

PRODUCTION COMPANY: 20/20 Productions
MOTION PICTURE: Orange Juice in Bishop's Garden, Season 5
START DATE: __June 27th, 2011_____
POSITION: _   -
VOLUNTEER or CREW MEMBER NAME: ___
ADDRESS: _____
PHONE: Home: _____ Cel: _   _____
SOCIAL SECURITY/FED I.D. NUMBER:_

**********(items below to be completed by production company only)**********

COMPENSATION:_   Volunteer   OR   Stipend_____
SCREEN CREDIT:

This Deal Memo shall confirm the agreement between the above-named volunteer or crew member ("CREW MEMBER") and   ("Company"), in connection with the motion picture presently entitled " Orange Juice in Bishop's Garden" ("the Picture"). For good and valuable consideration, the receipt of which is hereby acknowledged, Company and Crew Member agree as follows:

SERVICES: Crew Member shall render services hereunder from the Start Date, which are usual and customary of the services required of a person employed in this capacity in the motion picture industry, and shall render such services exclusively to Company thereafter through the completion of Crew Member's services as determined by Company. Crew Member's services in the position stated above shall be rendered to the best of Crew Member's ability and as Company directs in its sole discretion, including, without limitation, all matters of taste and judgment.

PAYMENT: Production services fees shall be paid to Crew Member within 30 days after Company's receipt of Crew Member's invoice. Pay date may be delayed by reason of an intervening federal or state holiday. Employee shall not receive any overtime, turnaround or other hourly payments. Paid work on a day off or a holiday must be approved in advance by Company and will be paid at the normal rate provided for by this Deal Memo.

PURCHASES: All purchases, rentals and other expenses incurred must be made with prior approval by Company.

Crew Deal Memo Page 1 of 4

PETTY CASH: If Crew Member is given a petty cash float, Crew Member is responsible for returning receipts, remaining cash, or a combination thereof upon completion of the job. A purchase order or check request is needed for all rentals or non-cash purchases. All purchase orders or check requests must be approved by Company in writing. If Crew Member is assigned a walkie-talkie, pager, or any other equipment, Crew Member shall be responsible for returning same to Company in good working order. Crew Member hereby authorizes Company to deduct from Crew Member's final payroll check any outstanding balance in Crew Member's petty cash advance fund and any costs of repair or replacement of any equipment assigned to Employee accrued as a result of Crew Member's negligence.

RENTALS: CREW MEMBER'S KIT/BOX AND EQUIPMENT IS SOLE RESPONSIBILITY OF CREW MEMBER. COMPANY ASSUMES NO RESPONSIBILITY FOR SAME. Any rentals from Crew Member must be approved by Company and must be documented at the time of hire with a rental agreement.

CREDIT: Unless otherwise specified in this Deal Memo, all aspects of screen credit are at Company's sole discretion.

TERM: Unless expressly provided elsewhere in this Deal Memo, Crew Member's employment hereunder shall not be for a "run of the show" or for any guaranteed period of employment. Company reserves the right to discharge Crew Member at any time, subject only to the obligation to pay the balance of any guaranteed compensation due provided that Crew Member is not in material breach of its obligations hereunder. Company will attempt to notify Crew Member a minimum of twenty-four (24) hours in advance of termination of employment. Use of alcohol or drugs during hours of employment will result in Crew Member's immediate termination. Crew Member confirms, by signing this agreement, that Crew Member does not have a sex offender record. This agreement is subject to immediate suspension and/or termination (at Company's election) without further obligation on the part of Company in the event of any incapacity or default of Crew Member or in the case of any suspension, postponement or interference with the production by reason of labor controversy, strike, earthquake, act of terrorism, act of God, governmental action, regulation, or decree or for any other customary force majeure reason. The expiration or termination of this Deal Memo shall not affect the ownership by Company of the rights granted herein.

WORK-FOR-HIRE: Company shall be the owner of all of the results and proceeds of Crew Member's services, including any copyright, trademark and any other intellectual property rights in any work or property created by Crew Member, or anyone under Crew Member's direction. Crew Member acknowledges that Crew Member's work is a "work

Crew Deal Memo Page 2 of 4

made for hire" within the scope of Crew Member's employment, and therefore Company shall be the author and copyright owner of any work created under the Deal Memo. Crew Member expressly waives any rights of droit moral that may be afforded Crew Member under the laws of any country in connection with the Picture. If Crew Member shall hereafter be deemed to own any rights in or to the Crew Member, Crew Member hereby assigns such rights to Company and further agrees to execute any documents required by Company to effectuate such intent.

PUBLICITY: Company shall have the right to use Crew Member's name, voice, picture and likeness in connection with the Picture, the advertising and publicizing thereof, and any promotional films or clips respecting the Picture without additional compensation therefore. Crew Member shall not directly or indirectly circulate, publish or otherwise disseminate any news story, article, book or other publicity concerning the Picture, or Crew Member's or others' services without Company's prior written consent, provided that Crew Member may issue personal publicity mentioning the Picture so long as such references are not derogatory. Crew Member has permission to show a videotape of Picture in connection with seeking future employment. Admittance of any guests to the set are at the sole discretion of Company.

AVAILABILITY: Crew Member will advise Company of Crew Member's whereabouts so that Crew Member may be reached at any reasonable hour of the night or day.

ENTIRE AGREEMENT: This Deal Memo sets forth the entire understanding of the parties regarding the subject matter and may not be amended except by a written instrument signed by the parties. Any added conditions on the front of this Deal Memo inconsistent with the conditions of employment detailed in the body of this agreement shall be null and void.

NO OBLIGATION TO PRODUCE: Company will not be obligated to produce or release the Picture, or to use the results of Crew Member's services.

ASSIGNMENT: Company shall have the right to transfer or assign its rights and obligations pursuant to this Deal Memo to any other person, firm, or corporation, and upon such assignment shall be relieved of its obligation to Crew Member.

HOLD HARMLESS: Crew Member shall indemnify and hold Company harmless from and against any and all loss, claim, liability, judgment, cost or expense suffered by Company for any breach or default of this Deal Memo by Crew Member. Company and its agents shall be free from all liabilities and claims for damages and/or suits for or by reason of any injury or death to any person or property of the Crew Member, its agents or employees, or third parties. Crew Member shall indemnify and hold harmless the Company from all liabilities/charges/expenses/costs on account of or by reason of any injuries/deaths/liabilities/claims/suits/losses.

Crew Member ACCEPTS ALL CONDITIONS OF EMPLOYMENT AS DESCRIBED ABOVE

AGREED TO AND ACCEPTED:

Date:

CREW MEMBER

Date:

PRODUCER

Crew Deal Memo Page 4 of 4

20/20 PRODUCTIONS

Work URL www.twentytwentyproductions.com

DATE: _____
NAME: _____
ADDRESS: _____

I, _____ (name), attest that I am an Independent Contractor for 20/20 productions. I am not an employee, and as such I am responsible for all taxes, insurance, & payroll (eg Social Security, Medicare, FICA, etc...)

My available work schedule is as follows:
_____
_____ (fill in blanks)

I have read and understand the Company Policy manual.

Sign here: _____

PRE-PRODUCTION AND ON-SET DOCUMENTS

Budget Sheet

Date:
Title:
Est. No. of Days:

Acct. No.	Category	Total
1	Script	$0.00
2	Producers	$0.00
3	Direction	$0.00
4	Cast	$0.00
5		
	Total Above-the-Line	$0.00
6	Production Staff	$0.00
7	Production Design	$0.00
8	Wardrobe	$0.00
9	Hair/Make-Up	$0.00
10	Set Operations	$0.00
11	Electrical	$0.00
12	Camera	$0.00
13	Sound	$0.00
14	Transportation	$0.00
15	Location Expenses	$0.00
16	Craft services	$0.00
	Total Production	$0.00
17	Editing	$0.00
18	Music	$0.00
19	Post Sound	$0.00
20	Titles/Graphics	$0.00
	Total Post Production	$0.00
21	Insurance	$0.00
22	Permits	$0.00
23	General/Administration	$0.00
	Total Other	$0.00
	Contingency: 10%	$0.00
	Grand Total	$0.00

Producer: Oressa Ghadar
Directors: Rebecca [redacted], Oressa Ghadar
UPM: Michelle [redacted]
Film Title: **ORANGE JUICE IN BISHOP'S GARDEN** Season 2   Episodes 1, 2, 3, 4
Log: The bad things we do, the things we get caught for—and how they are never the same. Like a Wonder Years for the 90's.

As of May 27th, 2009
Pg. 1 of 5 total

List of locations/Total shoot days:

1. School Classroom
2. School Auditorium
3. Back-steps - school
4. School Hallway
5. Chinatown
6. Kalorama Circle
7. Diana Spencer's Deck
8. Laura-the-Goth's bedroom
9. 29th St. Place cul-de-sac
10. Woodley Park
11. Rock Creek Park- water, bike-path
12. Rock Creek Park- glade
13. Rock Creek Park- glade
14. Sarah's Bedroom
15. Rox's Bedroom

#Total Cast: 19   #Total Minors: 6   #Total Extras: 2

EPISODE ONE

SCENE #	PAGE COUNT	INT/EXT DAY/	TIME PLOT	LOCATION	DESCRIPTION	CAST	EXTRAS	PROPS, ANIMAL, VEHICLES, STUNTS, EFX	Wardrobe: Costumes, accessories
1	4/8	INT/DAY	10am 6/15/95	School Classroom	Travis/Laura-the-Goth see Teaacher expell Jake/Trip	Travis, Laura, Teacher,	2 (stand-ins for Jake & Trip)	Black beanie, smurf hat, blue striped hoodie	
2	7/8	INT/DAY	NOON 6/15/95	School Auditorium	Principal berates school	ALL	10	flourescent lights	
3	1 & 7/8	EXT/DAY	2:07 PM 6/15/95	Back-Steps - School	Sarah & Gwen talk	Gwen, Sarah	0	back-steps	Sarah: Gwen:

Forms, Paperwork, and ImportantDocuments

Orange Juice in Bishop's Garden

Season 5 Call Sheet
Thursday, July 7, 2011

Call Time	Cast or Crew	People		Location
7:00 a.m.	Crew	Otessa Ashley Jorge Dylan	Crystal Lis Cheyenne Emily	▮▮▮▮▮▮▮▮▮▮
8:30 a.m.	Crew	Bim Drew	Connor	Awakening Sculpture
8:30 a.m.	Cast	Nick DeAndre	George	Awakening Sculpture
1:30 p.m.	Cast	Ellen	Rachel	41st & Belt
3:15 p.m.	Cast	Shawn Nick	Sam Otessa	Watermelon House

Location/shooting List
1. Awakening Sculpture- Ep. 10 Sc. 3
2. Car (on ride from Awakening Sculpture) - Ep. 10, Sc. 4
3. 41st & Belt- Ep. 9, Sc. 1
4. Comet Ping Pong- Ep. 11, Sc. 4
5. Watermelon House Alley- Ep. 9, Sc. 4
6. 20/20 Productions- Ep. 9, Sc. 6

Scene Information

Start Time	Episode/Scene	Description	Cast
8:30 am	Ep. 10, Sc. 3 (2/8 pg)	Ryan & Drew wake Adrian up	Adrian, Ryan, Drew
10:00 am	Ep. 10, Sc. 4 (7/8 pg)	Ryan & Drew give Adrian "tough love" speech	Adrian, Ryan, Drew
1:30 pm	Ep. 9, Sc. 1	EST of girls sing & tell Chloe to dump Adrian	Sarah, Alex
1:30 p.m. (B-cam)	Ep. 11, Sc. 4	EST Comet Ping Pong	n/a
3:15 p.m.	Ep. 9, Sc. 4 (5/8 pg)	Sailor & Adrian pick up mystery power, accost Stranger	Adrian, Gordon, Stranger, Dealer
7:00 am	Ep. 9, Sc. 6 (1/8 pg)	Adrian bleeds w/ broken glass, fleas	Adrian

Orange Juice in Bishop's Garden Season 5 Call Sheet
Thursday, July 7, 2011

Episode 10 Scene 3- Jeans on both, RYAN: brown stripe sweater w/ green grateful dead t-shirt. DREW: grey t-shirt w/ orange Orioles jersey. ADRIAN: white sailor hat, crackerjack uniform
Episode 10 Scene 4- Same as Scene 4
Episode 9 Scene 1- SARAH: green henley cardigan, ripped bellbottoms, hippypatchwork tanktop, converse (from pile of converses), ALEX: rio brazil shirt, tyedye slip dress, CASANDRA: pot shirt, blue cordoroy bellbottoms, converse
Episode 9 Scene 4- GORDON and ADRIAN: sailor uniforms and crackerjack hats, DEALER: orange corduroy high waters, blue work shirt, whatever shoes
Episode 9 Scene 6- ADRIAN: white sailor hat, crackerjack uniform

DIRECTIONS
20/20 Productions

███████████████████████████████

Awakening Sculpture (149 Waterfront St., Oxon Hill, MD)
NH1 bus from Branch Ave. Metro Station
Some Parking available, mostly in garages.

Nearest Bathroom:
Fleet St. Garage, one block away (Fleet St. & American Way)

41st St. NW & Belt Rd. NW (Near Dancing Crab: 4615 Wisconsin Ave. NW)
From Tenleytown-AU Metro Station on the Red Line
Exit station, Wisconsin ave. is right behind the escalators
Turn right and walk up Wisconsin
41st & Belt is 2 blocks up on the right.

Nearest Bathroom:
Dancing Crab

Watermelon House (1108 Q St. NW)
From Shaw-Howard University Metro on the Green or Yellow Line
Exit station using 7TH ST NW & R ST NW exit
Walk a short distance S on 7th St NW
Turn right on Rhode Island Ave NW
Walk approx. 3 blocks SW on Rhode Island Ave NW
Turn right on Q St NW
Walk a short distance NW on Q St NW

Nearest Bathrooms:
Starbucks or Whole Foods on 15th & P

Orange Juice in Bishop's Garden

Season 5 Call Sheet
Thursday, July 7, 2011

On-set Phone: ▮▮▮▮▮ UPM)

Additional Information
Breakfast: Ready to eat at call times indicated
Lunch: 2:30 pm- 3:15 pm
Day: 9 of 10
Weather: High 93 degrees. Low 72 degrees. Partial cloudiness early, with scattered showers & thunderstorms in the afternoon. A few storms may be severe. Winds light & variable. Chance of rain 50%.
wear sunscreen, dress appropriately for hot weather (light colors), wear comfortable, practical shoes
Sunrise: 5:50 a.m.
Sunset: 8:36 p.m.

Crew Directory

Title	Name	Phone	Email
Director/Producer	Ote▮		
UPM/PC	Ash▮		
1st AD/Sound	Jorg▮		
2nd AD	Dyl▮		
2nd AD	Crys▮		
DP	Bim▮		
1st AC	Dre▮		
Gaffer/Key Grip	Con▮		
Production Designer	Lis▮		
Art Director	Che▮		

20/20 Productions
Petty Cash Journal
Reporting Period: From _____ To _____   Balance _____

Date	To Whom Paid	Purpose	Amount	Amount Returned	Approved By	Total	Balance

Audited By
_____

Approved By
_____

Total Voucher Amount		
Total Receipts		
Cash on Hand		
Overage/Shortage		
Petty Cash Reimbursement		
Balance Forward		

Forms, Paperwork, and Important Documents

20/20 Productions

WALKIE-TALKIE SIGN-OUT SHEET

ITEM(S) & MODEL # INCLUDING ACCESSORIES	DEPARTMENT ASSIGNED TO	PRINT NAME	DATE & TIME OUT	DATE & TIME IN	SIGNATURE	DATE RETURNED TO 20/20

NOTES

CONTACT:

Ashley Mumford (UPM)
Phone: (301) 367-7937

Kathryn Beard (AD)
Phone: (703) 216-2475

CRAFT SERVICES

Here an example grocery list used for 1 week with a cast and crew of about 30.

Craft

Grocery List

~~paper plates~~ (100)
~~plastic forks~~ (50)
paper towels (3)
~~paper bowl~~ (30)
~~hot liquid cups~~ (30)
toilet paper (6-12)

Skim Milk (2)
~~Orange Juice~~ (2)
Lemonade (2)
~~Water~~ (4)
Coffee (1)
Diet Coke (4)
Coke (2)
Sprite (2)

~~Cereal (1-2)~~
White bagels (1)
Wheat bagels (2)
Everything bagels (1)
Cream cheese (1)
Eggs (1)
~~Hummus (2)~~
~~Cheese slice packs (5)~~

Oranges (1-2 bags)
Red Apples (10)
Green Apples (8)
Red Grapes (3)
Lemon (2)

Celery (6)
~~Carrots (5)~~
Cucumbers (5)
Tomatoes (2)
Onion (2)
Green Onion (1)
Iceberg (6)
Romaine (1)
Corn (3)
Green Beans (1 bag)
~~Kidney Beans~~ (8)
~~Black Beans~~ (4)
~~Chick Peas~~ (2)
Blackeyed Peas (2)
Green Chiles (1)
Cilantro (tiny bit)

Handwritten notes:
2 peanut butter
2 jelly
500 knives
Granola
Trail mix
Muffins

> Almonds (1 bag)
> Turkey lunch meat (3-4)
> Ham lunch meat (1)
> Tuna (10 small cans or 6 large cans)
>
> Ground Turkey meat (2lbs)
> Taco spices (2)
> Tortilla shells (4-5)
> Refried Beans (3)
> Rice (1)
>
> Chips Ahoy (2-3)
> *we have a lot of chips, pretzels, popcorn, and graham crackers from last time
> *we have a lot of bread (frozen) from last time

And here an easy-to-make recipe:

THE WIZARD'S FIESTA SALAD
(from Lis de Tuerk Ghadar, Production Designer)

3 32 oz. cans of cooked kidney beans, rinsed
3 Granny Smith apples, cored, chopped, and sprinkled with 3 tablespoons of lime juice
1 15 oz. can of sweet corn (vacuum packed if possible), drained
1 red onion, diced
1 red or yellow pepper, seeded and diced
3 - 4 tablespoons of rice vinegar
4 -5 tablespoons of sesame seed oil or vegetable oil
4 -5 tablespoons of dried, crushed herbs (choose either: tarragon, dill, or basil)

Add salt and pepper to taste

Combine first five ingredients. Add last three ingredients and mix gently. Add salt and pepper as needed. Chill. Serves 12. Serve with iceberg lettuce, iced tea, and Popsicles for dessert.